Early Manuscripts &
Modern Translations
of the New Testament

Other Books by the Author

The Complete Guide to Bible Versions
The Origin of the Bible
The Quest for the Original Text of the New Testament
Who's Who in Christian History (edited with J. D. Douglas)
I Am the Way: A Spiritual Journey through the Gospel of John
Opening the Gospel of John (with Wendell Hawley)

Philip Wesley Comfort (Ph.D., D.Litt. et Phil.) is senior editor of Bible Reference at Tyndale House Publishers and visiting professor at Wheaton College, where he teaches New Testament literature and interpretation. In addition to his many books, Dr. Comfort has written articles for *New Testament Studies, Tyndale Bulletin, Notes on Translation,* and *The Bible Translator.*

Early Manuscripts & Modern Translations of the New Testament

Philip Wesley Comfort

Wipf & Stock
PUBLISHERS
Eugene, Oregon

Wipf and Stock Publishers
199 W 8th Ave, Suite 3
Eugene, OR 97401

Early Manuscripts and Modern Translations of the New Testament
By Comfort, Philip Wesley
Copyright©1990 by Comfort, Philip Wesley
ISBN 13: 978-1-57910-838-0
ISBN 10: 1-57910-838-5
Publication date 12/17/2001
Previously published by Baker Books, 1990

Cover photo: A leaf from 𝔭46 (Chester Beatty Manuscript II) showing the end of Romans and beginning of Hebrews. The placing of Hebrews within the Pauline corpus may reflect an early opinion about the authorship of this book. *Photo courtesy of the Department of Rare Books and Special Collections, University of Michigan Library.*

To
my wife, Georgia

for the life and love

we share together

and

my sons, Jeremy, John, and Peter

for the joy

they give me

Contents

Foreword

A century has passed since the first early papyrus manuscript of the New Testament was discovered in Egypt. In 1889 Vincent Scheil discovered in Coptos, Egypt, a papyrus manuscript dated around 200 A.D., containing portions of Luke 1–4. A little later, in 1897, Grenfell and Hunt, two British archaeologists in search of ancient Biblical manuscripts, discovered a papyrus fragment written in Greek, showing Matthew 1:1-18. Since that time, nearly a hundred New Testament papyrus manuscripts or fragments of manuscripts have been discovered in Egypt. Many of these date between the second and fourth centuries A.D. Throughout the twentieth century these early papyri have had a significant impact on editions of the Greek New Testament as well as on the English translations based on them.

After years of painstakingly careful work, prompted by a deep love for the Scriptures, Dr. Comfort presents the fruit of his prodigious efforts in this book, *Early Manuscripts and Modern Translations of the New Testament*. It explores the effect that the early papyrus manuscripts had on critical editions of the Greek New Testament (especially upon the Nestle-Aland text) and upon twentieth-century English translations. Included among these translations are the Revised Standard Version, the New American Standard Bible, the New English Bible, the New International Version, and the New Revised Standard Version. Other translations are also referred to from time to time.

In the first section, Dr. Comfort gives a helpful introduction to the early New Testament papyrus manuscripts. In it he shows how these papyri have affected our understanding of the early transmission of the Greek New Testament and how, as a result, they produced changes in critical editions of the Greek New Testament. The second section provides a detailed description of each manuscript. The third section specifies the exact portions of Scripture (from Matthew to Revelation) where Greek texts and

English translations have been affected by these early manuscripts; this section is accompanied by textual commentary. The final section, then, gives an overview of how the papyri have created successive changes in modern translations of the New Testament: from the American Standard Version of 1901, to the New International Version of 1973, to the New Revised Standard Version of 1990.

This book will be a useful tool to pastor, student, teacher, scholar—to all those people who are seriously interested in understanding the history of the Greek text and the effect it has had on English versions.

Gerald F. Hawthorne
Professor of Greek Emeritus
Wheaton College

Preface to the Paperback Edition

I am grateful to Allan Fisher and Jim Weaver at Baker Book House for the opportunity to reissue this book in paperback. I have made some important revisions in this edition, especially with respect to the dating of some significant papyrus manuscripts (see comments on 𝔓4, 𝔓46, 𝔓64/67, and 𝔓66). I would like to have made more changes, but space did not permit. For instance, I would have added at least one more manuscript, 𝔓98, and I would have selected several more passages worthy of discussion. But these will have to wait for future publications with Baker Book House. In any event, I am thankful for this book in its present form, and I pray that it will continue to meet the needs of translators, scholars, and students.

Acknowledgments

Several people deserve recognition for the help and encouragement they gave me while I was writing this book. I am indebted to Professor Gerald Hawthorne and Professor Ralph Martin for their thorough review of the manuscript and many insightful suggestions. I also want to thank Professor Bruce Metzger and Professor Barbara Aland for several valuable suggestions, as well as Gordon Fee and Eldon Epp for their review of the last section of this book, which was the basis for a paper I presented at the Society of Biblical Literature Convention in November, 1988. Richard Comfort (my brother), Dan Elliott, and Phillip Hofinga offered their assistance in translating some articles written in French, Spanish, and German. Dan Simons and Vince Morris carefully read through the manuscript and offered several good stylistic suggestions. Others have been a great source of support and encouragement: Allen Jones of Fairfax University; Ken Taylor, Mark Taylor, Wendell Hawley, Robert Brown, and Mark Norton of Tyndale House Publishers; and those in my family—my parents, Richard and Dorothy Comfort, my brothers, Richard and Greg, my wife's parents, George and Joanne Riser, and my grandmother, Dorothy Bigham.

Finally, I must thank Karla Vandersypen, Assistant Rare Book Librarian of the University of Michigan Library, for her assistance on several occasions and for granting me permission to reproduce portions of the Chester Beatty manuscript, 𝔓46, and Dr. Hans E. Braun, Director of the Foundation Martin Bodmer (Cologny-Geneva), for giving my wife and me a personal tour of the foundation and for granting permission to reproduce portions of the Bodmer Papyri, 𝔓66 and 𝔓75. Others helped by granting permission to reproduce photographs of various manuscripts: Kathleen Houghton and Michael Boggan of the British Library for the Oxyrhynchus Papyrus, 𝔓13; Barbara Bohen, Director of the World Heritage Museum, for the Oxyrhynchus Papyrus, 𝔓23; Diana Yount, Librarian of Special Collections at Andover Newton Theological School, for the Oxyrhynchus Papyrus, 𝔓24; Wilfrid Lockwood, Director and Librarian of the Chester Beatty Library, for two leaves of the Chester Beatty manuscript, 𝔓46.

Abbreviations

ASV	American Standard Version
KJV	King James Version
LXX	Septuagint
mg	a variant reading noted in the margin of a translation
MS	Manuscript
MSS	Manuscripts
NA[26]	*Novum Testamentum Graece*, tweny-sixth edition
NASB	New American Standard Bible
NEB	New English Bible
NIV	New International Version
NJB	New Jerusalem Bible
NRSV	New Revised Standard Version
NT	New Testament
OT	Old Testament
RSV	Revised Standard Version
TEV	Today's English Version
TLB	The Living Bible
TR	Textus Receptus
UBS[3]	*Greek New Testament*, United Bible Society, third edition (corrected)
vid	Latin for "it appears [to read as such]"

Sigla used to denote specific manuscripts follow those found in NA[26] and UBS[3]; see lists in these two volumes.

Introduction

When some people think of manuscripts, even New Testament manuscripts, they think only of old, tattered parchments or papyrus leaves
inscribed with ancient, hard-to-decipher language. When I think of New
Testament manuscripts (hereafter abbreviated as NT MSS), I think of the
early Christians who wrote them and read them in their personal devotions
and in church meetings. These MSS were the God-inspired texts that gave
them life and light. No matter what differences in wording may have
existed in these early MSS (and this book will examine these in great
detail), the early Christians who had these MSS read the same basic mes-
sage about the Lord Jesus Christ, the Son of God, who died on the cross for
the remission of sins and rose again to give life to all who believe in him.
Nonetheless, the early MSS exhibit some very significant differences in the
wording of the NT text—differences pertaining to titles of the Lord Jesus,
Christian doctrine, and church practice, as well as other significant word
variations. It is the task of textual critics to determine which of the many
variant readings is the one most likely to be original, and it is the responsibility of any translator to follow a Greek text that accurately presents the
text of the original authors.

We who live at the end of the twentieth century have an advantage over
the early Christians with respect to the number of MSS and text-critical
methods that are available to us for ascertaining the original wording of the
NT text. Near the beginning of this century, some of the earliest NT
papyrus manuscripts were discovered in Egypt. Since then, almost one
hundred NT MSS have been recovered from the Egyptian sands and ruins.
Over half of these MSS are dated in the fourth century or earlier, and
several of the most important ones are dated nearly two hundred years
earlier than Codex Sinaiticus (ℵ) and Codex Vaticanus (B). These discoveries have brought us much closer to the original text of the Greek NT. It is

exciting to see how these early MSS have changed the major critical editions of the Greek NT and have had significant impact on the modern English translations of the NT. In this book I have described each of the early papyrus manuscripts (plus a few other manuscripts written on parchment), then examined how these MSS have actually affected critical editions of the Greek NT and modern English versions. (Since this book focuses on the twentieth-century discoveries of the papyrus MSS, primary attention is not given to the two fourth-century MSS, Codex Sinaiticus and Codex Vaticanus; but they, along with other noted MSS such as Codex Ephraemi Rescriptus and Codex Beza, are constantly cited for their textual readings.)

In doing this study, it was first necessary to see how the papyri have affected the theory and praxis of textual criticism and thus changed modern critical editions of the Greek NT. Then, I analyzed how the papyri have affected several modern translations of the NT: the American Standard Version (ASV), the Revised Standard Version (RSV), the New American Standard Bible (NASB), the New International Version (NIV), the New English Bible (NEB), Today's English Version (TEV), and the New Jerusalem Bible (NJB). Limited yet significant attention is also given to the NT of the New Revised Standard Version Bible (NRSV), especially in verses such as John 1:18; 1 Cor. 10:9; 13:3; and Heb. 4:2 (see section 3). (Because the NRSV is a 1990 publication, it was not possible to study this version with the same, full treatment given to the others.)

This book will also demonstrate the successive changes that have transpired from the ASV (1901), to the RSV (1946), to the NASB (1960), to the NIV (1973)—with comparative notes on the NEB (1961), TEV (1966), NJB (1985), as well as with some comments on the NRSV. The ASV is an excellent version to reflect the Greek text that was formulated by the end of the nineteenth century, a century that witnessed the discovery of Codex Siniaticus, the accessibility to Codex Vaticanus, and the deciphering of Codex Ephraemi Rescriptus, as well as the work of textual scholars such as Tregelles, Tischendorf, Westcott, and Hort. After the publication of the ASV (which shares essentially the same text as the English Revised Version, 1881), there were several important discoveries of early papyrus MSS—especially those found at Oxyrhynchus (early 1900s) and those in the Chester Beatty Collection (found in the 1930s). These discoveries were a motivation for the revision work that went into the Revised Standard

Version (see Preface to the NT in the Revised Standard Version). After the publication of the RSV, there were some other significant discoveries— most importantly, the papyri now in the Bodmer Collection (found in the 1950s and 1960s). These papyri might be expected to have had an impact on all modern English versions since 1960.

SECTION ONE

An Introduction to Early New Testament Papyrus Manuscripts

THE EARLY PAPYRUS MANUSCRIPTS AND
NEW TESTAMENT TEXTUAL TRANSMISSION

After the church began, the early believers relied on the words of the apostles to teach them about Jesus' life and ministry. This oral transmission about Jesus' life and ministry, together with the Septuagint, provided the verbal sustenance for the early church. Then certain individuals—either the apostles themselves (such as Matthew and John) or those who knew the apostles (Mark and Luke)—were inspired by God to write Gospel accounts to substantiate the oral tradition. Luke, for example, explained in the preface to his Gospel (Luke 1:1-4) that he wrote his account so as to confirm what had been taught catechetically about Jesus' life and ministry. Mark, tradition tells us, compiled a Gospel based on Peter's messages about Jesus' ministry. And many scholars believe that John first preached many of the chapters that later he weaved into a Gospel narrative. Thus, the Gospel was first published in oral form, then in written form. Most likely, the written publications were not published and circulated as trade books would be; rather, they were published for circulation in the churches. This would mean that a number of copies of the autograph would be made initially and then distributed to various churches. Ideally, each of the manuscripts constituting the first publication would be exactly the same, but it is possible that there was divergence from the autograph due to the manual copying procedure.

A number of epistles were also written during the days of the early church. Most of these were authored by Paul; but Peter, John, James, and Jude also contributed NT epistles. Several of these epistles were "dictated" to an amanuensis, and others were actually written by the author. The usual procedure for a "dictated" epistle was for the amanuensis to take down the

3

speaker's words in shorthand and then produce a transcript, which the author would then review, edit, and sign in his own handwriting (see Metzger's *The New Testament,* 215–217). Two NT epistles provide the name of the amamuensis: Tertius for Romans (16:22) and Silvanus for 1 Peter (5:12). Four of Paul's epistles indicate that he provided the concluding salutation in his own handwriting: 1 Corinthians (16:21), Galatians (6:11), Colossians (4:18), and 2 Thessalonians (3:17).

The Epistles were not "published," as were the Gospels; but they were soon copied by the churches to whom they were addressed and by neighboring churches. This is implicit in Col. 4:16, wherein Paul asks the church in Colossae to exchange epistles with the neighboring Laodicean church. (The epistle to the Laodiceans is now lost—unless it is the same epistle we call Ephesians.) This exchange implies that each church made a copy of their own epistle before sending it on. It is known that the authors of epistles would also keep copies of each epistle in a special letter-book (Metzger, ibid.). Perhaps Paul kept all of his epistles (2 Tim. 4:13 might contain an allusion to this). At any rate, the only epistles which might have been initially produced in multiple copies were Ephesians (written as an encyclical) and Revelation (see Rev. 1:11). Each of the other books was probably produced as one original manuscript, which was later reproduced in multiple copies. Thus, the various books of the NT, whether the Gospels (and Acts) or the Epistles, were written and/or published, then circulated within the Christian community, which then produced multiple copies.

Unfortunately, not one autograph of one NT book is extant. The closest copy we have to an autograph is a papyrus fragment (𝔓52) dated c. 100–115, containing a few verses of John 18 (31-34, 37-38). This scrap, only twenty to thirty years removed from the autograph, is a fragment of one of the first copies of John's Gospel. Other early and important papyrus MSS are 𝔓4 (second/third cent.), containing portions of Luke; 𝔓13 (third cent.), containing portions of Hebrews; 𝔓45 (third cent.), including portions of the Gospels and Acts; 𝔓46 (175–200), preserving almost all of Paul's Epistles; 𝔓47 (third cent.), containing half of Revelation; 𝔓66 (175–200), containing most of John; 𝔓72 (third cent.), preserving all of 1 and 2 Peter and Jude; and 𝔓75 (c. 200), containing most of Luke and John. These and several other early papyri (e.g., 𝔓64/67—c. 200, 𝔓77—c. 200, and 𝔓90—second cent.) discovered in this century provide positive proof that various NT books were being copied soon after the autographs were written. Another papyrus MS, called Egerton Papyrus 2, a fragment of what has been called

"The Unknown Gospel," displaying narrative portions that bear great resemblance to John (especially) and the synoptic Gospels, has been dated around 140-160—providing yet another early testimony to the Gospels (see *The New Gospel Fragments,* H. I. Bell).

Some of the early papyri also show that various books of the NT were being collected into groups—the Gospels (𝔓4/64/67—see comments on 𝔓4 and 𝔓75), the Gospels and Acts (𝔓45), Paul's Epistles (𝔓46), and General Epistles (𝔓72). Before the NT canon was fixed (367 in the eastern part of the church—viz., the Thirty-ninth Paschal Letter of Athanasius—and 397 in the western part of the church—viz., the Council at Carthage), Christians were copying parts of the NT text and compiling various NT books into separate volumes.

The early Christians were among the first to use the form of a book called a *codex,* instead of a roll or scroll (see C. H. Roberts's article, "Books in the Graeco-Roman World and in the New Testament" in *Cambridge History of the Bible,* Vol. 1). A codex was constructed by folding one or more sheets of papyrus or vellum in the middle and sewing them together at the spine. This construction was most advantageous because (1) it enabled the scribe to write on both sides (most scrolls had writing on one side only); (2) it facilitated easier access to particular passages (as opposed to a scroll, which had to be unrolled); (3) it enabled the Christians to bind together all four Gospels (or any combination thereof) or all of Paul's Epistles, etc.; and (4) it made it easier for any individual or local church to make its own volumes of the NT or any portion thereof (see Metzger's *The Text of the New Testament,* 6). Since papyrus was cheaper than vellum, it was used more often by individuals and local churches. Fortunately, the dry climate of Egypt has preserved many of these papyrus MSS.

Christians began to make copies of the autographs soon after they were written. Individuals would want a copy of a certain NT book (such as a Gospel, like John or Matthew), and various local churches, for example, would want to get a copy of Paul's letter to a neighboring church. From the first century into the second and third, various books of the NT were copied over and over again by some Christians—for personal use and use in local churches. Those made for personal use varied in quality of penmanship. Some papyrus MSS were written in a crude hand (such as 𝔓10, 22, 27); others bear the mark of better craftsmanship (such as 𝔓20, 21, 66); still others look nearly professional (such as 𝔓4, 38, 39, 75). For the most part, the NT papyri were written in what papyrologists call the "documentary" hand—that is, the handwriting reveals that the scribes were educated men—familiar with books and writing, but were not trained, professional scribes (see Roberts, op. cit., 63-64). Among some of the early papyri that have been discovered there appear to be those that were used by churches. For example, 𝔭30 was probably part of a church lectionary, for it contains markings for a reader. 𝔭24 "was once a large leaf of a papyrus codex, a church Bible" (Schofield, *The Papyrus Fragments of the Greek New Testament,* 203). And many scholars think that the Chester Beatty Papyri (𝔭45, 46, 47) and Bodmer Papyri (𝔭66, 72, 75) were discovered in a church library near Atfih or Panopolis, Egypt (see "Place of Discovery" under 𝔭45 and 𝔭66 in Section 2).

Since the earliest copies of the NT were not made by professional scribes, the MSS were rarely checked by a corrector (as would be done in a scriptorium) or proofread thoroughly (which was the normal responsibility of professional scribes). (There is one noteworthy exception among the papyri: the scribe of 𝔭66 made nearly five hundred corrections to his own manuscript.) Nonetheless, many of the papyri were produced by literate men who were working on a document that they knew would be used by a church for reading. With this knowledge, many such scribes did their best to produce a good copy. But when these Christian scribes made copies of various parts of the NT, it is quite unlikely that they had much thought of preserving a piece of literature for the future. Almost all the first-century Christians expected the imminent return of Jesus Christ. Furthermore, the early Christians did not necessarily treat the NT text as a "sacred" text— i.e., as a fixed, written, canonized text, sacred to the very letter. Some of the scribes may have considered themselves to have been inspired by the Spirit in making certain adjustments to the exemplar (a model text used for making other copies) before them. Most of the scribes felt free to express their individuality by creating their own punctuation, paragraph markings, and notation of certain words which they believed were (or were not) *nomina sacra* (i.e., divine titles)—although it must be noted that there was a high degree of regularity in writing words like "Jesus," "Christ," "God," "Lord," and "Savior" as *nomina sacra*. By contrast, the Jews had come to regard the OT text with deep reverence and therefore copied it with extreme fidelity. But not necessarily so with the early Christians. It took a while before certain books of the NT were even regarded as worthy of acceptance into the NT canon. Books like Hebrews, James, 2 Peter, 2 and 3 John, and

Revelation were not readily received by all the church. We must remember that the early church primarily used the OT (the Septuagint translation) as its text for exposition, recitation, and meditation when the believers assembled (see Acts 4:24-26; 15:13-18; Eph. 5:19; Col. 3:16; 1 Tim. 4:13; 2 Tim. 3:14-17). Writings of the NT were, at first, secondary to the OT text. With time, however, the order was reversed.

During this transition (which lasted from the end of the first century to the end of fourth century), the NT was copied again and again—with varying degrees of fidelity. In their analysis of the early papyri, Kurt and Barbara Aland have noted four kinds of textual fidelity, which they call "normal," "free," "strict," and "at least normal." I assume the Alands are speaking of textual fidelity to an exemplar and not to the original, for no one could know for certain how close a MS copy is to the original. And regarding textual fidelity to an exemplar—how can one know for sure if a scribe has produced a *strict* copy of his exemplar? Thus, the Alands' designations must be taken with caution. The Alands say the *normal* text is found in MSS in which the scribes transmitted the exemplar with a limited amount of variation characteristic of the NT textual tradition. The *normal* text is found in MSS like 𝔓4, 5, 12, 16, 18, 20, 28, 52, and 87. The *strict* text is found in those MSS in which the scribes reproduced the text of an exemplar with greater fidelity than in the *normal* text—although still with certain characteristic liberties.

In short, the *strict* text exhibits far less variation than the *normal* text. The *strict* text is found in MSS like 𝔓1, 23, 27, 35, 39, 64/67, 65, 70, and 75. Other papyri, however, display a very *free* rendition of the text—that is, they are characterized as having a greater degree of variation than the *normal* text. The *free* text is found in MSS like 𝔓9, 13, 37, 40, 45, 46, 66, 69, and 78. The fourth category, called *at least normal,* includes those MSS that are *normal* but also display a distinct tendency toward a *strict* text. The *at least normal* papyri are 𝔓15, 22, 30, 32, 72, and 77. The Alands have recognized another group of papyri that form a unit of their own, for they represent early precursors to the D-type text; there are three such papyri: 𝔓29, 38, and 48. (See Alands' *The Text of the New Testament,* 56ff., for a full discussion of the aforementioned categories.) Of course, all these designations of "kinds" of texts are spoken of with respect to fidelity to an exemplar, not necessarily to the original text; therefore, one cannot automatically think that the papyri with a *strict* text are those that best represent the original, even though there is a good chance that they do preserve a very ancient reading. All the facets of textual criticism must be at work to determine the original text.

During the early stages of the transmission of the NT text, certain changes began to be incorporated into the text—most unintentional but some intentional. The unintentional errors are mainly transcriptional mistakes, such as dittography, haplography, homoeoteleuton, and itacism. The intentional emendations fall into one of seven categories: (1) additions from oral tradition (such as the story about the adulteress in John 7:53–8:11 [see comments on this passage in Section 3]); (2) additions for liturgical use (such as the addition to the Lord's prayer at the end of Matt. 6:13); (3) additions due to the influence of certain ascetic practices (such as the addition of "and fasting" to "prayer" in Mark 9:29 and 1 Cor. 7:5 [see comments on these passages in Section 3]); (4) emendations due to the tamperings of heretics (such as the change in Luke 3:22 from "this is my beloved Son in whom I am well pleased" to "this is my Son; this day I have begotten you"—a statement used by the Adoptionists in support of the false notion that Jesus became God's Son at the time of his baptism [see comments on this verse in Section 3]); (5) emendations due to doctrinal biases, especially concerning the Spirit (see comments on John 7:39 in Section 3) and Jesus Christ (see comments on John 1:18; 1 Cor. 10:9; and Jude 5 in Section 3); (6) harmonization—especially among the Gospels; and (7) adjustments made by pious scribes who on occasion thought the readers might get the "wrong" idea about Jesus from the text. Unfortunately, many of the critical emendations (i.e., those affecting the meaning of the text) were incorporated into the NT text before the year 200. The oft-quoted comment made by Origen (born c. 202), probably the first NT textual critic, bears this out: "Nowadays, as is evident, there is a great diversity between the various MSS, either through the negligence of certain copyists, or the perverse audacity shown by some in correcting the text, or through the fault of those who, playing the part of correctors, lengthen or shorten it as they please" (*In Matth.* tom. 15, 14).

Since textual corruption happened at such an early date, it is very important that textual critics have access to the earliest MSS. The scholars of the nineteenth century had good MSS from the fourth century (Codex Vaticanus, Codex Sinaiticus, Codex Ephraemi Rescriptus). The scholars of the twentieth century have had access to several papyrus MSS dated in the second, third, or early fourth centuries. These MSS have greatly facilitated the task of recovering the original wording of the Greek NT. But not all the scholars agree as to how to interpret the data the early papyri provide. Although almost all scholars will admit that many of the major changes happened prior to the third century, not all agree as to how these changes were made. Some scholars have thought that there were purposed, "organized" recensions of the text (i.e., major recensions instigated by important church leaders or ecclesiastical centers); others have believed that the major emendations were the work of various scribes working independently from one another.

In the past, several scholars have attempted to identify specific recensions in the second or third century—both in the West and in (or around) Alexandria; but present-day scholars in the main have asserted that there is no substantial evidence to prove any second- or third-century recensions. The Alands have argued quite convincingly that there was no person in the West during the second and third centuries who would have been capable of organizing a recension or doing one himself (see *Text*, 54-55). And Gordon Fee has argued just as convincingly that there was not any kind of Alexandrian recension in the second or third century (see "𝔭66, 𝔭75, and Origen: The Myth of the Early Textual Recension in Alexandria" in *New Dimensions in New Testament Study*, 19-45).

To these assessments it could be added that there was not any kind of Egyptian (as distinct from Alexandrian) recension in the second or third century. An analysis of the early papyri—all discovered in Upper and Middle Egypt (Alexandria is in Lower Egypt)—affirms this. Several papyri, discovered in the same region (whether Oxyrhynchus or the Fayum) and dated about the same age (200–300), display significant differences in their texts. The papyri discovered in Oxyrhynchus (𝔭1, 5, 9, 10, 13, 15, 16, 17, 18, 19, 20, 21, 22, 23, 24, 26, 27, 28, 29, 30, 39, 51, 69, 70, 71, 77, 78, 90) do not show textual uniformity, nor do the papyri most likely discovered at the church library in Atfih/Panopolis (𝔭45, 46, 47, 66, 72, 75). This diversity shows that individual scribes in the same locality worked independently from one another. This diversity also shows that neither the church, scriptorium, nor catechetical school in Alexandria were exerting much influence on the rest of the churches in Egypt—especially with regard to the NT text.

This does not mean, however, that the churches in the Fayum and Oxyrhynchus were isolated from Alexandria and the rest of the Mediterranean world. Colin H. Roberts has argued in *Manuscript, Society, and Belief in Early Christian Egypt* that the evidence of all the papyri discovered in Oxyrhynchus and the Fayum show that there was a healthy flow of communication between scholars and others who lived in Upper and Middle Egypt and those who lived in Alexandria and beyond. E. G. Turner's studies of the papyri support this view. Turner has said that the various papyri discovered in Oxyrhynchus, Egypt (a site which has yielded many papyri, several of which have portions of the NT), and other sites in Upper and Middle Egypt, have disclosed, for example, that (1) scholars from Oxyrhynchus were exchanging notes with other Alexandrian scholars about how to procure works of scholarship; (2) several Alexandrians lived in cities in Middle and Upper Egypt; and (3) people from Rome brought books with them into Middle and Upper Egypt (*Greek Papyri*, 80–87). Furthermore, Roberts believes that some of the scribes in Middle and Upper Egypt probably knew of Alexandrian scriptorial practices (see *Manuscript*, 24)—perhaps as early as 180 (the time at which Pantaneus was first associated with the scriptorium at Alexandria).

Roberts also argued that all of the early MSS compiled by Christian scribes reveal an affinity in the use of *nomina sacra* (the abbreviation of divine titles—for example: $\overline{\Theta\Sigma} = \theta\epsilon o\varsigma$, $\overline{K\Sigma} = \kappa\upsilon\rho\iota o\varsigma$, $\overline{I\Sigma} = I\eta\sigma o\upsilon\varsigma$, $\overline{\Pi N A} = \pi\nu\epsilon\upsilon\mu\alpha$). Roberts believes that as early as A.D. 70 Christians invented a special way of writing out *nomina sacra* as a distinctive for Christian literature, as opposed to Jewish and secular literature. This practice could have been developed first in Jerusalem, Antioch, or Alexandria. From one of these localities, the practice of writing divine titles as *nomina sacra* in early Christian literature (the NT and other noncanonical books) spread throughout the Mediterranean world. Christian scribes everywhere, beginning from the end of the first century, were abbreviating the divine titles in the same way. This phenomenon reveals that there must have been a format which all Christian scribes could follow (see *Manuscript*, 44–48).

Furthermore, Roberts has posited the view that the early Christian churches in Egypt (outside of Alexandria) were fairly normal churches, affected by some Gnostic influences (but hardly as much as was thought before), existing with local autonomy, and living in independence from any hierarchical dominance such as could have come from Alexandria—but really did not come until the fourth century. The papyri that have been discovered reveal that the early Christians in Egypt read the OT and various portions of the NT. The NT they read was not emended by Gnostic influence—for even the earliest African Gnostics, such as Basilides and Valentinus, did not alter the text; rather, they gave it a new interpretation (see Hort's *Two Dissertations*, 9ff.). Since all of our papyri have come from Middle and Upper Egypt, it is helpful to know that the situation in early Christian Egypt was not atypical of the situation in the rest of the Christian church at that time.

All this tells us that the NT papyri discovered in this part of the world present a fair sampling of what might be found in early papyri all over the Graeco-Roman world. In fact, some scholars have thought that several of the NT papyri discovered in Egypt may actually have been transported there from other countries. We know that books were taken into Middle Egypt from as far as Rome (see Turner, *Greek Papyri*, 86–87)—why not copies of the NT also? The third-century NT MS 𝔓13 (discovered in Oxyrhynchus) is a prime example of a transported NT MS. In the case of 𝔓13 the text of Hebrews was written on the back of the papyrus containing the new epitome of Livy. Therefore, it is likely that this MS was brought to Egypt by a Roman official and left behind when he left his post. (An auxiliary Roman cohort was stationed in Oxyrhynchus as early as the second century A.D.—ibid., 81–82.) Most likely, some other NT papyri are not indigenous to Egypt—even though all the NT papyri have been discovered there.

Wherever the early papyri originated, some of the NT papyri that have been discovered show remarkable similarities with later MSS. In fact, several of the extant early papyri are related to many later MSS (fourth century and beyond)—or at least share a common ancestor. We know this because many of the later MSS have distinct textual affinities with specific early papyrus MSS. For example, 𝔓75 (or the like) was a precursor to Codex Vaticanus in Luke and John—for both MSS seem to have shared a common ancestor, 𝔓46 (or the like) a precursor to Codex Vaticanus in some of the Pauline Epistles (like Ephesians and Colossians), 𝔓66 a relative of Codex Sinaiticus in portions of John, 𝔓72 a distant relative to B in 1 Peter, and 𝔓38 a precursor to the D-type text (or Codex Bezae). (See comments on "Textual Character" under each of the papyri just mentioned.) With respect to the Gospel of John, for which we have the most extant papyri—twenty-two to date (𝔓2, 5, 6, 22, 28, 36, 39, 44, 45, 52, 55, 59, 60, 63, 66, 75, 76, 80, 84, 90, 93, 95)—several of the early papyri (early second to early fourth century) appear to have been precursors to specific fourth- and fifth-century codices. 𝔓6, 𝔓28, 𝔓39, and especially 𝔓75 are related to B; 𝔓5, 𝔓22 (in part), and 𝔓66 are related to ℵ; and 𝔓22 (in part) and 𝔓45 (in part) are related to D.

Eldon Epp has suggested that we look upon the history of the textual transmission of the NT from the early papyri to later MSS as forming trajectories or textual streams. He sees one line (called "Alexandrian" or "Neutral"—the designation given by Westcott and Hort to B and then ℵ) as "plotted first from 𝔓75, then perhaps through 𝔓23, 𝔓20, 0220, 𝔓50, etc. to Codex B and thence on through the centuries, e.g., to Codex L (eighth century), MSS 33 (ninth century), 1739 (tenth century), and 579 (thirteenth century)." He sees another line (called "Western" or D-type) as beginning from "𝔓5 and 𝔓29 through 𝔓48, 38, 37, and 0171, then to codices D and Dp and thence on through the centuries to Fp and Gp (ninth century) and MSS 614 and 383 (thirteenth century)." Several other papyri (such as 𝔓46 and 𝔓66), Epp says, stand midway between the aforementioned trajectories and do not develop textual streams of their own—with the exception of 𝔓45, which leads abortively to W (see "The Twentieth Century Interlude in New Testament Textual Criticism," the W. H. P. Hatch Memorial Lecture, The Society of Biblical Literature, November, 1973).

Epp's trajectories are not the same as stemmas (a genealogical list of direct relationships); he makes it very clear that we cannot, as of yet, reproduce a genealogical lineage back to the originals. Thus, his trajectory model is an attempt to show that there was the beginning of two distinct textual streams in the early periods of textual transmission—one leading to an Alexandrian type text and another to a "Western" or D-type text. Besides the later Syrian or Byzantine text type, these are the only two early text types that scholars continue to recognize—and even at that, there is debate about whether there is such a thing as a "Western" text.

The scribes at Alexandria must have used early papyri (much like those now known to us) in composing their NT texts. Probably they functioned somewhat like textual critics in selecting the best reading where variants occurred—so as to produce what might be called a good, edited text. Most likely, a definite Alexandrian recension of the text did not begin until the third and fourth centuries—and this recension was more in line with what we would now call "copyediting" (as opposed to "substantive editing") and minor textual criticism. In other words, it seems that the Alexandrian scribes did not greatly change the substance or meaning of the text; rather, they polished it grammatically and stylistically. Thus, an Alexandrian MS reflects a fairly accurate text. Bruce Metzger said that scholars "are still inclined to regard the Alexandrian text as on the whole the best ancient recension and the one most nearly approximating the original" (*The Text of the Greek New Testament*, 216).

The so-called "Western" form of text is as early as the Alexandrian, for it was used by Marcion, Irenaeus, Tertullian, and Cyprian—all of whom were alive in the second century. Unfortunately, we do not possess as many early "Western" MSS as those called "Alexandrian." (The climate of the western regions of the Mediterannean is hardly as good as that of Egypt for perserving ancient documents.) Though the "Western" text was early, it is characterized as being an uncontrolled, popular text—a type of text that incorporates many interpolations. Westcott and Hort characterized the "Western" text as one in which the scribes had a "disposition to enrich the text at the cost of its purity by alterations or additions taken from traditional and perhaps from apocryphal and other non-biblical sources" (*The New Testament in the Original Greek*, 134). The "Western" text was given its name because this type of text circulated in western countries like North Africa, Italy, and Gaul. However, "Western" is a misnomer inasmuch as MSS that have been classified "Western" are so named usually on the basis that they are non-Alexandrian. E. C. Colwell has said, "The so-called Western text or Delta type text is the uncontrolled, popular edition of the second century. It has no unity and should not be referred to as the 'Western text'" (*Studies in Methodology in Textual Criticism of the New Testament*, 53). Nonetheless, a number of papyrus MSS have been discovered in Egypt that have been labeled "Western" by various scholars—for example, Metzger labels 𝔭29, 38, and 48 as "Western" (*Text*, 214).

Scholars are more certain about the development of another text type called "Syrian," "Byzantine," or "Koine." Once the Diocletian persecution passed (c. 311), which was a persecution noted for its destruction of many copies of the NT, the church was anxious to reproduce many copies of the Greek NT. In Syria, Lucian of Antioch labored toward this end. L. D. Twilley wrote, "Lucian carefully compared different readings of the New Testament with those with which he was acquainted and produced a revised form of the text. This 'revised text' soon became very popular, not only at Antioch, where Lucian worked, but also at Constantinople, and, before long, all over the Mediterranean area" (*The Origin and Transmission of the New Testament*, 44–45).

As far as we know, Lucian's work was the first major recension of the Greek NT. This recension involved a great deal of harmonization (especially in the Gospels), emendation, and some interpolation. The Lucian recension seems to have relied more heavily on so-called "Western" MSS than "Alexandrian." From the fourth century onward, this recension became the most prevailing type of text throughout the Greek-speaking world. In fact, it became (with minor modifications) the received text of the Greek Orthodox Church.

From the fourth until the eighth century, the Byzantine text was revised even further until it was nearly standardized. From then on, almost all MSS followed the Byzantine text, including those MSS that were used by Erasmus in compiling the text that would eventually become the Textus Receptus (TR). The majority of the MSS, therefore, are Byzantine. Although a few textual scholars have argued for the trustworthiness of the "Majority Text" (as it has been called by Hodges and Farstad—see their introduction to *The Greek New Testament According to the Majority Text*), most scholars look to the earlier and fewer MSS in their work to recover the original wording of the Greek text. This is not to say that the same textual scholars altogether discount late MSS—for several late MSS have in fact preserved very early readings.

With respect to the foregoing discussion, it is important for us to remember that we have been speaking about the relationship between the early papyri and later MSS—MSS which have been classified as Alexandrian, Western, and Byzantine by various scholars. The same designations have been given to the early papyri. This can be misleading, for while it is true that there are affinities between some of the early MSS and later ones, the early ones do not always fit the later designations. For example, $\mathfrak{P}66$ is not fully Alexandrian nor fully Western nor fully Byzantine. Scholars are hardpressed to give $\mathfrak{P}66$ a fitting label. Some have attempted to distinguish the early MSS from the later ones by appending the word *proto* or *pre* to the label. For example, Metzger calls $\mathfrak{P}45$ (in Acts), $\mathfrak{P}46$, $\mathfrak{P}66$, and $\mathfrak{P}75$ "Proto-Alexandrian" (*The Text of the New Testament*, 216), and the Alands call $\mathfrak{P}29$, $\mathfrak{P}38$, and $\mathfrak{P}48$ "precursors or branches of the D text" (*The Text of the New Testament*, 93). Another approach would be to create new classifications that still retain the associations with the standard text types yet give new identity to the early papyri in their own right. Eldon Epp, for example, has created four textual groups, which he calls the "A" group (for the "accepted" text—the Byzantine text, in which he places some later papyri: $\mathfrak{P}42$, 68, 74[?], 84), the "B" group (having associations with "B," Codex Vaticanus—in which he places most of the early papyri: $\mathfrak{P}1$, 4, 10, 13, 16,

15, 20, 23, 28, 39, 40, 46, 47, 49, 52, 53, 62, 64/67, 65, 66, 71, 72 [in Peter], 75, 86, 91, 92), the "C" group (having associations with the Caesarean text type—in which he places 𝔭45 [in Mark] and other papyri known to have mixtures of "B" and "D": 𝔭8, 27, 35, 37[?]), and the "D" group (having associations with the "D-text" and the Western text—in which he places 𝔭5, 19[?], 21[?], 25[?], 29, 37[?], 38, 48, 69, 72 [in Jude]). Obviously, these groupings call for further investigation—especially the "D" group (note how many MSS are in question), but they are the beginning of a new mode of classification of textual affinities—especially for the early papyri. Hopefully, such groupings can help us see the patterns of early textual transmission and aid us in the ongoing search to recover the original text of the NT. (For more on Epp's groupings, see "The Significance for Determining the Nature of the New Testament Text in the Second Century: A Dynamic View of Textual Transmission.")

As was stated earlier, most of the significant theological changes in the NT text occurred prior to any kind of organized recension. These changes, however, tended to be isolated and then perpetuated in various MSS belonging to a particular text type. By identifying a MS with a particular text type, a textual critic can more readily value the worth of various readings in that MS. Generally speaking, a reading present in a MS belonging to the Alexandrian text type is given considerable weight—more so than a reading found in a MS belonging to the Western text type, and definitely more so than a reading found in a Byzantine MS. A reading found in several early MSS belonging to the Alexandrian text type and the Western text type has a good chance of being original.

The current praxis of textual critics attempting to reconstruct the text of the Greek NT is to examine each variation unit. According to Epp, a variation unit "is that length of the text (1) where our Greek New Testament MSS present at least two variant forms *and* (2) where each variant form is supported by at least two Greek manuscripts" ("Toward the Clarification of the Term 'Textual Variant,'" in *Studies in New Testament Language and Text*, 156). The textual critic must have knowledge of the MSS, knowledge of the NT book and the proclivities of the writer, and knowledge of the praxis of textual criticism before he or she can determine the reading most likely written by the original author. The textual critic today cannot adopt a reading just because it is supported by Codex Vaticanus (as did Westcott and Hort) or just because it is supported by an early papyrus MS or two. The situation is too complex for such a simplistic approach; there is too much evidence that must be weighed. Nevertheless, the papyri still figure very heavily in any evaluation because they represent, in many cases, the earliest extant readings. And most scholars still consider that the earliest reading is very often the best reading.

This approach to textual criticism has been called "eclectic"—inasmuch as the critic picks and chooses one reading from the rest on a case by case basis. The critic does not come to his task ready to follow rigidly a predetermined stemma or to adhere to a particular MS or group of MSS. He examines all the variations in each variation unit to determine what reading is the one from which the others most likely deviated. The resultant text, therefore, will not necessarily be a "Western" type text or an "Alexandrian" type text per se, but an eclectic text. This eclecticism is clearly manifest in recent critical editions of the Greek NT.

Eclecticism in textual criticism has spilled over into the praxis of producing English translations of the NT. In recent years, most English translators do not rigidly follow any particular edition of the Greek NT. For example, some translators may have used a specific edition of the Nestle text as a working base, but they deviated from the text at will—choosing rather to follow, here and there, a variant reading cited in the apparatus. This was the case with the RSV, NASB, NIV, and TEV. With respect to this book, it is important to note the places in which the translators may have been influenced by the evidence of the papyri in selecting one reading over against another.

THE EFFECT OF EARLY NEW TESTAMENT PAPYRUS MANUSCRIPTS ON CRITICAL EDITIONS OF THE GREEK NEW TESTAMENT (ESPECIALLY THE NESTLE TEXT)

With few exceptions, the NT papyri have all been discovered (and published) in the last one hundred years. In 1868 Tischendorf published the first papyrus MS, which is now designated 𝔓11 (from the seventh century, containing portions of 1 Cor.). Shortly thereafter, two more papyri were published by Gregory (who wrote the Prolegomena for Tischendorf's eighth edition of the Greek NT) and Tischendorf: 𝔓7 (fourth to sixth century, containing Luke 4:1-2) and 𝔓8 (sixth century, retaining portions of Acts 4, 5, and 6). In 1889 Vincent Scheil discovered 𝔓4 (third century, containing portions of Luke 1-4) in Coptos, Egypt. Around 1898 Carl Wessely and J. Rendel Harris published two papyri: 𝔓3 (sixth century, displaying portions of Luke 7 and 10) and 𝔭14 (fifth century, containing portions of 1 Cor. 1-3). All the rest of the papyri (of which there are now ninety-six) were discovered since 1897.

In 1897 Grenfell and Hunt went to Oxyrhynchus, Egypt, in search of ancient Christian documents. They picked Oxyrhynchus (now called El-Bahnasa) because Christianity had taken a firm foothold in Oxyrhynchus both before and after the Diocletian persecution (303), and it was supposed that the citizens would be able to afford libraries of literary texts and that the rubbish heaps of this city would contain ancient Christian texts (Schofield, *The Papyrus Fragments of the Greek New Testament*, 7ff.). A text found in a rubbish heap does not indicate that it was indeed "rubbish" or defective. When a copy of a piece of literature became old and worn, it was customary to replace it with a fresh copy and then discard the old one. The Egyptians are known to have disposed of such copies, not by burning them, but by putting them into rubbish heaps. Excavators looking for ancient Egyptian papyri would search for ancient rubbish heaps in deserted town sites on ground higher than the Nile. Excavators would also look in tombs, cemeteries, funerary shrines, monasteries, and church buildings. Grenfell and Hunt were very fortunate in their choice of the ancient rubbish heap at Oxyrhynchus, for it is the largest cache of papyri ever discovered (Turner, *Greek Papyri*, 26 and 33).

On the second day of the dig, Grenfell and Hunt unearthed (among many papyri fragments) the apocryphal "Sayings of Jesus" or "Logia" and a papyrus leaf containing Matthew 1 on the recto and verso. At the time of this discovery, this was the earliest extant copy of any NT portion—at least one hundred years earlier than Codex Vaticanus. In 1898 the first volume of *Oxyrhynchus Papyri* was published, including "Logia" (later identified as belonging to the "Gospel according to Thomas") and 𝔭1 (displaying Matt. 1). The discovery of 𝔭1 proved to be an auspicious beginning of many more discoveries. Grenfell and Hunt continued to excavate Oxyrhynchus until 1907; thereafter, the Italian exploration society (under G. Vitelli) continued the work there (from 1910 to 1913, and 1927 to 1934). In total, twenty-eight papyrus MSS containing portions of the NT were found at Oxyrhynchus—almost all of which date between 200 and 400. Although most of the Oxyrhynchus papyri are quite fragmentary (usually containing only one or two leaves), they have provided a broad sampling of many verses from several NT books at an early date. Twenty-one of these papyri were published by 1922: 𝔭1, 5, 9, 10, 13, 15, 16, 17, 18, 19, 20, 21, 22,

23, 24, 26, 27, 28, 29, 30, and 39 (see descriptions of each papyrus in Section 2). One Oxyrhynchus papyrus was published in 1941—p51; three more were published in 1957—p69, 70, and 71; two more in 1968—p77 and 78; one more in 1983—p90 (see descriptions of each papyrus in Section 2). Undoubtedly, more Oxyrhynchus NT papyri will be published, for the papyrologists have not yet worked their way through all the papyri discovered there.

In addition to the Oxyrhynchus papyri, several other papyri were discovered and published before 1930—making a total of forty-two, twenty-three of which are third/fourth century. But the papyri discovered before this time did not have much of an effect on critical editions of the Greek NT. The eighth edition of Tischendorf's Greek NT was not affected by the few papyri he published. Westcott and Hort did not even mention the papyri in their companion volume to their Greek NT (*An Introduction to the Greek New Testament*). The Greek text edited by von Soden (1913) lists only twelve papyri in the apparatus. The Nestle text did not include any citations from the papyri until the thirteenth edition (1927), which was the year Nestle's son, Erwin, took over the work. This edition included a few citations from a few papyri like p1 and p13. Before the 1930s, the papyri were considered too fragmentary and too insignificant (especially by comparison to the stature of the great codices, Vaticanus and Sinaiticus) to be of much import. Speaking of these papyri, Frederic G. Kenyon said these small fragments were individually of "almost no importance, but collectively they have some value as giving us a glimpse into the condition of the New Testament text in Egypt in the early centuries" (*Recent Developments in the Textual Criticism of the Greek Bible*, 33).

In the early 1930s, three papyrus MSS—p45, 46, and 47, known as the Chester Beatty Papyri (named after the owner, Chester Beatty of Dublin)—were discovered and published. These were the greatest discoveries since Codex Siniaticus and the Freer Gospels. The exact provenance of the Chester Beatty Papyri is unknown since the MSS came through the hands of native dealers by a purchase made in 1930/1931. Quite possibly they came from the ruins of the library of some church or library of a Christian scholar or monastery—perhaps in the Fayum or the east bank of the Nile about Atfih, the ancient Aphroditopolis, from which Antony, the founder of Egyptian monasticism, came (Schofield, *Papyrus Fragments*, 302–303). E. G. Turner, however, has suggested that the Chester Beatty Papyri (and the Bodmer Papyri) came from Panopolis (modern Akmim) because he has noticed several associations between MSS known to have come from Pano-polis and those in the Beatty and Bodmer collections (see his arguments in *Greek Papyri,* 52–53). ℘45 contains portions of each of the four Gospels and Acts; this third-century MS displays the work of an independent scribe (see comments on ℘45 in Section II). ℘46, a MS dated around 200, contains all of Paul's Epistles except 1 and 2 Thessalonians and the Pastoral Epis-tles. ℘47, a third-century text, contains about half the book of Revelation—from Revelation 9 to 17.

The evidence of the Chester Beatty Papyri was added to the critical apparatus of the sixteenth edition of the Nestle text (1936). The RSV (based upon the seventeenth edition of the Nestle text, 1941) was affected by the Chester Beatty Papyri. The RSV's Introduction to the NT (published in 1946) says, "The revisers in the 1870s had most of the evidence we now have for the Greek text, though the most ancient of all extant manuscripts of the Greek New Testament were not discovered until 1931."

The MSS so alluded to are, of course, the Chester Beatty Papyri. F. C. Grant in *An Introduction to the Revised Standard Version of the New Testament* explicitly states how influential the Chester Beatty Papyri were on the revisers of the NT. Speaking for the revisers, he said, "We have made considerable use of the Chester Beatty fragments; in fact we have consulted them constantly, and have occasionally adopted readings from that source, when supported by others. Usually, the Beatty fragments range themselves with Aleph and B, i.e., Sinaiticus and Vaticanus" (41–42). Grant then goes on to give a small list of some important verses in which the RSV differs from the ASV because the revisers followed readings supported by B-Aleph-Chester Beatty (see p. 42 for his list). This study will show exactly how much effect the Chester Beatty Papyri had upon the RSV in all the verses where there is significant textual variation.

After the 1930s, several other early papyri were discovered and pub-lished: namely, ℘48, 49, 50, 51, 52 and 62 (see descriptions of each papyrus MS in Section 2). Among these papyri, ℘52 (containing John 18:31-33, 37-38, in the Rylands collection) received the most attention be-cause it is the earliest copy of any NT fragment—dated between 110–125, only twenty to thirty years after the time John wrote his Gospel, if we accept the date of writing to be c. A.D. 85. The other papyri, though early, are quite fragmentary.

The evidence of the papyri was slowly added to the apparatuses of critical editions of the Greek NT. The twenty-first edition of the Nestle text

(1952) contained citations from twenty-seven papyri (𝔓1, 8, 10, 11, 13, 15, 16, 18, 20, 22, 23, 27, 28, 30, 37, 38, 41, 45, 46, 47, 48, 49, 50, 51, 52, 53, 54); the twenty-second edition (1956) added two more (𝔓25, 40); the twenty-third (1957), three more (𝔓64, 65, 66); the twenty-fourth (1960), two more (𝔓69, 72); the twenty-fifth (1963), three more (𝔓5, 74, 75); and the twenty-sixth (1979), fifty more—for it was in the twenty-sixth edition that Aland supplied a complete listing of all the papyri, even though not all of them were cited in the apparatus (see Eldon Epp's article, "The New Testament Papyrus in Historical Perspective," in *To Touch the Text: Studies in Honor of Joseph A. Fitzmyer, S.J.*). In between the twenty-fifth and twenty-sixth editions of the Nestle text, Kurt Aland joined some other scholars (Black, Metzger, and Wikgren) in producing the United Bible Societies' first edition of the *Greek New Testament* (1966). In this edition, nineteen more papyri were added to what were previously cited in Nestle's twenty-fifth edition: 𝔓2, 4, 6, 21, 24, 26, 33, 36, 39, 58, 59, 60, 61, 63, 67, 68, 70, 71, 76.

In the 1950s and early 1960s, another group of papyri—known as the Bodmer Papyri (named after the owner, Martin Bodmer of Geneva)—were discovered and published. There are five NT papyri in this collection: 𝔓66 (c. 175-200, containing most of John), 𝔓72 (third century, preserving all of 1 and 2 Peter and Jude), 𝔓73 (seventh century, containing a few verses in Matthew 25 and 26), 𝔓74 (seventh century, containing portions of Acts and the General Epistles), and 𝔓75 (c. 200, containing most of Luke and over half of John). Of course, the early papyri, 𝔓66, 72, and 75, are the most important. The Bodmer Papyri aroused significant scholarly inquiry into the NT papyri.

𝔓66, like 𝔓46, is primarily a proto-Alexandrian text, but with many independent readings. The copyist of 𝔓66 corrected his own MS nearly five hundred times—either using another exemplar to make the emendations or adjusting his errant text to his primary exemplar. The copyist of 𝔓72 produced an Alexandrian text—especially in 1 and 2 Peter, while Jude contains many independent readings. The text produced by the scribe of 𝔓75, however, is a very "strict," accurate MS. In fact, it seems to have been the kind of MS used in formulating Codex Vaticanus—for the readings of 𝔓75 and B are remarkably similar (see "Papyrus Bodmer XV (𝔓75) and the Text of Codex Vaticanus" by Calvin Porter in the *Journal of Biblical Literature*, 81 [1962], 363–376). Prior to the discovery of 𝔓75, certain scholars thought Codex Vaticanus was the work of a fourth-century recension; others (chiefly Hort) thought it must trace back to a very early and accurate copy. Hort said that Codex Vaticanus preserves "not only a very ancient text, but a very pure line of a very ancient text" (*Introduction*, 250–251). 𝔓75 appears to have shown that Hort was right.

Prior to the discovery of 𝔓75, many textual scholars were convinced that the second- and third-century papyri displayed a text in flux, a text characterized only by individual independence. The Chester Beatty Papyri (𝔓45, 46, 47) and even the Bodmer Papyri, 𝔓66 and 𝔓72 (in 2 Peter and Jude), show this kind of independence (see comments concerning textual character under each of these papyri). Scholars thought that scribes at Alexandria must have used such texts to produce a good recension—as is exhibited in Codex Vaticanus. But 𝔓75 has proven this theory wrong. What is quite clear now is that Codex Vaticanus was simply a copy (with some modifications) of a MS much like 𝔓75, not a fourth-century recension. This does not automatically mean, however, that 𝔓75 and B represent the original text. What it does mean is that we have a second-century MS showing great affinity with a fourth-century MS whose quality has been highly esteemed.

For now—until we have more discoveries—these are among the best MSS and probably the best representatives of the autographs. But this is still debated by some scholars who think that the esteem given to B and 𝔓75 is based on a subjective appreciation of the kind of text they contain (as over against the D-type text) rather than on any kind of theoretical reconstruction of the early transmission of the text (see Epp's article, "The Twentieth Century Interlude in New Testament Textual Criticism," 390ff.). This same subjective estimation was at work when Hort decided that B was intrinsically superior to D (see *Introduction*, 32–42). But textual critics have not been able to advance beyond Hort in formulating a theory for the early transmission of the text (see, for example, Colwell's "Hort Redivivus: A Plea and a Program," in *Studies in Methodology in Textual Criticism*). This has troubled certain textual scholars, while other scholars have argued that 𝔓75 and other papyri have simply shown that Hort was right—at least about the ancestry of Codex Vaticanus. But the papyri have not solved the problem as to why there were two competing texts as early as the second century: one represented by 𝔓75 etc., leading to B; and the other represented by 𝔓38 etc., leading to D. And so the debate continues, as does the search for the original text.

While the debate goes on, the editors of critical editions of the Greek NT have included the evidence of the papyri in the apparatus and adopted papyrus-supported readings in the text. The Nestle text became more and more influenced by the papyri. When Eberhard Nestle's work was continued by his son, Erwin, beginning in 1927 (the time of the thirteenth edition), he began to add evidence to the critical apparatus from various MSS in successive editions of the text. Kurt Aland became associated with the work in 1950; he began to add the evidence of more papyri to the critical apparatus beginning with the twenty-first edition (1951) until the twenty-fifth edition (1963). But the text itself was not changed until the twenty-sixth edition (1979). During the eighty years of its existence, through twenty-five editions, the text "remained the same (apart from a few minor changes adapted by Erwin Nestle—no more than a dozen at most)" (Aland and Aland, *The Text of the New Testament,* 26). The latest edition (the twenty-sixth) of Nestle-Aland's *Novum Testamentum Graece* involved a number of changes in the text—many due to the evidence of the papyri.

Kurt Aland, probably more than any other twentieth-century NT scholar, has been the champion of the NT papyri. Aland has headed up an institute in Münster, West Germany, called Institut für Neutestamentliche Textforschung. At this institute, Aland and his associates have collected, photographed, documented, and studied hundreds of MSS—including papyri, uncials, and miniscules. Aland himself has given special attention to the papyri. In the most recent edition of the Nestle text, now called the Nestle-Aland text (the twenty-sixth edition, 1979), eighty-eight papyri were used in formulating the text and/or were cited in the apparatus. Among these eighty-eight papyri are several early MSS that were discovered and/or published after the time of the Bodmer Papyri. Thus, the twenty-sixth edition of the Nestle-Aland text includes such papyri as $\mathfrak{P}$64/67 (c. 200, containing portions of Matt. 3, 5, and 26), $\mathfrak{P}$70 (third century, containing portions of Matt. 2, 11, 12, and 24), $\mathfrak{P}$77 (c. 200, containing a few verses from Matt. 23), $\mathfrak{P}$78 (third/fourth century, preserving four verses from Jude), $\mathfrak{P}$81 (fourth century, displaying parts of 1 Peter 2 and 3), $\mathfrak{P}$85 (fourth/fifth century, showing parts of Rev. 9 and 10), $\mathfrak{P}$86 (fourth century, containing a few verses in Matt. 5), $\mathfrak{P}$87 (third century, preserving five verses of Philemon), and $\mathfrak{P}$88 (fourth century, displaying most of Mark 2). In the eighth printing of this edition (1985), two more papyri were added—namely, $\mathfrak{P}$89 (fourth century, containing Heb. 6:7-9, 15-17) and $\mathfrak{P}$92 (third/fourth century, containing portions of Eph. 1 and 2 Thess. 1). As new papyri are found and published, the Institute studies each document and then Aland sees to it that any pertinent evidence is added to the next printing of the Nestle-Aland text. In future printings, we should see the inclusion of 𝔭90 (second century, containing John 18:36–19:7), 𝔭91 (c. 200, a fragment displaying parts of Acts 2:30-37, 46–3:2), 𝔭93 (fourth/ fifth century, containing John 13:15-17), 𝔭94 (third century, displaying parts of Acts 2:30-37, 46–3:2), and 𝔭95 (third century, containing John 5:26-29, 36-38).

As was stated earlier, many of the modern English translations generally followed one edition or another of the Nestle text—usually following the reading of the text and sometimes choosing a reading in the apparatus. Realizing that translators (of any language) use this eclectic approach and that they therefore need a critical apparatus that gives variant readings which affect the text only with respect to significant changes in meaning, the United Bible Societies prepared an edition of the *Greek New Testament* in which a full citation is given in the critical apparatus for select, significant variants. After the United Bible Societies had published two editions of the *Greek New Testament,* they decided to unite with the work being done on a new edition of the Nestle-Aland text—and so produce two volumes containing virtually the same text. Now, the United Bible Societies' third edition of the *Greek New Testament* and the Nestle-Aland twenty-sixth edition have the same basic text. Each, however, has different punctuation and a different critical apparatus. The United Bible Societies' text has a plenary listing of the MSS for select variation units; the Nestle-Aland text has a condensed listing of the MS evidence for almost all the variation units.

Since most of the translations I analyzed were based on a particular edition of the Nestle text—or its kindred text produced by the United Bible Societies—it is possible to ascertain which papyri were available to the translators. It is not possible, however, to see how NA[26]—the edition which incorporates the new changes based on the papyri—affected the translations because this text came out after all the translations had already been made. Nonetheless, the translators using the various editions could refer to the evidence in the papyri, whether cited in support of the text or a variant reading.

This Greek text—the UBS[3]/NA[26]—came to be recognized as the text accepted by most of the academic community as representing the best attempt at reconstructing the original text of the Greek NT. This text, however, is by no means "inspired" or infallible—as many scholars will readily attest. In fact, some scholars have openly criticized the UBS[3]/NA[26] as trying to gain the reputation of being the new "Textus Receptus"; and other scholars are discouraged that this new text still looks so much like the Westcott-Hort text. These sentiments are well worth our attention; they caution us to come to this new text with perspicuity. But whatever the criticisms, the UBS[3]/NA[26] is the best critical Greek NT available today. Several new revisions of existing English translations will base their revision on this text. The New Revised Standard Version (appearing in 1990), the revision of Today's English Version, and the revision of The Living Bible will all reflect the text of UBS[3]/NA[26].

A METHOD FOR ANALYZING THE EFFECT OF EARLY PAPYRUS MANUSCRIPTS ON MODERN ENGLISH TRANSLATIONS OF THE NEW TESTAMENT

In proceeding with the analysis of how the NT papyri have affected modern translations of the Greek NT, I found it was essential to set forth certain guidelines to be generally followed, of which there are four:

1. Only readings with "significant" variations are to be analyzed, and those readings must contain evidence from at least one of the early papyri. A "significant" variant is one that substantially changes the meaning of the text; this usually excludes variations of word order and spelling, grammatical aberrations, and variant readings supported only by a few and/or very late MSS. The United Bible Societies' *Greek New Testament* was especially designed to display a full critical apparatus for all "significant" variant readings. The Introduction to this volume says, "The variant readings cited in the textual apparatus are primarily those which are significant for translators or necessary for establishing the text" (xii). There are approximately 1,700 such variations cited; about 725 of these involve the early papyri. In this analysis, I examined each of these variation units. However, I did not proceed with the examination if and when I discovered that all of the English translations followed one reading against another (without even noting the variant reading in the margin) or when only one version cited a variant reading not supported by a papyrus MS. I did not proceed with the examination when I discovered that the translators had chosen the more common spelling of a person's name (regardless of the better-attested variant—as in Matthew's genealogy: "Asa" instead of "Asaph" and "Amon" instead of

"Amos") or that the translators had chosen a particular verb tense (regardless of a better-attested variant) in order to make the English read better.

2. A variation unit is worth examining if there is not concordance among the translations—whether in the text or in the margin.

3. As a prerequisite to the analysis, it is important to note when the evidence of the particular papyrus or papyri was included in a specific edition of the Nestle Greek text. Since several of the most modern, standard English translations basically followed one or another edition of the Nestle text, one can determine if the evidence of a particular papyrus was available to the translators.

4. The final goal of this analysis is to determine where and how the papyri affected modern English translations of the NT.

The marginal notes that pertain to textual variations are very helpful in this sort of study, for they often reveal that the translators were uncertain about which reading was the correct one. Of course, other textual notes are provided to show that the translators have broken with a particular textual tradition. Harold P. Scanlin, in his analysis of textual notes in English translations of the NT, observed the same practice. He said, "These notes were motivated by one of two reasons. At times, there was a concern to acknowledge the existence of a traditional reading that the translators chose not to follow. Sometimes the textual note is a frank recognition on the part of the translators that it is not altogether certain which is the preferred reading" ("Bible Translation as a Means of Communicating New Testament Textual Criticism to the Public," *The Bible Translator,* 39 [Jan. 1988], 111). Unfortunately, these two kinds of notes are not usually differentiated—so that the reader who is not schooled in textual criticism could come to the wrong conclusions, especially about readings that are now generally rejected but are included in the margin because of their place in the tradition of the English Bible. According to Scanlin's count, the Jerusalem Bible has 602 marginal notes pertaining to textual variants, the NEB 269, the RSV 239, the NASB 209, TEV 129, and the NIV 129 (ibid., 113). The difference in number can be partially accounted for by the translators' various views about textual variants: some (as NJB and NEB) were compelled to provide as many alternate readings as possible—even if they thought the readings in the margin could not be the original reading. Others (as TEV and NIV) gave alternate readings only when their translation diverged from a traditional reading or when they thought the marginal reading was possibly the original reading.

THE GREEK TEXTS UNDERLYING THE ENGLISH TRANSLATIONS

The analysis of the effect of the papyri on modern English translations of the NT focuses on four major versions—the American Standard Version (ASV, 1901), the Revised Standard Version (RSV, 1946 for the NT), the New American Standard Bible (NASB, 1971), the New International Version (NIV, 1973), and three others: the New English Bible (NEB, 1970), Today's English Version (TEV, 1969), and the New Jerusalem Bible (NJB, 1986)—with a few select comments on the New Revised Standard Version (NRSV, 1990).

The ASV (which has essentially the same text as the English Revised Version, 1881, with the exception of minor changes made for the American public) serves as the best English translation to reflect the Greek text produced by the end of nineteenth century through the labors of men like Tregelles, Tischendorf, Westcott, and Hort. These men were greatly influenced by Codex Siniaticus and Codex Vaticanus when they compiled a critical edition of the Greek NT, but were hardly influenced by the papyri (for only a few had been discovered and published by then). Thus, the ASV will reflect the influence of these two great uncial MSS and at the same time serve as a point of comparison for the other versions—all of which could have benefited from the papyri.

The RSV is based on the seventeenth edition of the Nestle text (1941), and the NASB on the twenty-third edition (1957). The NIV basically follows the United Bible Societies' first edition of the *Greek New Testament* (1966), as does TEV. Of course, none of these translations slavishly followed the printed text of any of these editions, for the translators operated according to the principle of eclectism—usually choosing a reading from a particular text and occasionally adopting a reading from the critical apparatus.

The RSV should reflect the influence of the papyri discovered before 1940—of which the most important are the Chester Beatty Papyri (𝔓45, 46, 47). In the introduction to the NT of the RSV, the translators alluded to the Chester Beatty Papyri (discovered in the 1930s) as providing a motivation for revising the work done by the English and American revisers in the 1870s. In this introduction they said, "We now possess many more ancient MSS of the New Testament, and are far better equipped to seek to recover the original wording of the Greek text. . . . The revisers in the 1870s had most of the evidence that we now have for the Greek text, though the most ancient of all extant manuscripts of the Greek New Testament were not discovered until 1931." In this study, I gave special attention to analyzing the effect of the Chester Beatty Papyri (as well as other papyri discovered and published before 1940) on the RSV.

Because of the time of their publication, both the NASB and the NIV had opportunity to reflect the effects of papyri discovered after the Chester Beatty Papyri—especially the Bodmer Papyri. In this study, I tried to determine the effect of the Bodmer Papyri (as well as other papyri discovered after the 1940s) on these two translations.

I selected three other versions to analyze—TEV, NEB, and NJB—because these three particular versions are frequently used side-by-side with the other standard versions and because each of these versions displays a different text.

TEV was the first English translation to be based on the United Bible Societies' *Greek New Testament,* first edition (1966). Robert Bratcher, the leading translator of TEV, wrote an article, "The T.E.V. and the Greek Text" (*The Bible Translator* 18 [Oct. 1967], 167–174), in which he describes the places in which the TEV varied from the United Bible Societies' first edition. Currently, TEV is undergoing a revision based on the third edition (1975) of the same Greek text.

The NEB (NT, 1961) is worthwhile to study because it reflects a very eclectic Greek text. In fact, the Greek text for the New English Bible was produced by R. V. G. Tasker after the English translation came out in order to reflect the underlying text decided upon by the translation committee (on a verse-by-verse basis). To say the least, the resultant text is very uneven and yet very interesting. The translators adopted readings never before adopted by English translators—some of them based upon the papyri.

The NJB (NT, 1986) is also worthy of analysis because it, too, displays an eclectic text—especially in the book of Acts, where many "Western" readings were adopted. Furthermore, the papyri have shown their effect on this translation—as can be seen in various marginal notes pertaining to variant readings.

SECTION TWO

A Description of Early
New Testament Manuscripts

A few works are cited throughout this entire second section for which only
the author's last name is provided. (The last name "Aland" signifies both
Kurt and Barbara Aland.) They are as follows:

Kurt and Barbara Aland, *The Text of the New Testament* (1987), "Descrip-
tive List of Papyri," 96–101 and pages displaying photos.

Philip W. Comfort, "Guide to the Ancient Manuscripts" in *Eight Translation New Testament* (eighth printing, 1987).

Jack Finegan, *Encountering New Testament Manuscripts,* 1974.

Frederick C. Grant, "The Greek Text of the New Testament," in *An Introduction to the Revised Standard Version of the New Testament*, 37–43.

W. H. P. Hatch, *The Principal Uncial Manuscripts of the New Testament.*

Bruce M. Metzger, *The Text of the New Testament* (1968; seventh printing,
1980), "Check-list of the Greek Papyri of the New Testament,"
247–256.

Ellwood M. Schofield, "The Papyrus Fragments of the Greek New Testament" (unpublished dissertation, Southern Baptist Theological Seminary, 1936).

R. V. G. Tasker, "Notes on Variant Readings" in *The Greek New Testament*
(being the text translated in the New English Bible, 1961), 411–445.

Karl Wessely, "Les plus anciens monuments du christianisme," in *Patrologia Orientalis* 4/2 (1907).

Every MS listed below is fourth century or earlier. The dates assigned by
Grenfell and Hunt to the MSS discovered in Oxyrhynchus are conservative;
for the most part, the dates could be earlier. See Turner's discussion of this
in *The Typology of the Early Codex* (11). The entry listed as "Photo(s)" is

31

given only for those MSS that are reproduced (whether in whole or part) in the literature known to me. The map of Egypt at the end of the book shows places in Egypt where some of the early papyri were discovered.

EARLY NEW TESTAMENT PAPYRI

Name: 𝔓1 (Pap. Oxy. 2)

Content: Matthew 1:1-9, 12, 14-20

Date: Third century

Place of discovery: Grenfell and Hunt in the winter of 1896-7 went to Oxyrhynchus (now called El-Bahnasa) in search of ancient Christian documents. 𝔓1 was discovered on the second day of the dig. At the time of this discovery, this was considered the earliest extant copy of any NT portion—at least 100 years earlier than Codex Vaticanus. (But see comments on "Date" under 𝔓4.)

Date of publication: 1898

Housing location: Philadelphia, Pennsylvania: University Museum, University of Pennsylvania (E 2746)

Bibliography: Grenfell and Hunt, *Oxyrhynchus Papyri* Vol. 1 (1898), 4–7.
Wessely, 142–44.
Schofield, 89–91.

Photo: Hatch, plate XI, Matt. 1:1-9, 12-13

Inclusion in Greek text: Nestle, 13th edition (1927)

Textual character: The copyist of 𝔓1 seems to have faithfully followed a very reliable exemplar. Where there are major variants, 𝔓1 agrees with the best Alexandrian witnesses, especially Codex Vaticanus (B)—from which it rarely varies.

Significance for text and translations: See Matt. 1:16, 18 (Section 3).

Name: 𝔓4

Content: Luke 1:58-59; 1:62–2:1, 6-7; 3:8–4:2, 29-32, 34-35; 5:3-8; 5:30–6:16

Date: Until recently, 𝔓4 has been dated as a third century (c. 250) MS, but 𝔓4 is either part of the same MS as 𝔓64/67 or the work of the same scribe (see comments there). Since 𝔓64/67 is dated in the early second century, 𝔓4 would also have to have a similar date.

Place of discovery: Coptos (modern name, Qift), Egypt, on the east bank of the Nile, by Fr. Vincent Scheil during his expedition to Upper Egypt in 1889. According to Roberts, 𝔭4 "was used as stuffing for the binding of a codex of Philo, written in the later third century, and found in a jar which had been walled up in a house at Coptos" (*Manuscript, Society, and Belief in Early Christian Egypt,* 7).

Housing location: Paris, France: Bibliothèque Nationale (Suppl. Gr. 1120)

Date of publication: 1892, 1938

Bibliography: Vincent Scheil, "Archéologie, Varia," *Revue Biblique* 1 (1892): 113–115. Jean Merell, "Nouveaux fragments papyrus IV," in *Revue Biblique* 47 (1938): 5–22. Philip Comfort, "Exploring the Common Identification of Three New Testament Manuscripts: 𝔭4, 𝔭64 and 𝔭67," in *Tyndale Bulletin* 46 (1995): 43–54.

Photos: Merell, Luke 1:58-73; 3:20–4:2

Inclusion in Greek text: UBS[1] (1966), NA[26] (1979)

Textual character: Like 𝔭1, 𝔭4 displays a text which was very much like the exemplar used for Codex Vaticanus (B). More often that not, 𝔭4 concurs with B as against ℵ, rather than vice versa. Aland calls this text a "normal" text; Metzger, "proto-Alexandrian."

Significance for text and translations: See Luke 1:68, 78; 3:22, 32-33; 6:1 (Section 3).

Name: 𝔭5 (Pap. Oxy. 208, 1781)

Content: John 1:23-31, 33-40; 16:14-30; 20:11-17, 19-20, 22-25

Date: Third century

Place of discovery: Oxyrhynchus, Egypt, by Grenfell and Hunt. Two separate portions were unearthed from Oxyrhynchus, both from the same papyrus manuscript. The first portion contained John 1:23-31, 33-40 on one fragment and John 20:11-17 on another—probably on the first and last inside quire of a MS containing only the Gospel of John. (The outside quire must have had the very first part and last chapter of John.) This portion was published in volume 2 of *Oxyrhynchus Papyri* in 1899 (no. 208); the second portion—containing John 16:14-30—was not published until 1922 in volume 15 of *Oxyrhynchus Papyri.*

Housing location: London, England: British Library (inv. nos. 782, 2484)

Date of publication: 1899, 1922 (see above under **Place of discovery**)

Bibliography: Grenfell and Hunt, *Oxyrhynchus Papyri* Vol. 2 (1899), 1–8;
   15 (1922), 8–12.
   Schofield, 107–117.
   Wessely, 145–148.

Photo: Hatch, plate VIII, John 16:14-22

Inclusion in Greek text: Nestle, 25th edition (1963)

Textual character: After examining the first portion, Grenfell and Hunt
   said, "The text is a good one, and appears to have affinities with that of
   Codex Sinaiticus, with which the papyrus agrees in several readings not
   found elsewhere." The agreement of 𝔭5 with ℵ against B is evident in
   critical passages (see comments on John 1:34; 16:22; 16:27; 16:28 in
   Section 3). This impression, however, was slightly modified after their
   inspection of the second portion. The affinity between 𝔭5 and ℵ is still
   there, but it is less pronounced. Grenfell and Hunt also noted that
   various corrections were entered on the manuscript by a corrector who
   was not the original scribe but must have been a contemporary. Furthermore, the papyrus is marked for its brevity. Schofield said, "The tendency
   to brevity, especially in omitting unnecessary pronouns, conjunctions,
   etc., is an outstanding feature of the fragment." In short, the text is a
   good example of what Aland would call a "normal" text—i.e., a relatively accurate text manifesting a normal amount of error and idiosyn-
   crasy.

Significance for text and translations: See John 1:34; 16:22, 23, 27
   (Section 3).

Name: 𝔭6

Content: Bilingual—Coptic and Greek. The Greek portion contains John
   10:1-2, 4-7, 9-10; 11:1-8, 45-52.

Date: Fourth century

Place of discovery: Since the kind of Coptic used in this MS belongs to the
   Achmimic dialect, "it is reasonable to suppose it was found in the
   vicinity of Akmim [Panopolis], and possibly from the town itself, where
   important finds of Coptic and Greek manuscripts were made in 1906
   and later" (Schofield).

Housing location: Strasbourg, France: Bibliothèque Nationale et Universitaire (P. Copt. 379, 381, 382, 384)

Date of publication: 1910

Bibliography: Friedrich Rösch, ed., *Bruchstücke des ersten Clemensbrief nach dem achmimischen Papyrus der Strassburger Universitäts- und Landesbibliothek* (Strasbourg, 1910).
Schofield, 118–125.

Inclusion in Greek text: UBS[1] (1966), NA[26] (1979)

Textual character: Metzger says 𝔭6 agrees with B and Θ, which means it is not proto-Alexandrian. Aland calls it a "free text."

Significance for text and translations: See John 11:45 (Section 3).

Name: 𝔭8

Content: Acts 4:31-37; 5:2-9; 6:1-6, 8-15

Date: Fourth century

Place of discovery: Egypt (1903)

Housing location: Berlin, Germany: Staatliche Museen (inv. no. 8683)

Date of publication: 1909

Bibliography: Caspar R. Gregory, *Textkritik des Neuen Testaments III* (Leipzig, 1909), 1087–1090.
Schofield, 128–133.

Inclusion in Greek text: Nestle, 16th edition (1936)

Textual character: The MS contains a mixture of Alexandrian and Western readings; Aland says it displays an independent text. Concerning major variants, 𝔭8 agrees with ℵ and B (see Acts 4:33 and 6:3 in Section 3 and see Acts 5:3 in UBS[3], where 𝔭8 agrees with ℵ[c] B and 0189—a second-century MS).

Significance for text and translations: See Acts 4:33; 6:3 (Section 3).

Name: 𝔭9 (Pap. Oxy. 402)

Content: 1 John 4:11-12, 15-17

Date: Fourth century

Place of discovery: Oxyrhynchus, Egypt, by Grenfell and Hunt

Housing location: Cambridge, Massachusetts: Harvard University, Semitic Museum (no. 3736)

Date of publication: 1903

Bibiliography: Grenfell and Hunt, *Oxyrhynchus Papyri* Vol. 3 (1903), 2–3.

Inclusion in Greek text: NA[26] (1979)

35

Textual character: The MS was written very carelessly. The handwriting is crude and irregular, and the copy contains many unintelligible word spellings.

Significance for text and translations: none (see comments under **Textual character**)

Name: 𝔓10 (Pap. Oxy. 209)

Content: Romans 1:1-7

Date: c. 320

Place of discovery: Oxyrhynchus, Egypt, by Grenfell and Hunt

Housing location: Cambridge, Massachusetts: Harvard University, Semitic Museum (no. 2218)

Date of publication: 1899

Bibliography: Grenfell and Hunt, *Oxyrhynchus Papyri* Vol. 2 (1899), 8–9.
Wessely, 148–150.
Schofield, 137–140.

Photo: Grenfell and Hunt, plate II, Rom. 1:1-7

Inclusion in Greek text: Nestle, 16th edition (1936)

Textual character: Grenfell and Hunt thought this papyrus MS was the exercise of a schoolboy; Deissmann thought it was an amulet. In either case, the text is proto-Alexandrian, or what Aland would call "strict."

Significance for text and translations: See Rom. 1:1 (Section 3).

Name: 𝔓12

Content: Hebrews 1:1

Date: c. 285

Place of discovery: Arsinoite Nome, the Fayum in 1897

Housing location: New York, New York: Pierpont Morgan Library (no. G. 3)

Date of publication: 1900

Bibliography: Grenfell and Hunt, *The Amherst Papyri* Vol. 1 (London, 1900).
Schofield, 152–154.

Inclusion in Greek text: NA[26] (1979)

Textual character: The MS contains three lines of the beginning of Hebrews written on the top of a letter by an Egyptian traveling in Rome between 265–282.

Significance for text and translations: See Heb. 1:1 (Section 3).

Name: 𝔓13 (Pap. Oxy. 657)

Content: Hebrews 2:14–5:5; 10:8-22; 10:29–11:13; 11:28–12:7

Date: Third century

Place of discovery: Oxyrhynchus, Egypt, by Grenfell and Hunt

Housing location: London, England: British Library (inv. no. 1532v)

Date of publication: 1904

Bibliography: Grenfell and Hunt. *Oxyrhynchus Papyri* Vol. 4 (1904), 36–48.

Schofield, 155–167.

Photos: *Illustrated Bible Dictionary,* Vol. 2, 628, Heb. 2:14–3:9.

Wycliffe Bible Encyclopedia, Vol. 1, 774, Heb. 12:1-11.

In this book see photo 11.

Inclusion in Greek text: Nestle, 13th edition (1927)

Textual character: Grenfell and Hunt said that 𝔓13 is a good and interesting text. 𝔓13 very often agrees with 𝔓46 and B, and it supplements B where it is lacking—namely, from Heb. 9:14 to the end of Hebrews. The text of Hebrews was written on the back of the papyrus containing the new epitome of Livy. For this reason, some scholars think the MS was possibly brought to Egypt by a Roman official and left behind when he left his post.

Significance for text and translations: See Heb. 3:2, 6; 4:2; 10:38; 11:4, 11; 12:1, 3 (Section 3).

Name: 𝔓15 (Pap. Oxy. 1008)

Content: 1 Corinthians 7:18–8:4

Date: Third century

Place of discovery: Oxyrhynchus, Egypt, by Grenfell and Hunt

Housing location: Cairo, Egypt: Egyptian Museum of Antiquities (JE 47423)

Date of publication: 1910

Bibliography: Grenfell and Hunt, *Oxyrhynchus Papyri* Vol. 7 (1910), 4–8.

Schofield, 171–174.

Inclusion in Greek text: Nestle, 16th edition (1936)

Textual character: Metzger called this MS "proto-Alexandrian," as did Schofield, who said also that 𝔓15 probably represented the best tradition of that time in Egypt. Aland has classified 𝔓15 as being somewhere between "normal" and "strict." In important variants (1 Cor. 7:34; 8:2,

8:3a, 3b—as listed in UBS[3]), 𝔓15 agrees with B four times against 𝔓46, and agrees three times with ℵ (or ℵ^c) A D against 𝔓46. In every case, 𝔓15 et al. represents the best text.

Significance for text and translations: See 1 Cor. 7:33-34, 40; 8:3 (Section 3). 𝔓15 is the work of the same scribe as 𝔓16 (see below).

Name: 𝔓16 (Pap. Oxy. 1009)

Content: Philippians 3:10-17; 4:2-8

Date: Third century

Place of discovery: Oxyrhynchus, Egypt, by Grenfell and Hunt

Housing location: Cairo, Egypt: Egyptian Museum of Antiquities (JE 47424)

Date of publication: 1910

Bibliography: Grenfell and Hunt, *Oxyrhynchus Papyri* Vol. 7 (1910), 8–11.

Schofield, 175–178.

Inclusion in Greek text: Nestle, 21st edition (1952)

Textual character: 𝔓16 was discovered together with 𝔓15. Grenfell and Hunt conjectured that 𝔓16 and 𝔓15 might have been parts of the same MS. Both MSS have the same formation of letters, line space, and punctuation. But the color of the ink is different. A careful study of the calligraphic features of both MSS shows that they are the work of one scribe.

𝔓16 shows the greatest agreement with ℵ, with which it agrees on almost every variation unit. It has less agreement with B than does 𝔓15, and yet more agreement with 𝔓46 than does 𝔓15.

Significance for text and translations: See Phil. 3:13; 4:3 (Section 3).

Name: 𝔓17 (Pap. Oxy. 1078)

Content: Hebrews 9:12-19

Date: Fourth century

Place of discovery: Oxyrhynchus, Egypt, by Grenfell and Hunt

Housing location: Cambridge, England: University Library (Add. 5893)

Date of publication: 1911

Bibliography: Grenfell and Hunt, *Oxyrhynchus Papyri* Vol. 8 (1911), 11–13.

Schofield, 179-181.

Inclusion in Greek text: NA²⁶ (1979)

Textual character: 𝔓17 displays an independent text, related to two later text types—Alexandrian and Byzantine.

Significance for text and translations: None of the variants exhibited in 𝔓17 have been significant enough to warrant any changes in the Greek text or English translations. However, in Heb. 9:14, 𝔓17ᵛⁱᵈ, with 𝔓46 ℵ* A B D², has confirmed the reading "the eternal Spirit" (followed by all versions) as opposed to the reading in ℵ² D*, "the eternal Holy Spirit" (followed by TLB—which displays a tendency to add "Holy" before "Spirit" in an attempt to identify the Spirit for the reader).

Name: 𝔓18 (Pap. Oxy. 1079)

Content: Revelation 1:4-7

Date: Third century

Place of discovery: Oxyrhynchus, Egypt, by Grenfell and Hunt

Housing location: London, England: British Library (inv. no. 2053v)

Date of publication: 1911

Bibliography: Grenfell and Hunt, *Oxyrhynchus Papyri* Vol. 8 (1911), 13–14.

Schofield, 182–185.

Inclusion in Greek text: Nestle, 21st edition (1952)

Textual character: Aland says 𝔓18 has a "normal" text; Metzger says it agrees with ℵ A C, the best witnesses to Revelation. Schofield asserted that in ten of the most important variation units, 𝔓18 concurs with ℵ seven times, A eight times, and C eight times.

Significance for text and translations: See Rev. 1:5 (Section 3).

Name: 𝔓20 (Pap. Oxy. 1171)

Content: James 2:19–3:9

Date: Third century

Place of discovery: Oxyrhynchus, Egypt, by Grenfell and Hunt

Housing location: Princeton, New Jersey: University Library (AM 4117)

Date of publication: 1912

Bibliography: Grenfell and Hunt, *Oxyrhynchus Papyri* Vol. 9 (1912), 9–11.

Schofield, 190–193.

Photos: Hatch, plate VI, James 2:19–3:2; 3:3-9

Inclusion in Greek text: Nestle, 21st edition (1952)

Textual character: Most scholars concede that 𝔓20 generally agrees with B, and then with ℵ C. Metzger calls it Alexandrian, and Aland calls it "normal." According to Schofield, 𝔓20 diverges from the B-group only twice (in 2:23 and 3:7). 𝔓20 and 𝔓27 were done by the same scribe.

Significance for text and translations: 𝔓20 does not offer any noteworthy variations. In fact, 𝔓20 is not once cited in the critical apparatus of UBS[3].

Name: 𝔓21 (Oxy. Pap. 1227)

Content: Matthew 12:24-26, 32-33

Date: Fourth century

Place of discovery: Oxyrhynchus, Egypt, by Grenfell and Hunt

Date of publication: 1914

Housing location: Allentown, Pennsylvania: Muhlenburg College (Theol. Pap. 3)

Bibliography: Grenfell and Hunt, *Oxyrhynchus Papyri* Vol. 10 (1914), 12–14.

Schofield, 194–195.

Inclusion in Greek text: UBS[1] (1966), NA[26] (1979)

Textual character: 𝔓21 shows agreement with ℵ[c] and D.

Significance for text and translations: See Matt. 12:25 (Section 3).

Name: 𝔓22 (Pap. Oxy. 1228)

Content: John 15:25–16:2, 21-32

Date: Third century

Place of discovery: Oxyrhynchus, Egypt, by Grenfell and Hunt

Housing location: Glasgow, Scotland: University Library (Ms. 2-X, 1)

Date of publication: 1914

Bibiliography: Grenfell and Hunt, *Oxyrhynchus Papyri* Vol. 10 (1914), 14–16.

Schofield, 196–199.

Photos: Hatch, plate VII, John 15:25–16:2; 16:21-32

Inclusion in Greek text: Nestle, 16th edition (1936)

Textual character: Grenfell and Hunt said that 𝔓22 is "a good and interesting text, but does not at all agree consistently with any one of the chief authorities." Following Grenfell and Hunt, Schofield indicated that 𝔓22's "textual affinities are not strongly marked; it does not agree with any one group of the MSS. The fragment rather represents the eclecticism of the early papyri before the crystalizing of the textual families had taken place." In significant variation units, 𝔭22 rarely agrees with 𝔭5. This shows that two MSS existing side by side in the same locality (Oxyrynchus) at the same time (third century) contained significantly different texts. The only MS 𝔭22 has an affinity with is ℵ.

Significance for text and translations: See John 16:22a, 22b, 23 (Section 3).

Name: 𝔭23 (Pap. Oxy. 1229)

Content: James 1:10-12, 15-18

Date: Third century

Place of discovery: Oxyrhynchus, Egypt, by Grenfell and Hunt

Housing location: Urbana, Illinois: University of Illinois (G. P. 1229)

Date of publication: 1914

Bibliography: Grenfell and Hunt, *Oxyrhynchus Papyri* Vol. 10 (1914), 16–18.

Photos: In this book see photo 12.

Inclusion in Greek text: Nestle, 16th edition (1936)

Textual character: 𝔭23 displays what Aland calls a "strict" text. For example, in James 1:17 𝔭23, together with ℵ and B, contains the genitive, ἀποσκιάσματος, where one would normally expect a nominative (see discussion in Section 3). This shows strict adherence to a common exemplar. In general, 𝔭23 agrees with ℵ B C, which represent the best text of the General Epistles.

Significance for text and translations: See James 1:12, 17 (Section 3).

Name: 𝔭24 (Pap. Oxy. 1230)

Content: Revelation 5:5-8; 6:5-8

Date: Third century

Place of discovery: Oxyrhynchus, Egypt, by Grenfell and Hunt

Housing location: Newton Centre, Massachusetts: Andover Newton Theological School, Franklin Trask Library (O.P. 1230)

Date of publication: 1914

Bibliography: Grenfell and Hunt, *Oxyrhynchus Papyri* Vol. 10 (1914), 18–19.

Schofield, 203–205.

Photos: In this book see photos 13 and 14.

Inclusion in Greek text: UBS[1] (1966), NA[26] (1979)

Textual character: Grenfell and Hunt said that 𝔓24 does not follow any one MS or group of MSS rigidly, although its closest agreement is with ℵ and A. Actually, the papyrus departs from A only three times (all in 5:6). Schofield noted that the text was written on a large leaf—part of a church Bible—and that the penmanship was the work of an untrained scribe.

Significance for text and translations: See Rev. 5:6 (Section 3).

Name: 𝔓25
Content: Matthew 18:32-34; 19:1-3, 5-7, 9-10
Date: Fourth century
Place of discovery: Unknown
Housing location: 𝔓25 was in Berlin, Germany in the Staatliche Museen (inv. no. 16388), but the MS is now lost.
Date of publication: 1938
Bibliography: Otto Stegmuller, "Ein Bruchstück aus dem griechischen Diatessaron," in *Zeitschrift für Papyrologie und Epigraphik* 37 (1938): 223–229.
Inclusion in Greek text: Nestle, 22nd edition (1956)
Textual character: 𝔓25 displays an independent text.
Significance for text and translations: See Matt. 19:9 (Section 3).

Name: 𝔓27 (Pap. Oxy. 1355)
Content: Romans 8:12-22, 24-27; 8:33–9:3, 5-9
Date: Third century
Place of discovery: Oxyrhynchus, Egypt, by Grenfell and Hunt
Housing location: Cambridge, England: University Library (Add. 7211)
Date of publication: 1915
Bibliography: Grenfell and Hunt, *Oxyrhynchus Papyri* Vol. 11 (1915), 9–12.
Schofield, 219–222.
Photo: Hatch, plate IX, Rom. 8:33–9:3
Inclusion in Greek text: Nestle, 21st edition (1952)
Textual character: The text of 𝔓27 (a very mutilated MS) is a "strict" text according to Aland; it shows general agreement with B and other Alexandrian witnesses. 𝔓27 and 𝔓20 are the work of one scribe.
Significance for text and translations: See Rom. 8:34 (Section 3).

Name: 𝔓28 (Pap. Oxy. 1596)

Content: John 6:8-12, 17-22

Date: Third century

Place of discovery: Oxyrhynchus, Egypt, by Grenfell and Hunt

Housing location: Berkeley, California: Pacific School of Religion, Palestine Institute Museum (Pap. 2)

Date of publication: 1919

Bibliography: Grenfell and Hunt, *Oxyrhynchus Papyri* Vol. 13 (1919), 8–10.

Schofield, 223–225.

Photo: Finegan, 108

Inclusion in Greek text: Nestle, 21st edition (1952)

Textual character: Aland has called 𝔓28 a "normal" text; Metzger and Schofield, "Alexandrian"; and Grenfell and Hunt said it was "eclectic"—showing more agreement with B than ℵ.

Significance for text and translations: 𝔓28 does not contain any significant textual variants; thus, it is not once cited in UBS[3].

Name: 𝔓29 (Pap. Oxy. 1597)

Content: Acts 26:7-8, 20

Date: Late third century

Place of discovery: Oxyrhynchus, Egypt, by Grenfell and Hunt

Housing location: Oxford, England: Bodleian Library (Gr. bibl. g. 4 [P])

Date of publication: 1919

Bibliography: Grenfell and Hunt, *Oxyrhynchus Papyri* Vol. 13 (1919), 10–12.

Schofield, 226–228.

Inclusion in Greek text: 𝔓29 was first listed in the NA[26] (1979) but was not cited in the critical apparatus.

Textual character: Metzger thinks 𝔓29 might be "Western," and Aland says it is related to the D-type text; but the fragment is too small for anyone to be certain of its textual character.

Significance for text and translations: The text of 𝔓29 is very brief and fragmented; it has not affected any readings in modern editions of the Greek NT or modern English translations.

Name: 𝔓30 (Pap. Oxy. 1598)

Content: 1 Thessalonians 4:12-13, 16-17; 5:3, 8-10, 12-18, 25-28; 2 Thessalonians 1:1-2

Date: Third century

Place of discovery: Oxyrhynchus, Egypt, by Grenfell and Hunt

Housing location: Ghent, Belgium: Rijksuniversiteit, Bibliotheek (inv. 61)

Date of publication: 1919

Bibliography: Grenfell and Hunt, *Oxyrhynchus Papyri* Vol. 13 (1919), 12–14.

Schofield, 229–233.

Photos: Hatch, plate V, 1 Thess. 4:12—2 Thess. 1:2 (with lacunae)

Inclusion in Greek text: Nestle, 21st edition (1952)

Textual character: Aland says 𝔓30 has a text that is "at least normal" (i.e., a text somewhere between "normal" and "strict"). Schofield thought it may have been part of a private church lectionary.

Significance for text and translations: See 1 Thess. 5:9, 25 (Section 3).

Name: 𝔓32 (Papyrus Ryland 5)

Content: Titus 1:11-15; 2:3-8

Date: c. 200

Place of discovery: Probably Oxyrhynchus, Egypt

Date of publication: 1911

Housing location: Manchester, England: John Rylands Library (Gr. P. 5)

Bibliography: A. S. Hunt, *Catalogue of the Greek Papyri in the John Rylands Library* Vol. 1 (Manchester, 1911), 10–11.

Schofield, 238–241.

Photos: Hunt, plate III, Titus 1:11-15; 2:3-8

Inclusion in Greek text: Nestle, 16th edition (1936)

Textual character: Metzger says 𝔓32 shows agreement with ℵ and with F and G. For example, 𝔓32 shows a reading in Titus 2:7 that was previously contained only in F and G (and a few other late MSS): ἀφθονίαν ("without envy"), against the testimony of all other MSS, which read ἀφθορίαν ("without corruption"). Since F and G (nearly identical MSS) go back to the same archetype, it is quite possible that 𝔓32 could be linked to the same source (Schofield). Aland has stated that 𝔓32 is "at least normal" (i.e., the text is somewhere between "normal" and "strict").

Significance for text and translations: none

Name: 𝔓35

Content: Matthew 25:12-15, 20-23

Date: Fourth century (?)

Place of discovery: Oxyrhynchus, Egypt, by the Società Italiana per la ricerca dei Papiri greci e latini in Egitto

Housing location: Florence, Italy: Biblioteca Laurenziana

Date of publication: 1912

Bibliography: E. Pistelli, *Papiri greci e latini della Società Italiana* Vol. 1 (1912), 1–2.

Schofield, 253–255.

Inclusion in Greek text: NA²⁶ (1979)

Textual character: Aland has called 𝔓35 a "strict" text. In significant variation units (Matt. 25:20, 21, 22a, 22b—see critical apparatus of NA²⁶), 𝔓35 always agrees with B and disagrees with ℵ only once.

Significance for text and translations: Although 𝔓35 shows good textual affinity with B and ℵ and is often cited in NA²⁶, it does not affect any readings significant to translations (thus, it is never cited in UBS³).

Name: 𝔓37

Content: Matthew 26:19-52

Date: Late third century

Place of discovery: 𝔓37 was purchased in Cairo, Egypt, in 1924. Its exact provenance is unknown, but it is likely that it came from the Fayum because many of the documents in the purchase came from there.

Housing location: Ann Arbor, Michigan: University of Michigan (inv. no. 1570)

Date of publication:1926

Bibliography: Henry A. Sanders, "An Early Papyrus Fragment of the Gospel of Matthew in the Michigan Collection," in *Harvard Theological Review,* 19 (1926): 215–226.

Schofield, 259–265.

Photo: Hatch, plate XIII, Matt. 26:19-52

Inclusion in Greek text: Nestle, 16th edition (1936)

Textual character: Sanders described 𝔭37 as having a so-called "Western" text with some variants peculiar to Egypt. Schofield said that 𝔭37's text "probably represents quite accurately the type of uncorrected text that circulated in Egypt before the time of the great recensions." (Schofield also added that 𝔭37 has the script of an educated man, but not of a professional scribe.) 𝔭37 shows great affinity with 𝔭45 (see verses below). Both MSS used to be called "Caesarean" (see Metzger), but are now more appropriately described as "free" texts (see Aland).

Significance for text and translations: See Matt. 26:20, 27, 28 (Section 3).

Name: 𝔭38

Content: Acts 18:27–19:6, 12-16

Date: c. 300

Place of discovery: 𝔭38 was purchased in Cairo, Egypt, in 1924. Although its exact provenance is unknown, it probably came from the Fayum because many of the manuscripts sold at this time came from there. Various fragments were allotted to contributing institutions by Dr. H. I. Bell of the British Museum.

Housing location: Ann Arbor, Michigan: University of Michigan Library (inv. no. 1571)

Date of publication: 1927

Bibliography: Henry A. Sanders, "A Papyrus Fragment of Acts in the Michigan Collection," in *Harvard Theological Review* 20 (1927), 1–19. Schofield, 266–272.

Inclusion in Greek text: Nestle, 16th edition (1936)

Textual character: 𝔭38, as with 𝔭29, 𝔭48, and especially D, is a representative of the "Western" form of the book of Acts.

Significance for text and translations: Since no modern translations follow the Western text in this portion of Acts, 𝔭38 does not evidence any effect on modern English translations. Nevertheless, one significant variant reading is worth noting. In Acts 19:2, 𝔭38, without any support from any other MS, reads, εἶπεν τε πρὸς αὐτοὺς εἰ πνεῦμα ἅγιον ἐλάβετε πιστεύσαντες τὸ ἴδιο τοῦ κυρίου εἶναι. No other MS contains the last five words—which even in this MS are very difficult to read. (Nevertheless, I was able to read these words when I examined the MS at the library of the University of Michigan—thus verifying Sanders' transcription, with but a few minor adjustments that are not worth mentioning.) The text in ℘38 could be rendered, "And he said to them, 'Have you received the Holy Spirit, having believed the same [Spirit] to be of the Lord?'" The last part of this question could also be rendered, "having believed the same [Spirit] of the Lord to exist?" or "having believed that it [the Holy Spirit] is the characteristic quality of the Lord?" (this last rendering was provided by Sanders). The scribe of ℘38 thought it necessary to show the identification of the Spirit with the Lord.

Name: ℘39 (Pap. Oxy. 1780)

Content: John 8:14-22

Date: Third century

Place of discovery: Oxyrhynchus, Egypt, by Grenfell and Hunt (acquired in 1922)

Housing location: Rochester, New York: Ambrose Swabey Library (inv. no. 8864)

Date of publication: 1922

Bibliography: Grenfell and Hunt, *Oxyrhynchus Papyri* Vol. 15 (1922), 7–8.

Schofield, 273–277.

Inclusion in Greek text: UBS[1] (1966), NA[26] (1979)

Textual character: Grenfell and Hunt said ℘39 generally agrees with B; in fact, Schofield said it "never once leaves B." As would be expected, Aland considers ℘39 to have a "strict" text.

Significance for text and translations: See John 8:16 (Section 3).

Name: ℘40

Content: Romans 1:24-27, 31–2:3; 3:21–4:8; 6:4-5; 9:17, 27

Date: Third century

Place of discovery: ℘40 was discovered near the obscure village of Qarara, Egypt, on the site of a monastery, by a joint expedition of the Heidelberger Akademie der Wissenschaften and the Freiburger Wissenschaftliche Gesellschaft, between January 1 and March 29, 1914 (Schofield).

Housing location: Heidelberg, Germany: Papyrussammlung der Universität (inv. no. 645)

Date of publication: 1924

Bibliography: Friedrich Bilabel, "Römerbrieffragmente" in *Veröffentlichungen aus den Badischen Papyrussammlungen* Vol. 4 (1924), 28–31, 124–127 (P. Baden 57).

Schofield, 278–284.

Inclusion in Greek text: Nestle, 22nd edition (1956)

Textual character: Although the scribe was careless in his work, the text manifests an Alexandrian exemplar. Schofield called 𝔓40 "strongly Alexandrian"; Metzger, "Alexandrian"; and Aland, "free."

Significance for text and translations: 𝔓40 does not have much to offer in the way of significant variants. One reading worth mentioning is that found in Rom. 3:22—"unto all them that believe." 𝔓40 with ℵ* A B C supports this reading (a reading which is followed by all the translations) versus the reading, "unto all and upon all them that believe," found in ℵᶜ D and noted in ASVmg. 𝔓40 provides the earliest testimony to the first reading—which, as the shortest, is the one Paul most likely wrote.

Name: 𝔓45 (Chester Beatty Papyrus I)

Content: Matthew 20:24-32; 21:13-19; 25:41–26:39; Mark 4:36–9:31; 11:27–12:28; Luke 6:31–7:7; 9:26–14:33; John 10:7-25; 10:30–11:10, 18-36, 42-57; Acts 4:27–17:17 (with many lacunae). According to Kenyon, the order of books in the original intact MS was probably as follows: Matthew, John, Luke, Mark, Acts (the so-called Western order). Since the MS came to London from Egypt in separate portions, this cannot be fully affirmed; however, since Mark and Acts arrived together, it is a fair assumption.

Date: Third century

Place of discovery: The exact provenance of 𝔓45 is unknown since the MS came through the hands of native dealers by a purchase made in 1930/1931. Quite possibly 𝔓45 came from the ruins of the library of some church or library of a Christian scholar or monastery—perhaps in the Fayum or the east bank of the Nile about Atfih, the ancient Aphroditopolis, from which Antony, the founder of Egyptian monasticism, came (Schofield). According to Colin H. Roberts, "Carl Schmidt was told in 1934 that the Chester Beatty Papyri had been found in a pitcher in the ruins of a church or monastery near Atfih (Aphroditopolis)"—see *Manuscript, Society, and Belief in Early Christian Egypt*, 7. Turner, however, has suggested that the Chester Beatty Papyri (and the Bodmer

Papyri) came from Panopolis (modern Akmim) because he has noticed several associations between MSS known to have come from Panopolis and those in the Beatty and Bodmer collections (see his arguments in *Greek Papyri,* 52–53).

Housing location: 𝔓45 was purchased by Chester Beatty of Dublin, Ireland, in 1931. This papyrus MS, along with two other very important MSS, 𝔓46 (Chester Beatty Papyrus II) and 𝔓47 (Chester Beatty Papyrus III), are kept in Beatty's private collection. (The discovery and purchase of these papyri were first announced in *The London Times* on November 19, 1931.)

Date of publication: 1933–34, 1951 (see bibliography)

Bibliography: Frederic G. Kenyon, *Chester Beatty Biblical Papyri* II/1: *The Gospels and Acts, Text* (London, 1933); II/2: *The Gospels and Acts, Plates* (London, 1934).

Hans Gerstinger, "Ein Fragment des Chester Beatty-Evangelienkodex in der Papyrussammlung der Nationalbibliothek in Wien," *Aegyptus* 13 (1933): 67–72.

Augustin Merk, "Codex Evangeliorum et Actum ex collectione P Chester Beatty," *Miscellanea Biblica* II (1934): 375–406.

Günther Zuntz, "Reconstruction of one Leaf of the Chester Beatty Papyrus of the Gospels and Acts (Mt 25:41–26:39)," *Chronique d'Egypte* 26 (1951): 191–211.

Ernest C. Colwell, "Method in Evaluating Scribal Habits: A Study of 𝔓45, 𝔓66, 𝔓75," in *Studies in Methodology in Textual Criticism of the New Testament* (Grand Rapids: Eerdmans, 1969).

Photos: Kenyon, plates for entire MS

Inclusion in Greek text: Nestle, 16th edition (1936)

Textual character: According to an excellent study done by Colwell, the scribe of 𝔓45 worked "without any intention of exactly reproducing his source." He wrote with a great amount of freedom—"harmonizing, smoothing out, substituting almost whimsically." It was apparent to Colwell that the scribe of 𝔓45 copied his exemplar phrase by phrase and clause by clause (as opposed to more careful copyists who transcribe the text letter by letter [as in 𝔓75]). While copying phrases and clauses, he worked at reproducing what he imagined to be the thought of each phrase. Thus, he transposed and omitted many words and deleted several phrases. Colwell said, "The most striking aspect of his style is its conciseness. The dispensable word is dispensed with. He omits

49

adverbs, adjectives, nouns, participles, verbs, personal pronouns—without any compensating habit of addition."

The text of ⅌45 varies with each book. According to Kenyon, ⅌45 in Mark shows a strong affinity with those MSS that used to be called Caesarean (i.e., W [in Mark] f¹ f¹³ 565 700). In Matthew, Luke, and John, ⅌45 stands midway between the "Alexandrian" MSS and so-called "Western" MSS. In Acts, ⅌45 shows the greatest affinity with the Alexandrian uncials (ℵ A B C)—as over against the MSS with a D-text. The general textual character of ⅌45 is explained by Kenyon as follows:

> [T]his MS. is a witness to the existence in Egypt in the first half of the third century of a type of text distinct from that found predominantly in B, and with a strong infusion of readings found in the early authorities which are grouped together as 'Western', though with none of the large divergences which are found in some of these authorities. Further, it is closely akin (at any rate in Mark) to the type which found a home in Caesarea. The fact that this type of text is found in a MS. written in Egypt during the lifetime of Origen (or not much later) is some evidence that the type did not originate in any editorial revision undertaken at Caesarea, but existed already in Egypt, whence it was taken (it may be by Origen himself) to Caesarea, where it was adopted by the great scholars who used the library of Pamphilus. Its 'Western' features do not imply any connexion with either Rome or the Syriac Church. It only confirms the conclusion as to the misleading character of the term 'Western' (xviii).

Significance for text and translations: See Matt. 26:20; Mark 5:21; 6:3, 23, 44; 7:4, 28, 35; 8:15, 38a, 38b; 9:24, 29; Luke 6:48; 9:26, 35, 54, 55b-56a, 62; 10:17, 21, 22, 38, 42; 11:11, 33; 14:5; John 10:16, 18; 11:25, 45; Acts 8:18, 37; 11:11, 12; 13:33, 48; 15:20a, 20b, 20c; 16:32, 36 (Section 3).

Name: ⅌46 (Chester Beatty Papyrus II)
Content: The papyrus has most of Paul's Epistles (excluding the Pastorals) in this order: Romans 5:17–6:14; 8:15–15:9; 15:11–16:27; Hebrews 1:1–13:25; 1 Corinthians 1:1–16:22; 2 Corinthians 1:1–13:13; Ephesians 1:1–6:24; Galatians 1:1–6:18; Philippians 1:1–4:23; Colossians

1:1–4:18; 1 Thessalonians 1:1; 1:9–2:3; 5:5-9, 23-28 (with minor lacunae in each of the books). The position of Hebrews following Romans shows that Hebrews was considered Pauline (see cover photo).

Date: Usually dated c. 200, but assigned a late-first-century date by Kim in *Biblica* 69 (1988): 248–257.

Place of discovery: 𝔓46 was discovered (along with 𝔓45 and 𝔓47) somewhere in the Fayum of Egypt, or perhaps in the ruins of a church or monastery near Atfih—ancient Aphroditopolis, or perhaps in Akmim—ancient Panopolis (see comments on 𝔓45). A dealer from Cairo sold the MS in different batches to two different parties—Chester Beatty and the University of Michigan. Chester Beatty purchased ten leaves of the MS (in 1930-31), and the University of Michigan six leaves (in 1930–31). The University of Michigan acquired twenty-four more leaves in the winter of 1932-33. The ten leaves in the Beatty collection were first published in fasciculus III of *The Chester Beatty Papyri* (1936). The thirty leaves in the Michigan collection were published in 1935 by H. A. Sanders in *A Third-century Papyrus Codex of the Epistles of Paul*. Soon after this publication, Chester Beatty announced that he had obtained forty-six more leaves of the same MS. Through collaboration, the entire MS was published in 1936 (see bibliography below).

Housing location: The University of Michigan library has thirty leaves, containing the following portions: Romans 11:35–14:8; Romans 15:11—Hebrews 8:8; Hebrews 9:10-26; 1 Corinthians 2:3–3:5; 2 Corinthians 9:7–13:13; Ephesians; Galatians 1:1–6:10. The Chester Beatty Collection has fifty-six leaves, containing Romans 5:17–6:14; 8:15–11:35; 14:19–15:11; Hebrews 8:9–9:10; Hebrews 9:26—1 Corinthians 2:3; 1 Corinthians 3:6—2 Corinthians 9:7; Galatians 6:10-18; Philippians; Colossians; 1 Thessalonians 1:1–2:3; 5:5-28. (The MS originally had 104 leaves; eighteen are still missing.)

Date of publication: 1934, 1936, 1937

Bibliography: Frederic G. Kenyon, *The Chester Beatty Biblical Papyri* III/1: *Pauline Epistles and Revelation, Text* (London, 1934); III/3 (Supplement): *Pauline Epistles, Text* (London, 1936); III/4: *Pauline Epistles, Plates* (London, 1937).

Henry A. Sanders, *A Third-century Papyrus Codex of the Epistles of Paul* (Ann Arbor: University of Michigan Press, 1935).

Photos: Kenyon, plates for entire MS.

In this book see photos 7, 8, 9, 10.

Inclusion in Greek text: Nestle, 16th edition (1936)

Textual character: The text of 𝔓46 shows a strong affinity with B (although less in Rom. and 1 Cor. than in the other epistles) and next with ℵ. 𝔓46 agrees much less with the later representatives of the Alexandrian text (namely, A C P 33). In short, 𝔓46 is proto-Alexandrian—that is, it contains an uncorrected text (with a number of peculiar readings), which must have been the kind used in the Alexandrian recension.

In Hebrews, 𝔓46 and 𝔓13 display nearly the same text. Out of a total of eighty-eight variation units, there are seventy-one agreements and only seventeen disagreements. (The copyists of 𝔓13 and 𝔓46 made similar use of double points for punctuation, and the pagination of both documents indicates that Romans preceded Hebrews in 𝔓13 as well as in 𝔓46.) 𝔓13 and 𝔓46 both represent the text current in Egypt during the early third century. Both were relatively free from correction and must have been the kind of exemplar used for the Alexandrian recensions. Other early papyri display general agreement with 𝔓46—namely, 𝔓17 and 𝔓27.

Textual critics have observed that when 𝔓46 agrees with B *and* with D F G, the reading is usually "Western." (A reading with the combination of B D F G was usually rejected by Westcott and Hort.) However, a number of readings supported by 𝔓46 and B by themselves or with MSS of all text types show themselves to be most likely Pauline.

Significance for text and translations: See Rom. 8:21, 23, 24, 28; 9:4; 11:17, 31; 12:11, 14; 15:19, 33; 16:7, 20, 24, 25-27; 1 Cor. 1:13, 28; 2:1; 5:5; 7:15, 33-34; 8:3a, 3b, 12; 10:2, 9; 11:24; 13:3; 14:38; 15:49; 2 Cor. 1:10a, 10b, 11, 12; 2:1, 17; 3:2, 9; 8:7; 11:3; Gal. 1:3, 6, 15; 2:5, 12; 4:25, 28; 6:2, 13; Eph. 1:1, 14, 15; 2:5; 3:9; 4:8, 9, 28, 32; 5:2, 5, 9; 6:1; Phil. 1:14; 2:30; 3:3, 13; 4:3, 16; Col. 1:7; 2:2, 18; 3:4, 6, 16; Heb. 1:8, 12; 2:7, 9; 3:2, 6; 4:2; 6:1-2; 9:11; 10:1, 38; 11:11, 37; 12:1, 3; 13:21a, 21b (Section 3).

Name: 𝔓47 (Chester Beatty Papyrus III)

Content: Revelation 9:10–17:2

Date: Second half of the third century (the handwriting is similar to that of 𝔓5 and 𝔓18)

Place of discovery: 𝔓47 (along with 𝔓45 and 𝔓46) was discovered in the Fayum of Egypt, or perhaps in the ruins of a church or monastery near

Atfih—ancient Aphroditopolis—or in Akmim—ancient Panopolis (see comments on ℙ45).

Housing location: Dublin, Ireland: Chester Beatty Collection

Date of publication: 1934

Bibliography: Frederic G. Kenyon, *Chester Biblical Papyri* III/1: *Pauline Epistles and Revelation, Text* (London: 1934); III/2: *Revelation, Plates* (London: 1936).

Photos: Kenyon, plates for entire MS

Inclusion in Greek text: Nestle, 16th edition (1936)

Textual character: When this MS was first examined by Kenyon, he said that "it is on the whole closest to ℵ and C, with P next, and A rather further away" (xiii). In Metzger's handbook, he said that ℙ47 agrees with A C and ℵ (*Text*, 252). Aland, in his handbook, counters Metzger; he says that ℙ47 is allied to ℵ, but not to A and C, which are of a different text type (*Text*, 59). Actually, Metzger clarified the matter earlier in the same handbook; he wrote, "In general the text of ℙ47 agrees more often with that of Codex Sinaiticus than with any other, though it often shows a remarkable independence" (*Text*, 38).

Significance for texts and translations: See Rev. 10:6; 11:12; 12:18; 13:1; 13:6, 7, 18; 14:3; 15:3, 6; 16:4 (Section 3).

Name: ℙ48

Content: Acts 23:11-17, 23-29

Date: Third century (around the same time as ℙ13, for the two MSS bear a close resemblance in handwriting)

Place of discovery: Oxyrhynchus, Egypt, by the Società Italiana per la ricerca dei Papiri greci e latini in Egitto.

Date of publication: 1932

Housing location: Florence, Italy: Biblioteca Laurenziana (no. 1165)

Bibliography: G. Vitelli and S. G. Mercati, *Pubblicazioni della Società Italiana, Papiri Greci e Latini* Vol. 10 (1932), 112–118.

Schofield, 326–329.

Albert C. Clark, *The Acts of the Apostles* (Oxford, 1933), 409–413.

Photos: Hatch, plate XII, Acts 23:11-17; 23:24-29.

Aland, plate 16, Acts 23:11-17.

Inclusion in Greek text: Nestle, 16th edition (1936)

Textual character: Aland and Metzger, following Vitelli, have classified ℙ48 as "Western." Schofield said, "This papyrus shows a text in Egypt in the latter part of the third century which was not merely non-Alexandrian, but definitely Western in the full sense of that term as it is applied to D and the African Latin." (See comments on Acts 23:29 in Section 3 for a particular association between ℘48 and other Western MSS.) Unfortunately, ℘48 cannot be compared with D because D ends at Acts 22:29.

Significance for text and translations: See Acts 23:12, 29 (Section 3).

Name: ℘49

Content: Ephesians 4:16-29; 4:31–5:13

Date: Early third century

Place of discovery: The MS was purchased in February, 1931, in Cairo for Yale University. Its provenance prior to Cairo is not known.

Housing location: New Haven, Connecticut: Yale University Library (P. 415 + 531)

Date of publication: 1949 and 1958

Bibliography: W. H. P. Hatch and C. B. Wells, "A Hitherto Unpublished Fragment of the Epistle to the Ephesians," in *Harvard Theological Review* 51 (1958): 33-37. The MS was given notice earlier by G. Maldfeld and Bruce Metzger in the *Journal of Biblical Literature* 68 (1949): 368.

Photos: Hatch and Wells, Eph. 4:16-29; 4:31–5:13

Inclusion in Greek text: Nestle, 21st edition (1952)

Textual character: Aland has called this MS "at least normal"; Metzger identifies it as Alexandrian; Hatch and Wells also identify it as an Alexandrian MS, having the greatest affinity with B, then A, then ℘46 and ℵ.

Significance for text and translations: See Eph. 4:28, 32; 5:5, 9 (Section 3).

Name: ℘50

Content: Acts 8:26-32; 10:26-31

Date: Late fourth century/early fifth century according to some scholars (Metzger, Aland); Kraeling dates it middle fourth century.

Place of discovery: Egypt—Kraeling said the "document . . . was acquired by Yale University at Paris in 1933, together with a number of other texts of Egyptian provenance."

Date of publication: 1937

Housing location: New Haven, Connecticut: Yale University Library (P. 1543).

Bibliography: Carl H. Kraeling, "℗50: Two Selections from Acts," in *Quantulacumque: Studies Presented to Kirsopp Lake*, R. Casey, S. Lake, A. K. Lake, eds. (London: 1937): 163–172.

Photos: Kraeling, Acts 8:26-32; 10:26-31

Inclusion in Greek text: Nestle, 17th edition (1941)

Textual character: Kraeling says that ℗50 agrees generally with B and ℵ—and that when B and ℵ disagree, ℗50 agrees with B in preference to ℵ. (Metzger simply says ℗50 agrees chiefly with B.) What have been otherwise noticed as Western affinites in this MS are, for the most part, actually nothing more than errors or orthographic peculiarites (see Kraeling and Aland)—of which there are many, for the scribe (though educated) did a hasty job in producing this MS.

Significance for text and translations: See Acts 10:30 (Section 3).

Name: ℗51 (Pap. Oxy. 2157)

Content: Galatians 1:2-10, 13, 16-20

Date: c. 400

Place of discovery: Oxyrhynchus, Egypt

Housing location: Oxford, England: Ashmolean Museum (P. Oxy. 2157)

Date of publication: 1941

Bibliography: Edgar Lobel, Colin H. Roberts, E. P. Wegener, *Oxyrhynchus Papyri* Vol. 18 (1941), 1–3.

Inclusion in Greek text: Nestle, 21st edition (1952)

Textual character: According to the editors, the text of ℗51 is "eclectic in character; its closest affinities seem to be with B, but an agreement with D F G against ℵ A B ℗46 in v. 19 is worth noticing. None of the three peculiar readings of the Chester Beatty codex of the Pauline Epistles (℗46) find support here, nor does it ever agree with ℗46 except when the latter is supporting B."

Significance for text and translations: See Gal. 1:3, 6, 8 (Section 3).

Name: ℗52

Content: John 18:31-34, 37-38

Date: c. 110–125. This is the earliest extant NT papyrus. Many scholars (Kenyon, H. I. Bell, Deissmann, and W. H. P. Hatch) have confirmed this dating. Deissmann was convinced that ℗52 was written at least

55

during the reign of Hadrian (117–138) and perhaps even during the reign of Trajan (98–117). Deissmann wrote an article on this: "Ein Evangelienblatt aus den Tagen Hadrians" (in *Deutsche allgemeine Zeitung* 564, [3 Dec. 1935]), which was translated in the *British Weekly*, 12 Dec. 1935, p. 219. In recent discussions about 𝔓52, scholars tend to date it closer to 100 than to 125 (see Aland, 84–87).

Place of discovery: Fayum or Oxyrhnchus, Egypt—it may have circulated in both areas, according to Roberts. It was acquired in 1920 by Grenfell, but "it remained unnoticed among hundreds of similar shreds of papyri until 1934. In that year C. H. Roberts, Fellow of St. John's College, while sorting over the unpublished papyri belonging to the John Rylands Library at Manchester, recognized that this scrap preserves several sentences from John's Gospel" (Metzger, *Text*, 38). Roberts immediately published a booklet describing this papyrus (see first listing in bibliography below).

Date of publication: 1935

Housing location: Manchester, England: John Rylands Library (Gr. P. 457)

Bibliography: C. H. Roberts, *An Unpublished Fragment of the Fourth Gospel in the John Rylands Library* (Manchester: 1935). This was republished with a few alterations in the *Bulletin of the John Rylands Library* 20 (1936): 45–55; and then again in the *Catalogue of the Greek and Latin Papyri in the John Rylands Library* Vol. 3 (Manchester: 1938), 1–3. The last publication contains critical notes and a bibliography of scholarly reviews.

Photos: Aland, plate 19, John 18:31-33; 18:37-38
Illustrated Bible Dictionary, Vol. 2, 582, John 18:31-33.
Finegan, 85, John 18:31-33; 18:37-38.

Inclusion in Greek text: Nestle, 17th edition (1941)

Textual character: Though the amount of text in 𝔓52 is hardly enough to make a positive judgment about its textual character, the text seems to be "Alexandrian" (Metzger), or what Aland would call "normal."

Significance for text and translations: Since the text in 𝔓52 is so small and does not contain any significant variations, it has not directly affected modern English translations of the NT. Its greatest value is its early date, for it testifies to the fact that the autograph of John's Gospel must have been written before the close of the first century.

Name: 𝔓53

Content: Matthew 26:29-40; Acts 9:33–10:1 (Sanders said the two fragments are probably part of the same MS. This was confirmed by H. I.
Bell. The two fragments were found together; they were part of a codex
containing the four Gospels and Acts or just Matthew and Acts.)

Date: c. 260

Place of discovery: Most likely an Egyptian dealer obtained 𝔓53 from the
Fayum, Egypt.

Housing location: Ann Arbor, Michigan: University of Michigan Library
(inv. no. 6652). The University of Michigan obtained the papyrus in the
summer of 1934 through the British Museum, which had obtained the
fragments from an Egyptian dealer.

Date of publication: 1937

Bibliography: Henry A. Sanders, "A Third Century Papyrus of Matthew
and Acts," in *Quantulacumque: Studies Presented to Kirsopp Lake*, R.
Casey, S. Lake, A. K. Lake, eds. (London: 1937), 151–161.

Photos: Sanders, Matt. 26:29-35; 26:36-40; Acts 9:33-38; 9:41–10:1

Inclusion in Greek text: Nestle, 17th edition (1941)

Textual character: Sanders says 𝔓53 is another example of the characteristic third-century text of Egypt. The early third-century Egyptian MSS
present a text quite similar to but not exactly the same as the notable
Alexandrian MSS. Sanders remarked, "The closeness of agreement
between the older papyri and the Alexandrian text may be interpreted to
mean that the basic Egyptian text was less corrupt than the text that
circulated in other provinces and that the editors were in the main
conservative."

Significance for text and translations: The UBS[3], known for its apparatus
that contains variants that are significant for translators, does not once
cite a variant reading supported by 𝔓53. This is because 𝔓53 confirms
the basic text and does not present support for variants that would create
significant variation in modern English translations.

Name: 𝔓62

Content: Matthew 11:25-30

Date: Fourth century

Place of discovery: According to Amundsen, this papyrus fragment came
from a small lot of papyri fragments obtained in Egypt (inv. 1653–1661),

which belonged to Dr. A. Fonahn and were transferred to the Oslo collection after his death (1940).

Housing location: Oslo, Norway: University Library (P. Osloensis 1661)

Date of publication: 1945

Bibliography: Leiv Amundsen, "Christian Papyri from the Oslo Collection" in *Symbolae Osloenses* 24 (1945): 121–147.

Inclusion in Greek text: NA[26] (1979)

Textual character: Though the fragment is quite small, 𝔓62 appears to be Alexandrian. In the only instance in which 𝔓62 is cited in NA[26] (namely Matt. 11:25), the reading of 𝔓62 (ἔκρυψας) agrees with ℵ B D 33 as against the reading of C L W Θ 𝔐 (ἀπέκρυψας). Elsewhere, the text concurs with Alexandrian MSS.

Significance for text and translations: The UBS[3], known for its apparatus that contains variants that are significant for translators, does not once cite a variant reading supported by 𝔓62. This is because 𝔓62 does not present support for variants that would create significant variation in modern English translations.

Name: 𝔓64/67

Content: Matthew 3:9, 15; 5:20-22, 25-28; 26:7-8, 10, 14-15, 22-23, 31-33. 𝔓64 contains the verses from ch. 26; 𝔓67, the verses from chs. 3 and 5. It was later discovered that both portions are from the same MS.

Date: Usually dated c. 200, but dated c. 100 by Thiede, *Tyn Bul* 46 (1995): 29–42.

Place of discovery: The portion designated 𝔓64 was first purchased by Rev. Charles B. Huleatt in Luxor in 1901 and then given to the Magdalen College Library in Oxford, where it was examined by Colin Roberts, who then published it in 1953. A few years later, P. Roca-Puig published a papyrus fragment known as 𝔓67. Colin Roberts realized that 𝔓67 was from the same MS as 𝔓64. Later, Colin Roberts came to the conclusion that 𝔓4 belongs to the same MS as do 𝔓64 and 𝔓67. If this is true, 𝔓4/64/67 are portions of a MS that was used as packing for the binding of a codex of Philo, which was found walled up in a house in Coptos (see Roberts's *Manuscript, Society and Belief in Early Christian Egypt*, 8).

Housing location: 𝔓64 is housed in the Magdalen College Library, Oxford, England (Gr. 18). 𝔓67 is housed in Fundación San Lucas Evangelista, Barcelona, Spain (inv. no. 1).

Date of publication: 1953 and 1957 (see discussion under bibliography)

Bibliography: 𝔓64 was first published by Colin Roberts in "An Early Papyrus of the First Gospel" (*Harvard Theological Review* 46 [1953], 233-237). 𝔓67 was first published by P. Roca-Puig in a booklet called *Un Papiro Griego del Evangelio de San Mateo* (Barcelona, 1957). After Colin Roberts realized that 𝔓64 and 𝔓67 were two parts of the same MS and then confirmed this with Roca-Puig, the latter published another article entitled, "Nueva publicación del papiro número uno de Barcelona" in *Helmantica* 37 (1961), 5–20, in which he gives a full presentation of the entire MS. Colin Roberts appended a note to this article, explaining how he had discovered that 𝔓64 and 𝔓67 were part of the same MS. Still later, Roberts came to the conclusion that 𝔓4 belongs to the same MS as 𝔓64/67 (*Manuscript,* 13).

See also Thiede's article in *Tyndale Bulletin* 46 (1995): 29–42.

Photos: Roberts, Matt. 26:7-8, 10, 14-15, 22-23, 31-33 (𝔓64).

Roca-Puig, Matt. 3:9, 15; 5:20-22, 25-28 (𝔓67).

Inclusion in Greek text: 𝔓64 was first cited in the Nestle 23rd edition (1957); 𝔓67 was first cited in UBS[1] (1966) and NA[26] (1979).

Textual character: Aland said 𝔓64/67 has "a strict text"; Roberts noted the Alexandrian character of 𝔓64; Roca-Puig demonstrated 𝔓67's close affinity with ℵ.

Significance for text and translations: See Matt. 5:22, 25 (Section 3).

Name: 𝔓65
Content: 1 Thessalonians 1:3-10; 2:1, 6-13
Date: Third century (the handwriting is quite similar to that found in 𝔓49, dated third century)
Place of discovery: unknown
Housing location: Florence, Italy: Istituto di Papirologia G. Vitelli (PSI 1373).
Date of publication: 1957
Bibliography: Vittorio Bartoletti, *Pubblicazioni della Società Italiana, Papiri Greci e Latini* Vol. 14 (1957), 5-7.
Inclusion in Greek text: Nestle, 23rd edition (1957)
Textual character: According to Metzger, 𝔓65 is Alexandrian. Aland considers it most likely to be a "strict" text, though the text is too brief for certainty.
Significance for text and translations: See 1 Thess. 2:7 (Section 3).

Name: 𝔓66 (Papyrus Bodmer II)

Content: John 1:1–6:11; 6:35–14:26, 29-30; 15:2-26; 16:2-4, 6-7; 16:10–20:20, 22-23; 20:25–21:9

Date: Usually dated c. 175–200, but dated c. 125 by Hunger in *Anzeiger der österreichischen Akademie der Wissenschaften,* phil.-hist. Klasse, 1960, no. 4:12–23.

Place of discovery: The Bodmer Papyri were purchased by M. Martin Bodmer (founder of the Bodmer Library of World Literature in Cologny, a suburb of Geneva) from a dealer in Cairo, Egypt. Along with the rest of the Bodmer Papyri, 𝔓66 was discovered in 1952 in Jabal Abu Mana seven years after the Nag Hammadi codices were found nearby. It is quite likely that all these manuscripts were part of the library of a Pachomian monastery (Robinson in *Roots of Egyptian Christianity,* ed. Pearson and Goehring [Philadelphia: Fortress, 1986], 4–5).

Housing location: Geneva/Cologny, Switzerland: Bibliotheca Bodmeriana

Date of publication: 1956, 1958, 1962 (see bibliography below)

Bibliography: Victor Martin, *Papyrus Bodmer II: Evangile de Jean, 1–14* (Cologny/Geneva, 1956); *Papyrus Bodmer II: Supplément, Evangile de Jean, 14–21* (Cologny/Geneva, 1958).

Victor Martin and J. W. B. Barns, *Papyrus Bodmer II: Supplément, Evangile de Jean, 14-21* (Cologny/Geneva, 1962).

Kurt Aland, "Neue neutestamentliche Papyri III," in *New Testament Studies* 20 (1974), 357-381 (a publication containing previously unidentified fragments belonging to the same MS).

Gordon Fee, *Papyrus Bodmer II (𝔓66): Its Textual Relationships and Scribal Characteristics* in *Studies and Documents* 34 (1968), University of Utah Press. J. N. Birdsall, *The Bodmer Papyrus of the Gospel of John* (1960), The Tyndale Press.

Photos: Martin and Barns, plates of entire MS. Finegan, 92 (John 18:29-33), 93 (John 18:37–19:1), 103 (John 6:5-11), 114 (John 1:1-14), 115 (John 1:14-21). In this book see photos 1, 3, 4, 5.

Inclusion in Greek text: Nestle, 23rd edition (1957)

Textual character: 𝔓66 displays an independent text with both Alexandrian and Western affinities. The scribe of 𝔓66 corrected himself nearly 500 times. More than half of these were corrections of scribal blunders, but the other half "involve alterations to the text in which both the original and corrected readings are shared by other important manuscripts" (Fee, *Studies and Documents,* 37). The scribe of 𝔓66 most likely used at least one other manuscript besides his primary exemplar in order to improve his text.

Significance for text and translations: See John 1:18, 34, 41; 3:13, 25, 31; 4:1, 9; 5:1, 2, 3b-4, 44; 6:36; 7:8, 39, 52; 7:53–8:11; 8:16, 39, 57; 9:35; 10:16, 18, 29; 11:25; 12:17, 41; 13:2, 10, 32; 14:4, 7, 14; 16:22, 27; 17:11, 12; 19:35; 20:31 (Section 3).

Name: Ᵽ69 (Pap. Oxy. 2383)

Content: Luke 22:41, 45-48, 58-61

Date: Third century

Place of discovery: Oxyrhynchus, Egypt

Housing location: Oxford, England: Ashmolean Museum (P. Oxy. 2383)

Date of publication: 1957

Bibliography: Lobel, Roberts, Turner, Barns, *Oxyrhynchus Papyri* Vol. 24 (London, 1957), 1–4.

Inclusion in Greek text: Nestle, 24th edition (1960)

Textual character: Ᵽ69 displays an independent text, "similar but unrelated to D" (Aland)—i.e., it contains three examples of characteristic D-type readings, but these are counterbalanced with eight disagreements with D (Lobel et al., 2).

Significance for text and translations: See Luke 22:43-44 (Section 3).

Name: Ᵽ70 (Pap. Oxy. 2384)

Content: Matthew 2:13-16; 2:22–3:1; 11:26-27; 12:4-5; 24:3-6, 12-15

Date: Third century

Place of discovery: Oxyrhynchus, Egypt

Housing location: Oxford, England: Ashmolean Museum (P. Oxy. 2384)—portion with Matt. 11 and 12 ; Florence, Italy: Istituto di Papirologia, G. Vitelli (CNR 419, 420)—portion with Matt. 2–3, 24.

Date of publication: 1957

Bibliography: Lobel, Roberts, Turner, Barns, *Oxyrhynchus Papyri* Vol. 24 (London, 1957), 4–5.

M. Naldini, "Nuovi frammenti del vangelo di Matteo," in *Prometheus* Vol. 1 (1975), 195-200. (After the Istituto di Papirologia realized that they possessed another part of the same MS previously published in *Oxyrhynchus Papyri*, Naldini made this publication.)

Photos: Naldini, Matt. 2:13-16; 2:22–3:1; 24:3-6, 12-15

Inclusion in Greek text: UBS[1] (1966), NA[26] (1979)

Textual character: According to Aland, 𝔓70 has "a strict text," though somewhat carelessly written.

Significance for text and translations: See Matt. 2:23 (Section 3).

Name: 𝔓71 (Pap. Oxy. 2385)

Content: Matthew 19:10-11, 17-18

Date: Fourth century

Place of discovery: Oxyrhynchus, Egypt

Housing location: Oxford, England: Ashmolean Museum (P. Oxy. 2385)

Date of publication: 1957

Bibliography: Lobel, Roberts, Turner, Barns, *Oxyrhynchus Papyri* Vol. 24 (London, 1957), 5–6.

Inclusion in Greek text: UBS[1] (1966), NA[26] (1979)

Textual character: Though this fragment is quite small, it appears that 𝔓71 agrees with B (so Metzger). For example, in Matt. 19:10 𝔓71[vid] agrees with B (and ℵ) in reading οἱ μαθηταί ("the disciples") versus the reading in 𝔓25 C D L W Z, οἱ μαθηταί αὐτοῦ ("his disciples").

Significance for text and translations: See comments on Matt. 19:10 under textual character above.

Name: 𝔓72 (Papyrus Bodmer VII-VIII)

Content: 1 Peter 1:1–5:14; 2 Peter 1:1–3:18; Jude 1-25 (which are in the same document as are the Nativity of Mary, the apocryphal correspondence of Paul to the Corinthians, the eleventh ode of Solomon, Melito's Homily on the Passover, a fragment of a hymn, the Apology of Phileas, and Psalms 33 and 34)

Date: Late third/early fourth century

Place of discovery: See comments on 𝔓66.

Housing location: Geneva/Cologny, Switzerland: Bibliotheca Bodmeriana (1 and 2 Peter now in Biblioteca Vaticana)

Publication date: 1959

Bibliography: Michael Testuz, *Papyrus Bodmer VII-IX: L'Epître de Jude, Les deux Epîtres de Pierre, Les Psaumes 33 et 34* (Cologny/Geneva, 1959).

Carlo M. Martini, *Beati Petri Apostoloi Epistulae, Ex Papyro Bodmeriano VIII* (Milan, 1968).

Sakae Kubo, 𝔓72 and the Codex Vaticanus in *Studies and Documents* 27 (1965), University of Utah Press.

Photos: Testuz, plates of entire MS

Inclusion in Greek text: Nestle, 24th edition (1960)

Textual character: 𝔓72 is a small codex made for private use and not for church meetings. Scholars think that four scribes took part in producing the entire MS (for contents, see above). First Peter has clear Alexandrian affinities—especially with B and then with A. Second Peter and (especially) Jude display more of an uncontrolled type of text (usually associated with the "Western" text), with several independent readings. Nonetheless, Kubo said, "Exclusive of singular variants, 𝔓72 has as a whole a text superior to that of B" (52).

Significance for text and translations: See 1 Peter 1:22; 2:21, 25; 3:7, 18; 4:14; 5:2a, 2b, 10, 13; 2 Peter 1:1, 3; 2:4, 13, 20; 3:10; Jude 5, 22-23 (Section 3).

Name: 𝔓75 (Papyrus Bodmer XIV-XV)

Content: Luke 3:18–4:2; 4:34–5:10; 5:37–18:18; 22:4–24:53; John 1:1–11:45, 48-57; 12:3–13:1, 8-9; 14:8-30; 15:7-8

Date: c. 200

Place of discovery: See comments on 𝔓66.

Housing location: Cologny/Geneva, Switzerland: Bibliotheca Bodmeriana.

Date of publication: 1961

Bibliography: Rudolf Kasser and Victor Martin, *Papyrus Bodmer XIV-XV, I: XIV: Luc chap. 3-24; II: XV: Jean chap. 1-15,* (Cologny/Geneva, 1961).

Kurt Aland, "Neue neutestamentliche Papyri III," in *New Testament Studies* 22 (1976): 375-396 (a publication containing previously unidentified fragments of the same MS).

Calvin Porter, "Papyrus Bodmer XV (𝔓75) and the Text of Codex Vaticanus." In *Journal of Biblical Literature* 81 (1962): 363-376.

Photos: Kasser and Martin, plates of entire MS.

Finegan, 105 (John 6:7-22), 119 (Luke 24:51-53 and John 1:1-16), 120 (John 1:16-33).

In this book see photos 2 and 6.

Inclusion in Greek text: Nestle, 25th edition (1963)

Textual character: Calvin Porter clearly established the fact that 𝔓75 displays the kind of text that was used in making Codex Vaticanus. In short, 𝔓75 is either an ancestor of B or a precursor of B. Scholars have a high regard for 𝔓75's textual fidelity. Metzger called it "proto-Alexandrian"; Aland said it has a "strict text." (For a further discussion concerning the textual character of 𝔓75 and its effect on the present view of the early transmission of the NT text, see Section 1.)

Significance for text and translations: See Luke 4:44; 6:1, 48; 7:11; 8:26, 43; 9:26, 35, 54, 55, 62; 10:1, 17, 22, 42; 11:2a, 2b, 2c, 4, 11, 23, 33, 42; 12:21, 27, 39; 14:5; 15:21; 17:24, 36; 18:11; 22:19b-20, 43-44, 62; 23:17, 34, 42; 24:3, 6, 12, 13, 32, 36, 40, 51, 52; John 1:18, 28, 34, 41; 3:13, 25; 4:1, 9; 5:1, 2, 3b-4, 44; 6:23a, 23b, 36; 7:8, 37-38, 39, 52; 7:53–8:11; 8:16, 39, 57; 9:35; 10:29; 11:25; 12:8, 41; 14:17 (Section 3).

Name: 𝔓77 (Pap. Oxy. 2683)

Content: Matthew 23:30-39

Date: Late second century

Place of discovery: Oxyrhynchus, Egypt

Housing location: Oxford, England: Ashmolean Museum (P. Oxy. 2683)

Date of publication: 1968

Bibliography: Ingrams, Kingston, Parsons, Rea, *Oxyrhynchus Papyri* Vol. 34 (1968), 1–3.

Inclusion in Greek text: NA[26] (1979)

Textual character: According to Ingrams et al., 𝔓77 has the closest affinity with ℵ. Aland describes the MS as having at least a normal text, done by a careless scribe.

Significance for text and translations: See Matt. 23:38 (Section 3).

Name: 𝔓78 (Pap. Oxy. 2684)

Content: Jude 4-5, 7-8

Date: Third/fourth century

Place of discovery: Oxyrhynchus, Egypt

Housing location: Oxford, England: Ashmolean Museum (P. Oxy. 2684)

Date of publication: 1968

Bibliography: Ingrams, Kingston, Parsons, Rea, *Oxyrhynchus Papyri*, Vol. 34 (1968), 4–6.

Inclusion in Greek text: NA[26] (1979)

Textual character: According to the editors, 𝔓78 displays a free text; "in four verses it contains two unique and three rare readings, all of them in disagreement with the earliest witness [𝔓72]" (4). But see the comments on Jude 4 below.

Significance for text and translations: In Jude 4, ℙ78 agrees with ℙ72 (and ℵ A B C) in reading "our only Lord and Master, Jesus Christ" versus the variant reading, "God, the only Master, and our Lord Jesus Christ"—a reading found in 𝔐 and noted only in NJBmg. Unfortunately, ℙ78 does not show the portion pertaining to the significant variant in Jude 5 (see comments on this verse under ℙ72).

Name: ℙ80
Content: John 3:34
Date: Third century
Place of discovery: Unknown
Housing location: Barcelona, Spain: Fundación San Lucas Evangelista (inv. no. 83)
Date of publication: 1966
Bibliography: R. Roca-Puig, "Papiro del evangelio de San Juan con 'Hermeneia,'" in *Atti dell' XI Congresso Internazionale di Papirologia* (Milan, 1966), 226–236.
Photo: Roca-Puig, John 3:34
Inclusion in Greek text: NA²⁶ (1979)—but not cited in apparatus
Textual character: too fragmentary to determine
Significance for text and translations: none, too fragmentary

Name: ℙ81
Content: 1 Peter 2:20–3:1, 4-12
Date: Fourth century
Place of discovery: The MS, originating from Egypt, was purchased from an antiquity dealer.
Housing location: Trieste: Sergio Daris (inv. no. 20)
Date of publication: 1967
Bibiliography: Sergio Daris, "Uno nuovo frammento della prima lettera di Pietro," in *Papyrologica Castroctaviana: Studia et Textus* 2 (Barcelona, 1967): 11–37.
Inclusion in Greek text: NA²⁶ (1979)
Photos: Daris, 1 Pet. 2:20–3:1; 3:4-12
Textual character: ℙ81 is an Alexandrian MS, showing agreement with B, then with ℙ72.
Significance for text and translations: See 1 Peter 2:21, 24; 3:7 (Section 3).

Name: 𝔓82

Content: Luke 7:32-34, 37-38

Date: Fourth century or perhaps fifth

Place of discovery: Perhaps Oxyrhynchus, Egypt (according to Schwartz)

Housing location: Strasbourg, France: Bibliothèque Nationale et Universitaire (P. Gr. 2677)

Date of publication: 1968

Bibliography: J. Schwartz, "Fragment d'évangile sur papyrus," in *Zeitschrift für Papyrologie und Epigraphik* 3 (1968): 157–158.

Inclusion in Greek text: NA²⁶ (1979)—but not cited in apparatus

Textual character: too fragmentary to determine

Significance for text and translations: 𝔓82 contains no significant variants and is too small to make any effect on the Greek text or subsequent English translations.

Name: 𝔓85

Content: Revelation 9:19–10:1, 5-9

Date: Fourth century or perhaps fifth

Place of discovery: perhaps Oxyrhynchus, Egypt

Housing location: Strasbourg, France: Bibliothèque Nationale et Universitaire (P. Gr. 1028)

Date of publication: 1969

Bibliography: J. Schwartz, "Papyrus et tradition manuscrite," in *Zeitschrift für Papyrologie und Epigraphik* 4 (1969): 178–182.

Inclusion in Greek text: NA²⁶ (1979)

Textual character: 𝔓85 displays remarkable agreement with 𝔓47 and with ℵ, as over against A and C. In the three variation units in which 𝔓85 is cited in NA²⁶, 𝔓85 agrees with 𝔓47 in every instance—and twice also with ℵ, against A and C (see Rev. 9:20; 10:7, 9 in the critical apparatus of NA²⁶).

Significance for text and translations: None of the variations in 𝔓85 have been adopted by the translators. Nonetheless, it would seem that the variant in Rev. 10:7 is worth at least a note in the margin. 𝔓47 𝔓85 ℵ 𝔐ᴷ read, "just as he announced to his servants and the prophets"; whereas A C 𝔐ᴬ read, "just as he announced to his servants, the prophets"—which is the reading followed by all the translators.

Name: 𝔓86
Content: Matthew 5:13-16, 22-25
Date: Beginning of the fourth century
Place of discovery: Unknown
Housing location: Cologne: Institut für Altertumskunde (P. Col. theol. 5516)
Date of publication: 1974
Bibliography: Charalambakis, Hagedorn, Kaimakis, Thüngen, "Vier literarische Papyri der Kölner Sammlung," in *Zeitschrift für Papyrologie und Epigraphik* 14 (1974): 37–40.
Inclusion in Greek text: NA[26] (1979)—but not cited in the apparatus. The one place where 𝔓86 could be added to the apparatus of NA[26] is at Matt. 5:13—where 𝔓86* (with א B C 33) supports the text, as opposed to the variant reading which reads βληθῆναι ἔξω καὶ καταπατεῖσθαι (supported by 𝔓86[c] [a second-hand corrector, according to the editors] D W 𝔐).
Textual character: The text of 𝔓86 contains very little variation from NA[26]; the editors have said that it agrees with א and B, the prominent members of the "Egyptian" text-type.
Significance for text and translations: See comments on Matt. 5:13 under "Inclusion in Greek text" above.

Name: 𝔓87
Content: Philemon 13-15, 24-25
Date: Early third century (the earliest extant fragment of Philemon)—the handwriting is very similar to that found in 𝔓46
Place of discovery: Unknown
Housing location: Cologne: Institut für Altertumskunde, P. Col. theol. 12
Date of publication: 1982
Bibliography: Kramer, Römer, Hagedorn, *Kölner Papyri 4: Papyrologica Coloniensa* Vol. 7 (1982), 28–31.
Inclusion in Greek text: NA[26] (1979)—but not cited in apparatus
Textual character: Aland has said that 𝔓87 has a "normal" text.
Significance for text and translations: See Philem. 25 (Section 3).

Name: 𝔓88
Content: Mark 2:1-26
Date: Fourth century

Place of discovery: Unknown

Housing location: Milan, Italy: Università Cattolica, P. Med. (inv. no. 69.24)

Date of publication: 1972

Bibliography: Sergio Daris, "Papiri letterari dell' Università Cattolica di Milano," in *Aegyptus* 52 (1972): 80–88.

Photos: Daris, Mark 2:2-8; 2:9-15; 2:15-19; 2:20-26

Inclusion in Greek text: NA[26] (1979)

Textual character: According to Daris, 𝔓88 is Alexandrian.

Significance for text and translations: See Mark 2:4, 10, 16a, 16b, 22 (Section 3).

Name: 𝔓89

Content: Hebrews 6:7-9, 15-17

Date: Second half of the fourth century

Place of discovery: Unknown

Housing location: Florence: Biblioteca Medicea Laurenziana (PL III/292)

Date of publication: 1981

Bibliography: Rosario Pintaudi, "N.T. Ad Hebraeos VI, 7-9; 15-17 (PL III/292)," in *Zeitschrift für Papyrologie und Epigraphik* 42 (1981): 42–45.

Photos: Pintaudi, Heb. 6:7-9; 6:15-17

Inclusion in Greek text: NA[26], 7th printing (1985)—incorrectly cited in appendix as containing Philemon 13-15, 24-25

Textual character: 𝔓89 is too fragmentary to determine its textual affinities.

Significance for text and translations: The portion that 𝔓89 contains does not have any variation units significant for translators (see UBS[3]), and 𝔓89 does not present any significant variant readings.

Name: 𝔓90 (Pap. Oxy. 3523)

Content: John 18:36–19:7

Date: Second century (150–175)

Place of discovery: Oxyrhynchus, Egypt

Housing location: Oxford, England: Ashmolean Museum (P. Oxy. 3523)

Date of publication: 1980

Bibliography: Theodore A. Skeat, *Oxyrhynchus Papyri* Vol. 50 (1983), 3–8. Kurt Aland, "Der Text des Johannesevangeliums im 2. Jahrhundert," in *Studien zum Text und zur Ethik des Neuen Testaments* (Berlin, 1986), 1-10.

Inclusion in Greek text: Not yet included in UBS³ or NA²⁶

Textual character: 𝔭90 has more affinity with 𝔭66 than with any other single MS, though it does not concur with 𝔭66 in its entirety.

Significance for text and translations: The portion of text surviving in 𝔭90 does not contain significant variant readings. The UBS³ does not have any textual notes for this portion, and none of the translations provide any marginal notes for textual variants in this portion.

Name: 𝔭91

Content: Acts 2:30-37, 46–3:2. Note: this MS was first published in two segments, one by Pickering and the other by Gallazzi (see bibliography below). It was later discovered by K. Treu that both fragments were part of the same MS; in fact, the two fragments fit side by side.

Date: Third century

Place of discovery: Unknown

Housing location: One portion (the larger one): Milan, Italy: Istituto di Papirologia, Università degli Studi di Milano (P. Mil. Vogl. Inv. 1224); the other portion (the smaller one): North Ryde, Australia: Ancient History Documentary Research Centre at Macquarie University (P. Macquarie inv. 360).

Date of publication: 1982, 1984

Bibliography: Claudio Gallazzi, "P. Mil. Vogl. Inv. 1224: Novum Testamentum, Act. 2,30-37 E 2,46-3,2" in *Bulletin of American Society of Papyrologists* 19 (1982): 39–45.

S. R. Pickering, "The Macquarie Papyrus of the Acts of the Apostles," a preliminary report (Aug. 30, 1984).

S. R. Pickering, "P. Macquarie Inv. 360 (+ P. Mil. Vogl. Inv. 1224): Acta Apostolorum 2.30-37, 2.46–3.2," in *Zeitschrift für Papyrologie und Epigraphik* 65 (1986): 76–79. In this publication, the transcription for both portions of the MS is given.

Photos: Gallazzi's article shows the larger portion of Acts 2:30-37; 2:46–3:2; Pickering's first article (above) shows the smaller portion of the same MS.

Inclusion in Greek text: Not yet included in UBS³ or NA²⁶

Textual character: According to Gallazzi, 𝔭91 agrees with ℵ and B and differs from Western MSS and D. According to Pickering, 𝔭91 contains no Western variants and appears to be in conformity with the Alexandrian text type—though the extant portion is too fragmentary to be absolutely sure.

Significance for text and translations: In Acts 2:47, 𝔭91^{vid} (with 𝔭74^{vid} ℵ A B C 095) supports the reading ἐπὶ τὸ αὐτό. Πέτρος δὲ (usually translated ". . . to their number. And Peter . . ."), as against the reading τῇ ἐκκλησίᾳ. Ἐπὶ τὸ αὐτό δὲ Πέτρος καὶ Ἰωάννης (". . . to the church. Now Peter and John together . . ."), supported by E P 𝔐, and followed by KJV. All the modern translations follow the reading of ℵ A B C, now supported by 𝔭91vid. Other than this portion, 𝔭91 does not present any evidence for other significant variant readings.

Name: 𝔭92
Content: Ephesians 1:11-13, 19-21; 2 Thessalonians 1:4-5, 11-12
Date: Late third/early fourth century
Place of discovery: The MS was found in the winter of 1969 near a race-course in Narmouthis (ancient Medinet Madi) near the Fayum, Egypt.
Housing location: Cairo, Egypt: Museo Egizio del Cairo (P. Narmuthis inv. 69.39a and 69.229a)
Date of publication: 1982
  Bibliography: Claudio Gallazzi, "Frammenti di un Codice con le Epistole di Paolo," in *Zeitschrift für Papyrologie und Epigraphik* 46 (1982): 117–122.
Inclusion in Greek text: NA^{26}, 7th printing (1983)
Textual character: According to Gallazzi, 𝔭92 shows a strong affinity with 𝔭46, ℵ, and B.
Significance for text and translations: The extant portion of 𝔭92 displays a text very similar to that found in NA^{26} and UBS^3, which is a portion that does not have significant variants (the UBS^3 text does not have any notes for these verses). Nonetheless, it is worthwhile to note that in Eph. 1:20 𝔭92^{vid} agrees with B in having the participle καθίσας ("seating")—as opposed to D F G 𝔐, which read ἐκαθίσεν ("seated") and ℵ A, which read καθίσας αὐτόν ("seating him").

Name: 𝔭95
Content: John 5:26-29, 36-38
Date: Early third century
Place of discovery: Unknown

Housing location: Florence: Biblioteca Medicea Laurenziana (PL II/31)

Date of publication: 1985

Bibliography: Jean Lenaerts, "Un papyrus l'Evangile de Jean: PL II/31," in *Chronique d'Egypte* 60 (1985): 117–120.

Photos: Lanaerts, John 5:26-29; 5:36-38

Inclusion in Greek text: Not yet included in UBS[3] or NA[26]

Textual character: 𝔓95 is too fragmentary to determine its textual affinities.

Significance for text and translations: The variant readings found in 𝔓95 are not significant enough to warrant any changes in modern English translations.

EARLY UNCIAL MANUSCRIPTS

Early MSS written on a material other than papyri (such as vellum or parchment) have been classified as "Uncial Manuscripts." A few Uncial MSS have been dated in the third century; thus, they should be considered along with all the early papyrus MSS as providing witness to the NT text prior to the time of ℵ and B.

Name: 0162 (Pap. Oxy. 847)

Content: John 2:11-22

Date: Third century

Place of discovery: Oxyrhynchus, Egypt

Housing location: New York: Metropolitan Museum of Art (09.182.43)

Date of publication: 1909

Bibliography: Grenfell and Hunt, *Oxyrhynchus Papyri* Vol. 5 (1909), 4–5.

Inclusion in Greek text: UBS[1] (1966), NA[26] (1979)

Textual character: 0162 shows great affinity with the papyri, 𝔓66 and 𝔓75, as well as with B (see John 2:12, 15a, 15b, 16 in the critical apparatus of NA[26]).

Significance for text and translations: See **Textual character** above.

Name: 0171

Content: Matthew 10:17-23, 25-32; Luke 22:44-56, 61-64

Date: c. 300

Place of discovery: Hermopolis Magna, Egypt

Housing location: Florence: Bibliotheca Laurenziana (PSI 2.124)

Date of publication: 1912, 1913

Bibliography: *Pubblicazioni della Società Italiana, Papiri Greci e Latini*
Vol. 1 (1912): 2–4; Vol. 2 (1913): 22–25.

Photo: Aland, plate 17, Luke 22:44-50

Inclusion in Greek text: UBS¹ (1966), NA²⁶ (1979)

Textual character: Aland considers 0171 to be an early or secondary form
of the D-text. Metzger says it is an important witness in Egypt to the
Western text (*Text*, 61). A transcription of the text is printed in *New
Documents Illustrating Early Christianity* (vol. 2), by G. H. R. Horsley,
ed., who says that 0171 "accords overall—although not everywhere—
with D, which embodies several readings influenced by phraseology in
the synoptic parallels" (127).

Significance for text and translations: See Luke 22:43-44, 62 (Section 3).

Name: 0189

Content: Acts 5:3-21

Date: Late second or early third century (the earliest parchment MS of the
NT)

Place of discovery: Unknown

Housing location: Berlin, Germany: Staatliche Museen (P. 11765)

Date of publication: 1981, 1987

Bibliography: A photograph of 0189, showing Acts 5:12-21, is included in
Aland's *Text of the New Testament*, 104.

Photo: See bibliography above.

Inclusion in Greek text: UBS¹ (1966), NA²⁶ (1979)

Textual character: Aland says it is "at least normal."

Significance for text and translations: In Acts 5:3, 0189 supports the
reading ἐπλήρωσεν ("has filled") versus ἐπείρασεν ("has hard-
ened"). See Metzger's discussion on this textual variation in *A Textual
Commentary on The Greek New Testament*, 327–328.

Name: 0212 (a fragment of Tatian's Diatessaron)

Content: Matthew 27:56-57; Mark 15:40, 42; Luke 23:49-51, 54; John
19:38

Date: Early third century (prior to A.D. 256–257, according to Metzger,
because Dura-Europos fell to the Persians then—*Text*, 90)

Place of discovery: In 1933 this small portion of the Diatessaron was "unearthed by archaeologists on the site of the ancient Roman fortress-town of Dura-Europos on the lower Euphrates" (Metzger, ibid.).

Housing location: New Haven, Connecticut: Yale University (P. Dura 10).

Date of publication: 1935

Bibliography: Carl H. Kraeling, *Studies and Documents*, Vol. 3 (London, 1935).

Photo: Aland, plate 13, entire MS

Inclusion in Greek text: NA[26] (1979)—but not cited in apparatus

Textual character: too fragmentary to determine

Significance for text and translations: See Metzger's English translation of the text (ibid.).

Name: 0220

Content: Romans 4:23–5:3, 8-13

Date: Third century

Place of discovery: Purchased in Cairo, Egypt, in 1950 by Dr. Leland C. Wyman, a Professor of Biology at Boston University.

Housing location: London: Quatrich

Date of publication: 1952

Bibliography: W. H. P. Hatch, *Harvard Theological Review* 45 (1952): 81–85.

Inclusion in Greek text: Nestle, 21st edition (1952)

Textual character: According to Metzger, 0220 is in agreement with B everywhere except in Rom. 5:1 (*Text*, 61). Aland says it has a "strict" text (*Text*, 95).

Significance for text and translations: See Rom. 5:1 (Section 3).

SECTION THREE

The Effect of Early Manuscripts on Modern English Translations of the New Testament

The following section contains all the passages from Matthew to Revelation in which the early MSS have had a significant influence on modern English translations of the NT. Of course, this section does not cover all the passages in the NT where there is significant variation because the early MSS do not cover the entire NT. Those who want to see a discussion on many such variations may find such in my work, "Guide to the Ancient Manuscripts" in *Eight Translation New Testament* (eighth printing, 1987); they may also consult Metzger's *Textual Commentary on the Greek New Testament*.

The first reading cited for each variation unit below is that found in the text of UBS³ and NA²⁶; the following readings are variants. When that first reading is one that was newly adopted for NA²⁶ (thus constituting a change from previous editions of the Nestle text), it has been marked with an asterisk (*) at the beginning of the reading. After each reading cited, I have provided a short list of MSS supporting the reading. This list includes the papyri and some major uncial MSS (such as ℵ A B C D Q L R W) and others (33 1739). A more complete listing for each variant can be found in UBS³ and NA²⁶. Whenever a papyrus MS is cited with the siglum *vid* (such as 𝔭45ᵛⁱᵈ), I have endeavored to verify the reading—either by looking at a photo, a facsimile, a microfiche, or the actual MS—which I have done on several occasions and mentioned when it was appropriate to do so. Some of these MSS are presented in photographic form at the back of the book.

A list of abbreviations used in the next section is found at the beginning of this book. Bibliographic information is also provided in abbreviated form in this section. Page numbers are not given for works that are formatted to the NT text, verse by verse. (The reader need only look up the verse being discussed to locate the comments quoted or referenced.) A few works are cited throughout this entire third section for which only the author's last name is provided. They are as follows:

Kurt and Barbara Aland, *The Text of the New Testament* (1987).

Philip W. Comfort, "Guide to the Ancient Manuscripts," in *Eight Translation New Testament* (eighth printing, 1987).

Frederick C. Grant, "The Greek Text of the New Testament" in *An Introduction to the Revised Standard Version of the New Testament*, 37-43.

Bruce M. Metzger, *A Textual Commentary on the Greek New Testament* (1971; corrected edition, 1975).

R. V. G. Tasker, "Notes on Variant Readings," in *The Greek New Testament* (being the Text Translated in the New English Bible, 1961), 411–445.

B. F. Westcott and F. J. A. Hort, *Introduction to the New Testament in the Original Greek: Notes on Selected Readings*, 1882.

Matthew

Early manuscripts containing portions of Matthew:

𝔓1: 1:1-18
𝔓21: 12:24-26, 32-33
𝔓25: 18:32-34; 19:1-3, 5-7, 9-10
𝔓35: 25:12-15, 20-23
𝔓37: 26:19-52
𝔓45: 20:24-32; 21:13-19; 25:41–26:39 (with lacunae)
𝔓53: 26:29-40
𝔓62: 11:25-30
𝔓64/67: 3:9, 15; 5:20-22, 25-28; 26:7-8, 10, 14-15, 22-23, 31-33
𝔓70: 2:13-16; 2:22–3:1; 11:26-27; 12:4-5; 24:3-6, 12-15
𝔓71: 19:10-11, 17-18
𝔓77: 23:30-39
𝔓86: 5:13-16, 22-25
0170: 10:17-23, 25-32

▶ Matthew 1:16

The NEBmg and NJBmg give two variant readings: "Joseph, to whom was betrothed Mary, a virgin, who gave birth to Jesus" and "Joseph, to whom Mary, a virgin, was betrothed, was the father of Jesus." The first reading is supported by some early Latin translations and a few later MSS; the second reading is supported by one Syriac MS. The NJBmg says that the Syriac reading must have arisen as a result of a misunderstanding of the first variant just mentioned. Since no Greek MSS contain the second reading, and all the early Greek MSS—including 𝔓1 ℵ B C L W—support the reading "Joseph, the husband of Mary of whom was born Jesus," the readings given in NEBmg and NJBmg could hardly have been part of the original text.

▶ Matthew 1:18

the birth of Jesus Christ 𝔓1 ℵ C: ASV RSV NASB NIV TEV NJB.
the birth of the Christ no Greek MSS; some Old Latin MSS and Syriac MSS: NEB ASVmg RSVmg. (B reads "Christ Jesus" and W reads "Jesus.")

The Greek expression supported by 𝔓1 et al. is difficult, for τοῦ δὲ Ἰησοῦ Χριστοῦ ἡ γένεσις literally means "now the birth of the Jesus Christ." The definite article before the title "Jesus Christ" does not appear in any other place in the NT except in inferior MSS: in Acts 8:37; 1 John 4:3; and Rev. 12:17 (Westcott and Hort, 7). This would give copyists cause to make the changes as noted above. However, all of the translations except the NEB followed the more difficult reading. The ASV translators had the testimony of ℵ and C; all the rest, the added testimony of 𝔓1.

▶ Matthew 2:23

𝔓70 is the only MS (and the earliest) to read Ναζαρά (contrary to the reading Ναζαρέτ in ℵ B D L 33 or Ναζαρέθ in C W). Ναζαρά is an Aramaic form of Ναζαρέτ, derived from the word *netser*, meaning "branch." Though this will not affect the translation of the name of the city in which Jesus lived, it does add weight to the argument that the last part of this verse ("that what was spoken by the prophets might be fulfilled, 'He shall be called a Nazarene' ") alludes to the messianic prophecy in Isaiah 11:1, where the Messiah is called *Netser* ("Branch"). The reason Jesus is called "a Nazarene" is that he, "the Branch," comes from the city whose name means "branch." (For a further explanation of this difficult passage, see "Matthew" by D. A. Carson in *The Expositor's Bible Commentary*, 96–97.)

▶ Matthew 5:22
angry with his brother 𝔭67 ℵ* B: all the translations.
angry with his brother without cause ℵ² D L W 33 𝔐: ASVmg RSVmg NASBmg NIVmg NEBmg TEVmg.

The UBS³ text cites 𝔭67ᵛⁱᵈ, but there is no need to affix the *vid* to this papyrus—for it clearly does not have the addition εἰκῆ ("without cause"). 𝔭67 strengthens the case for the shorter reading. The addition is an attempt to soften Jesus' bold assertion: "every one who is angry with his brother shall be liable to judgment" (RSV).

▶ Matthew 5:25
lest the adversary hand you over to the judge, and the judge to the officer 𝔭67ᵛⁱᵈ ℵ B: ASVmg RSV NASB NEB NJB.
lest the adversary hand you over to the judge, and the judge hand you over to the officer D L W 33 𝔐: ASV NIV TEV.

The difference between the two readings is that the second reading repeats σε παραδῷ ("hand you over"). This repetition could have been original and then later dropped in the Alexandrian MSS for the purpose of refinement, but it is more likely (and in keeping with the habits of copyists) for certain scribes to have repeated the phrase. Most of the translators followed the first reading, except the translators of two modern versions, NIV and TEV, to whom the testimony of 𝔭67 was available but not followed.

▶ Matthew 12:25
knowing their thoughts he said ℵ*,² B: ASV RSV NASB NEB NJB.
knowing their thoughts Jesus said C L W: NIV TEV.
seeing [or, perceiving] their thoughts he said 𝔭21 ℵ¹ D: none.

Not one translation followed the reading in 𝔭21 et al. or even listed this reading in the margin. Perhaps textual critics and translators alike thought it unlikely that Matthew would have described Jesus as "seeing" the thoughts of others. But it could be argued that the very unusualness of this expression caused certain scribes to change "seeing" to "knowing." The UBS[3] and NA[26] compilers opted for "seeing" over "knowing" in Matt. 9:4 in a very similar context. Why not here? Perhaps some translators should consider the reading in 𝔭21 et al.—and if not adopt it, at least note it in the margin as a viable option (cf. ASVmg and RSVmg for Matt. 9:4).

▶ Matthew 19:9

and marries another, he commits adultery ℵ C[3] D L: ASVmg RSV NASB NIV NEB TEV NJB.
and he who marries a divorced woman commits adultery (𝔭25) (B) C* W: ASV RSVmg NASBmg NEBmg.

𝔭25 and B, each with minor variations, have wording similar to that found in C* and W (translated above), a reading which asserts that a man commits adultery by marrying "a divorced woman." As in Matt. 19:9a, this added thought was probably borrowed from Matt. 5:32.

▶ Matthew 19:10

See comments on this verse in the description of 𝔭71 (Section 2).

▶ Matthew 23:38

***your house is left to you desolate** 𝔭77[vid] ℵ C D W 33 𝔐: ASV RSV NASB NIV NEBmg TEV NJB.
your house is left to you B L: ASVmg RSVmg NEB.

𝔭77[vid] provides the earliest witness to the presence of ἔρημος ("desolate") in Matt. 23:38. This witness, combined with that of several other MSS, was enough to prompt the UBS[3] and NA[26] editors to include the word in the text (a change from previous editions of the Nestle text) and to convince almost all the translators to do the same. The only argument against this reading is that scribes could have added the word ἔρημος to make it conform to Jer. 22:5, the OT passage behind this verse. But it is more likely that ἔρημος was dropped in MSS like B and L because the scribes thought the word ἔρημος was superfluous after ἀφίεται ("is left") (Metzger).

▶ Matthew 26:20

*with the twelve 𝔓37[vid] 𝔓45[vid] B D: ASVmg RSVmg NIV NJB.
with the twelve disciples ℵ A L W: ASV RSV NASB NEB TEV.

The testimony of the papyri along with B and D created a change in the Nestle text. Prior to NA[26], the Nestle text included the word μαθητῶν. But the early evidence shows that this must have been a later addition. But one wonders why the RSV, NASB, etc. did not follow the superior reading—unless, of course, the translators also felt obligated to add "disciples." But such an addition is not necessary in light of the fact that Jesus' closest followers were often designated by the gospel writers as simply "the Twelve."

▶ Matthew 26:27

a cup ℵ B L W: ASV RSV NASB NEB NJB.
the cup 𝔓37[vid] 𝔓45 A C D: ASVmg NIV TEV.

Given the fact that scribes would be more inclined to add a definite article before "cup" (especially since the cup here is the cup of the Lord's supper) than to delete an article, it is quite likely that ℵ B L W preserve the original wording. Most of the translations, accordingly, did not follow the second reading. Nevertheless, the testimony of 𝔓37[vid] and 𝔓45 may have encouraged the translators of NIV and TEV to add the definite article before "cup."

▶ Matthew 26:28

covenant 𝔓37 𝔓45[vid] ℵ B L: ASV RSV NASB NIV NEB TEV NJB.
new covenant A C D W: ASVmg RSVmg NIVmg NJBmg.

The first reading is most probably the one Matthew wrote. The four earliest MSS attest to this, and all the translations follow. Influenced by Luke 22:20, which contains the word "new" before "covenant," later scribes harmonized the Matthean account to Luke's.

Mark

Early manuscripts containing portions of Mark:

𝔭45: 4:36–9:31; 11:27–12:28 (with many lacunae)
𝔭88: 2:1-26
0212: 15:40, 42

▶ Mark 2:4

could not bring him 𝔭88 ℵ B L 33: ASVmg NASB NIV TEV NJB.
could not come near to him A C D 090: ASV RSV NEB.
could not come to him W: none.

𝔭88 joins with ℵ and B in giving the earliest witness to the shortest reading, "could not bring him," a reading that many of the more recent versions reflect.

▶ Mark 2:10

the authority the Son of man has to forgive sins on earth B: NJB.
the authority the Son of man has to forgive on earth sins A: none.
the Son of man has authority on earth to forgive sins 𝔭88 ℵ C D L 090 33: ASV RSV NASB NIV NEB TEV.

Each varying syntactical arrangement of this part of Mark 2:10 seems to convey a slightly different meaning. Almost all the translators preferred the reading supported by 𝔭88 et al., against the editors of UBS[3] and NA[26], who chose the arrangement found in B.

▶ Mark 2:16a

the scribes of the Pharisees 𝔭88 ℵ B L W 33: all the translations.
the scribes and the Pharisees A C D 𝔐: ASVmg RSVmg.

The first reading is the more difficult of the two and the one with earlier and better attestation. Mark was speaking of certain scribes who were also Pharisees. This is conveyed in all the translations.

▶ Mark 2:16b

why does he eat B D W: ASVmg RSV NIV NEB TEV NJB.
why does he eat and drink 𝔭88 A 33: ASV RSVmg NASB.

why do your disciples eat ℵ: none.
why do your disciples eat and drink C L: none.

The shorter reading, found in B D W, is probably the one from which all the others diverged. This is the reading followed by most of the modern versions, though the ASV and NASB preferred the expanded reading found in A and C, now supported by 𝔭88 (which could very likely have come from the parallel passage in Luke 5:30).

▶ Mark 2:22

but new wine into fresh wineskins ℵ* B: (ASV) (NASB) RSV NEB NJB.
but new wine into fresh wineskins is put 𝔭88 ℵ¹ A C 074 33: NIV TEV.
omit D and a few Old Latin MSS: RSVmg.

Most likely, scribes added the verb to complete a statement (intended to be parenthetical) lacking a predicate. Thus, the reading in ℵ* B displays the original text. Some of the translations followed this text strictly— i.e., they do not have a predicate, and other translations have a supplied verb (set in italics—as in ASV and NASB). The NIV and TEV, which do not have italicized words, by consequence reflect the reading of 𝔭88 et al.

▶ Mark 5:21

include **in the boat** ℵ A B C L: ASV RSV NASB NIV NEB NJB.
omit 𝔭45[vid] D: TEV.

Given the fact that the scribe of 𝔭45 had a proclivity for omitting words, it could be argued that the words "in the boat" are original. But it could also be argued that the words were added by scribes to fill out the sentence. Thus, the words "in the boat" appear in the texts of UBS[3] and NA[26] but are contained within brackets to signal some doubt about their authenticity. Either way, most of the translators included these words to fill out what would otherwise be a bare, nondescriptive statement: "Jesus went back across to the other side of the lake" (TEV).

▶ Mark 6:3

Is not this the carpenter, the son of Mary? א A B C D L W: all the translations.

Is not this the son of the carpenter, the son of Mary? $\mathfrak{P}$45[vid]: none.

Is not this the son of the carpenter and Mary 33[vid] several Old Latin MSS and Origen: NEBmg.

The first reading is undoubtedly the one Mark wrote. Certain scribes made emendations (as recorded above) either to harmonize Mark 6:3 with Matt. 13:55 or to soften what some might consider an offensive statement—i.e., Jesus was here said to be not just the son of a carpenter but a carpenter himself! Origen countered Celsus, a second-century anatagonist of Christianity who attacked its founder as being nothing but a carpenter, by saying that "in none of the Gospels current in the churches is Jesus himself ever described as a carpenter" (*Contra Celsum*, 6.34 and 36). Origen must have forgotten Mark 6:3 or deliberately favored a reading like that found in $\mathfrak{P}$45 f[13] and 33 (see Metzger).

Although the NEBmg notes the third reading above, the committee for the NEB did not incorporate this reading into the text on the grounds that it was "considered suspect, as a probable harmonization with Mt. 13.55" (Tasker).

▶ Mark 6:23

*with many [vows] **he swore to her** $\mathfrak{P}$45[vid] D: TEV.

he swore to her א A B C[cvid] 33: ASV RSV NASB NIV NEB NJB.

The Greek word for "many" ($\pi o \lambda \lambda \alpha$) is bracketed in UBS[3] and NA[26] because the word is a suspected addition to the Marcan original. Nonetheless, the word was included in deference to the testimony of $\mathfrak{P}$45[vid]. But most of the translations followed the second reading noted above.

▶ Mark 6:44

include **the bread** A B L 33: ASV RSV NASB NEB NJB.

omit $\mathfrak{P}$45 א D W: NIV TEV.

The Greek words for "the bread" ($\tauο\grave{υ}ς$ $\overset{\prime}{α}\rhoτους$) are bracketed in UBS[3] and NA[26] in deference to their omission in $\mathfrak{P}$45 et al. (see Metzger). The NIV and TEV translators must have been influenced by the testimony of $\mathfrak{P}$45 with א D W versus that of A and B.

▶ Mark 7:4

*bronze vessels and beds A D W 33: ASVmg RSVmg NIVmg TEV.
bronze vessels $\mathfrak{P}$45^{vid} ℵ B L: ASV RSV NIV NEB TEVmg.

The Greek words for "and beds" ($\kappa\alpha\grave{\iota}$ $\kappa\lambda\iota\nu\hat{\omega}\nu$) are included (for the first time in the Nestle text) yet bracketed in UBS[3] and NA[26] because the committee could not decide if these words "were added by copyists who were influenced by the legislation of Lv 15, or whether the words were omitted (*a*) accidentally because of homoeoteleuton or (*b*) deliberately because the idea of washing or sprinkling beds seemed to be quite incongruous" (Metzger). Most of the translations follow the reading without the words "and beds" on the basis of the testimony of $\mathfrak{P}$45^{vid}. Grant indicated that the RSV was specifically influenced by the testimony of $\mathfrak{P}$45 with B.

▶ Mark 7:28

*Lord [or, **Sir**] $\mathfrak{P}$45 D W: NEB TEV.
Yes, Lord [or, **Sir**] ℵ A B L W: ASV RSV NASB NIV NJB.

The first reading constitutes a change for the Nestle text, which prior to NA[26] retained the word $\nu\alpha\acute{\iota}$ ("yes")—per the testimony of ℵ A B. $\mathfrak{P}$45 helped to produce the change. But only two translations followed the reading in $\mathfrak{P}$45 D W—which probably is the original, because the second reading shows the marks of harmonization with Matt. 15:27.

▶ Mark 7:35

include **immediately** $\mathfrak{P}$45 A W: TEV.
omit ℵ B D L: ASV RSV NASB NIV NEB NJB.

The Greek word for "immediately" ($\epsilon\grave{\upsilon}\theta\acute{\epsilon}\omega\varsigma$) is bracketed in UBS[3] and NA[26] because the external testimony against its inclusion is so impressive. Quite likely, the scribe of $\mathfrak{P}$45, displaying his usual editorialization, added one of Mark's favorite words. As in Mark 6:23 and 7:28, TEV adhered to the text of UBS[3] as against almost all the other translations.

▶ Mark 8:15

Herod ℵ A B C D L 33: all the translations.
Herodians $\mathfrak{P}$45 W: RSVmg.

The translators of the RSV, influenced by the testimony of 𝔓45 and W (two MSS discovered after the publication of the ASV), provided the alternative reading in the margin (see Grant).

▶ Mark 8:38a

whoever is ashamed of me and my words ℵ A B C D L 33: ASV RSV NASB NIV NEBmg TEV NJB.

whoever is ashamed of me and mine (i.e., my disciples) 𝔓45[vid] W: NEB.

See comments on Mark 8:38b below.

▶ Mark 8:38b

the glory of his father with his holy angels ℵ A B C D L W 33: ASV RSV NASB NIV NEBmg TEV NJB.

the glory of his father and of the holy angels 𝔓45 W: NEB.

In both the parts of Mark 8:38 which contain textual variation, the translators of NEB followed the reading of 𝔓45 and W. Concerning Mark 8:38a, "the translators considered that the reference in context is more likely to be to Jesus and his *followers* than to Jesus and his *words*" (Tasker). Concerning Mark 8:38b, "καί [and] was read rather than μετά [with]" because "μετά was regarded as an assimilation to Mt. 16.27" (Tasker). Of course, the testimony of all the other early MSS—followed by all the other translations—speaks very well for the other reading.

▶ Mark 9:24

cried out 𝔓45 ℵ A* B C* L (W): all the translations.

cried out with tears A² C³ D 33: ASVmg RSVmg.

The first reading is so manifestly superior, one wonders why the translators of the ASV and RSV considered it worthwhile to note the second reading in the margin.

▶ Mark 9:29

prayer ℵ* B: all the translations.

prayer and fasting 𝔓45[vid] ℵ² A C D L W 33: margins of all the translations.

All the versions followed the shorter reading supported by the two venerable MSS, ℵ* B. This is a good choice because the second reading is a manifest expansion, added by scribes who associated prayer with fasting. (See also 1 Cor. 7:5 for the same kind of addition.) Nonetheless, the second reading was noted in all the versions out of respect for the testimony of 𝔓45ᵛⁱᵈ ℵ² A C D.

Luke

Early manuscripts containing portions of Luke:

𝔓4: 1:58-59; 1:62–2:1, 6-7; 3:8–4:2, 29-32, 34-35; 5:3-8; 5:30–6:16
𝔓45: 6:31–7:7; 9:26–14:33 (with many lacunae)
𝔓69: 22:41, 45-48, 58-61
𝔓75: 3:18–4:2; 4:34–5:10; 5:37–18:18; 22:4–24:53
𝔓82: 7:32-34, 37-38
0171: 22:44-56, 61-64
0212: 23:49-51, 54

▶ Luke 1:68
Blessed be [the] Lord, the God of Israel ℵ A B C D: ASV RSV NASB NIV TEV NJB.
Blessed be the God of Israel 𝔓4 W: NEB.

The first reading follows the wording found in Ps. 40:14 LXX and 105:48 LXX. The modern translations, except NEB, follow this reading. The NEB follows the reading found in 𝔓4 W and some early versions, a reading which omits "Lord"—hence the translation, "Blessed be the God of Israel." Although it could be argued that the word "Lord" (κύριος) was dropped due to homeoteleuton (the eye of the scribe passed from $\overline{ΟΣ}$ in ΕΥΛΟΓΗΤΟΣ$\overline{ΚΣ}$Ο$\overline{ΘΣ}$ to the final word $\overline{ΘΣ}$), it could also be argued that κύριος was added in order to make the quotation conform to the LXX.

▶ Luke 1:78
the dayspring will visit us 𝔓4ᵛⁱᵈ ℵ* B W: ASV RSV NASB NIV NEB TEV.

the dayspring has visited us ℵ² A C D R: ASVmg RSVmg NEBmg NJB.

Every version, except NJB, adopts the wording with the future tense; but several versions (ASV, RSV, NEB) note the past tense reading in the margin. The change from the future tense to the aorist (past) is more probable than vice versa because the same verb is aorist in Luke 1:68. Even though the verb is future, the expression in context points to Christ's first advent—his visitation as the sunrising or dayspring from the heights (Comfort).

It should be noted that $\mathfrak{p}4^{vid}$ is not listed in UBS³ or NA²⁶, probably because the MS is very difficult to read in this place. Having examined the actual MS in the Bibliothèque Nationale in Paris, I am fairly certain that the word in $\mathfrak{p}4$ is ἐπισκέψεται ("will visit"), not ἐπεσκέψατο, ("has visited") because the letter before the lacuna is a broken *iota*, not a broken *epsilon*.

▶ Luke 3:22

You are my beloved Son in whom I am well pleased $\mathfrak{p}4$ ℵ A B L W 0124 33: ASV RSV NASB NIV NEB TEV NJBmg.
You are my Son; this day I have begotten you D and some Old Latin MSS: RSVmg NEBmg NJB (which reads, "You are my Son; this day I have fathered you").

The translators of the NJB defended their text by saying that the first reading noted above was probably a harmonization to the baptism account in Matthew and Mark. They say that Luke shows him to be "the King-Messiah of the Ps. [2:7], enthroned at the Baptism to establish the rule of God in the world." But the argument posited by the NJB translators loses its force in light of the fact that this reading was included in the Gospel of the Ebionites (second century), the gospel created by the Ebionites, chief among the adoptionists. "They regarded Jesus as the son of Joseph and Mary, but elected Son of God at his baptism when he was united with the eternal Christ" (H.L. Ellison, "Ebionites," in *New International Dictionary of the Christian Church*). Due to this and to the fact that the earliest MSS ($\mathfrak{p}4$ ℵ A B) support the first reading, all the other translations contain the reading that appears in all three of the synoptic Gospels.

▶ Luke 3:32-33

𝕻4 (with א* and B) reads "Sala" instead of "Salmon" (supported by later MSS and found in Matt. 1:4-5). 𝕻4ᵛⁱᵈ (with א² and L) reads "the son of Amminadab, the son of Admin, the son of Arni" as opposed to the reading "the son of Amminadab, the son of Ram" (supported by A D 33 and found in Matt. 1:4). The RSV and NJB follow the readings in 𝕻4 et al., and the ASVmg and NIVmg note them. But all others follow the secondary readings, which are obviously harmonizations to the genealogy in Matthew.

▶ Luke 4:44

the synagogues of Judea 𝕻75 א B C L Q R W: ASVmg RSV NASB NIV NEB NJB.
the synagogues of Galilee A D 33 𝔐: ASV RSVmg NASBmg NIVmg NEBmg.

The first reading, having the more difficult and better-attested wording (especially from 𝕻75 א B), is most likely the original. Scribes harmonized Luke's account to Matt. 4:23 and Mark 1:39, and/or fixed what they believed to be a contradiction of facts in Luke's account (Luke 4:14 and 5:1 indicate that Jesus was in Galilee). However, Luke may have used "Judea" to cover all of Palestine, which includes Galilee (see Luke 7:17; 23:5).

All the translations since the ASV have followed the more difficult reading, and several have noted the variant in the margin. TEV avoided the problem altogether by translating this verse, "So he preached in the synagogues all over the country."

▶ Luke 6:1

on the sabbath 𝕻4 א B L W 33: all the translations.
on the second-first sabbath A C D R: ASVmg RSVmg NASBmg.

Although the second reading is the more difficult, the editors of NA²⁶ and UBS³ did not adopt this reading because the Greek word δευτεροπρώτῳ occurs nowhere else and appears to have been created by a transcriptional blunder (see Metzger). None of the translations followed the second, choosing rather to go with the reading having the earliest testimony—𝕻4 א B.

▶ Luke 6:48

because it was well built 𝔓75ᵛⁱᵈ ℵ B L W 33: all the translations.
for it was founded on the rock A C D: RSVmg.
omit 𝔓45ᵛⁱᵈ: none.

Since the second reading was most likely taken from Matt. 7:25 and the third reading a scribal error, the first reading (supported by 𝔓75ᵛⁱᵈ et al.) was the obvious choice for the editors of the Greek text and English translators.

▶ Luke 7:11

soon afterward 𝔓75 ℵᶜ A B L 33: all the translations.
on the next day ℵ* C D: ASVmg RSVmg NEBmg TEVmg.

All the translations followed the reading of 𝔓75 et al. because it has slightly better attestation—while the variant, also having good attestation, is noted in the margin of several versions.

▶ Luke 8:26

Gerasenes 𝔓75 B D: ASV RSV NASB NIV NEBmg TEV NJB.
Gergesenes ℵ L: ASVmg RSVmg NIVmg NEB TEVmg NJBmg.
Gadarenes A W: ASVmg RSVmg NIVmg NEBmg TEVmg NJBmg.

In every instance in the synoptic Gospels where the writer records Jesus' visit to the region on the eastern side of the Galilee (where he healed the demoniac), there is textual variation as to what this region is called. In Matt. 8:28, Mark 5:1, and here in Luke 8:26 all three readings occur: "Gerasenes," "Gergesenes," and "Gadarenes." In every instance, the editors of UBS³ and NA²⁶ adopted the reading with the earliest support. In Matt. 8:28 that reading is "Gadarenes" (supported by ℵ* B C); in Mark 5:1 (supported by ℵ B D) and Luke 8:26 that reading is "Gerasenes." For the most part, the translations reflect the same kind of thinking. In this verse, the testimony of the earliest MSS (𝔓75 and B) was followed by all but one version (NEB). (For a further discussion of this textual problem, see Tj. Baarda's article, "Gadarenes, Gerasenes, Gergesenes and the 'Diatessaron' Traditions," in *Neotestamentica et Semitica* [Studies in Honor of Matthew Black], 181–197.)

▶ Luke 8:43

include **who had spent all her living on physicians and** ℵ A C L W 33: ASV RSVmg NASBmg NIVmg NEBmg TEV NJBmg.

omit 𝔓75 B (D): ASVmg RSV NASB NIV NEB TEVmg NJB.

Though the above clause is included in UBS[3] and NA[26], it has been bracketed in the text to show the editors' doubts about it being genuinely Lukan. It is far more likely that the clause was borrowed from Mark 5:26. If it had been original, it is difficult to explain why the clause would have been dropped by the scribes of 𝔓75 B D. Most of the translators thought the clause did not belong as part of Luke's Gospel, and the testimony of 𝔓75 especially strengthens their position.

▶ Luke 9:26

whoever is ashamed of me and my words 𝔓45 𝔓75[vid] A B C L W: ASV RSV NASB NIV NEBmg TEV NJB.

whoever is ashamed of me and mine D and some Old Latin MSS: NEB.

Against such excellent external testimony, the translators of the NEB selected the second reading because they thought it suited the context better. The same thinking is behind the selection of the same variant reading in Mark 8:38a (see comments there).

▶ Luke 9:35

my Son, the chosen One 𝔓45 𝔓75 ℵ B L: all the translations.

my Son, the beloved A C* W 33: ASVmg RSVmg NJBmg.

my Son, the beloved in whom I am well pleased C[3] D: none.

The first reading, supported by the four earliest MSS (𝔓45 𝔓75 ℵ B) and followed by all the versions, is without question the one Luke wrote. The two variants show the work of harmonization with Mark 9:7 and/or Luke 3:22.

▶ Luke 9:54

omit **as Elijah did** 𝔓45 𝔓75 ℵ B: all the translations.

include A C D W 33: ASVmg RSVmg NIVmg NEBmg TEVmg NJBmg.

The words of James and John—"Lord, do you want us to bid fire come down from heaven and consume them?" (RSV)—would easily bring to mind Elijah's action of calling down fire from heaven (see 1 Kings 18). Thus, this allusion was added by later scribes to what James and John said. If the words had originally been in the text, there is no good reason why they would have been deleted in the four earliest extant MSS.

▶ Luke 9:55b-56a

omit verses 𝔭45 𝔭75 ℵ A B C L W: all the translations.

include verses D (which adds to verse 55, **You do not know what manner of spirit you are of**) and many later MSS (which add further, **for the Son of man came not to destroy men's lives but to save them**): margins of all the translations.

The best witnesses attest to the absence of the above-mentioned words. All the versions followed the best authorities, and all of them included the variant reading(s) in the margin. Unfortunately, however, the marginal notes do not specify that the MSS which support the variant are all late MSS and/or that the reading of the text is supported by all the earliest and most reliable MSS.

▶ Luke 9:62

no one putting his hand to the plow and looking back 𝔭75 ℵ A B C L W 0181: all the translations.

no one who looks backs as he puts his hand to the plow 𝔭45^{vid} D: NEBmg.

The second reading presents an interesting variation—though clearly secondary in light of the evidence in favor of the first reading. The variant is noted, however, in the NEB because of the testimony of 𝔭45, D, Old Latin MSS, and Clement (Tasker).

▶ Luke 10:1

seventy-two 𝔭75 B D 0181: ASVmg RSVmg NIV NEB TEV NJB.

seventy ℵ A C L W: ASV RSV NASB NIVmg NEBmg TEVmg NJBmg.

See comments on Luke 10:17.

▶ Luke 10:17

seventy-two 𝔓45 𝔓75 B D: ASVmg RSVmg NIV NEB TEV NJB.
seventy ℵ A C L W: ASV RSV NASB NIVmg NEBmg TEVmg
NJBmg.

The same kind of variation appears among the Greek MSS in Luke 10:1.
Some (including 𝔓75 B D) read "seventy-two," while others (including
ℵ A C L W) read "seventy." Thus, the pattern is the same for Luke 10:1
and 10:17—with one exception: 𝔓45 has a lacuna at Luke 10:1. But it
could easily be conjectured that it also read "seventy-two."

It appears that the most modern translations were influenced by the
combined testimony of 𝔓45 and 𝔓75. 𝔓45 (published in 1933) alone was
not enough to convince the RSV translators, but 𝔓45 and 𝔓75 (published
in 1961) must have influenced the NIV, TEV, and NJB.

▶ Luke 10:21

in [or, by] the Holy Spirit 𝔓75 ℵ B C L 33: all the translations.
in the Spirit [or, in his spirit] 𝔓45 A W: NEBmg TEVmg.

Since it appears that the first reading has better external support, Luke
most likely said that Jesus rejoiced "in the Holy Spirit." If the second
reading were original, Jesus could have been rejoicing in the divine
Spirit or in his spirit—the Greek can be taken either way (Comfort).

The translators of the NEB and TEV wisely noted the second reading
especially because of its presence in 𝔓45 and because scribes were
known for adding the word "Holy" before "Spirit."

▶ Luke 10:22

omit **and turning to his disciples said** 𝔓45 𝔓75 ℵ B D L: ASV RSV
NASB NIV TEV NJB.
include A C W: NEB.

Since nearly the same phrase appears in the next verse, it was quite likely
that scribes added it here. But Tasker, in defense of the NEB, argued for
the opposite: "The recurrence of the same words (but with the significant
addition of κατ᾽ ἰδίαν) in verse 23 may have led to their omission in
verse 22." But the textual evidence for the omission of the words far
outweighs such internal considerations.

► Luke 10:38

*received him 𝔓45 𝔓75 B: none.

received him into the house 𝔓3[vid] ℵ C*: none.

received him into her house ℵ[1] A C[2] D L W 33: all the translations.

Of the three readings, the first is the one most likely original because it is found in the three earliest MSS and because it is quite apparent that the other two readings display scribal additions—inserted to fill out the sentence. The papyri with B definitely caused the editors of NA[26] to adopt the first reading over the third, which used to be in previous editions of the Nestle text. However, none of the translators followed the superior reading because they, as did many scribes, felt compelled to expand on words to fill out the sense.

► Luke 10:42

but one thing is needful 𝔓45 𝔓75 C,3[vid]: ASV RSV NASBmg NIV NEB TEV NJBmg.

but few things are needful or only one 𝔓3 ℵ B L 33: ASVmg RSVmg NASB NIVmg NEBmg NJB.

Some later MSS (including D and some Old Latin MSS) omit the above mentioned clause and the preceding one—"you are anxious and troubled about many things" (Luke 10:41a): NEBmg.

The testimony of 𝔓45 with 𝔓75 offset the testimony of ℵ and B—so much so that the editors of NA[26] adopted the reading supported by 𝔓45 and 𝔓75 over against the one in previous editions of the Nestle text. Many of the translations (including the NIV and TEV, whose translators had knowledge of 𝔓45 *and* 𝔓75) followed the first reading, while the alternative reading is included in the margin of six of the seven translations—in deference to the witness of ℵ and B. (For a full discussion of the textual problem involved here, see Gordon Fee's chapter, "'One Thing is Needful'?, Luke 10:42" in *New Testament Textual Criticism: Its Significance for Exegesis*, 61–75, in which Fee argues for the second reading.)

► Luke 11:2a

Father 𝔓75 ℵ B: all the translations.

our Father in heaven A C D W 𝔐: ASVmg NASBmg NIVmg NEBmg.

See comments on Luke 11:4 below.

95

▶ Luke 11:2b

your kingdom come 𝔭75 ℵ A B C W 33: all the translations.

your kingdom come upon us D: NIVmg.

your Holy Spirit come upon us and cleanse us two late MSS (162 700) Marcion: NIVmg NJBmg.

See comments on Luke 11:4 below.

▶ Luke 11:2c

omit **your will be done on earth as in heaven** 𝔭75 B L: all the translations.

include ℵc A C D W 33: ASVmg NASBmg NIVmg NEBmg.

See comments on Luke 11:4 below.

▶ Luke 11:4

omit **but deliver us from evil** 𝔭75 ℵ* B L: all the translations.

include ℵc A C D W 33: ASVmg NASBmg NIVmg NEBmg.

In the above four instances (Luke 11:2a, 2b, 2c, 4), the longer readings are scribal expansions borrowed from that form of the Lord's prayer which is recorded in Matt. 6:9-10, 13 (with the exception of the third reading in Luke 11:2c). In every instance, the translations followed the shorter reading, which is always supported by 𝔭75 and B (with other MSS). The expanded readings, however, were noted in several versions; and two translations (NIV and NJB) noted an unusual variant in Luke 11:2b: "your Holy Spirit come upon us and cleanse us."

▶ Luke 11:11

omit **if his son asks for bread will he give him a stone?** 𝔭45 𝔭75 B: ASVmg RSV NASB NIV NEB TEV NJB.

include (ℵ) A C D (L) 33: ASV RSVmg NEBmg NJBmg.

Unquestionably, the papyri—supporting B—made all the difference here. The ASV translators, not having 𝔭45 and 𝔭75, could only note the omission, based on B. The succeeding translators had the benefit of the papyri. Undoubtedly, the expanded reading presents a harmonization with Matt. 7:9.

▶ Luke 11:33

puts it in a hidden place or under a bushel א A B C D W: ASV RSV NASB NIV NEBmg TEV NJB.
puts it in a hidden place 𝔭45 𝔭75 L 0124: NEB TEVmg.

The Greek words for "or under a bushel" (οὐδὲ ὑπὸ τὸν μόδιον) are bracketed in UBS³ and NA²⁶ because these words do not appear in the papyri and because they could very well have been borrowed from Matt. 5:5 and/or Mark 4:21. Despite these reasons, all the versions except the NEB followed the testimony of the longer reading. One would have expected that the translators who adopted the longer reading would have at least noted the shorter reading in the margin.

▶ Luke 12:39

omit **he would have watched and** 𝔭75 א* (D): RSV NASB NIV NEB TEV NJB.
include א¹ (A) B (Q) W 070 33: ASV RSVmg.

Though several early MSS include these words, they were probably assimilated from the parallel passage in Matt. 24:43. All of the translations since the ASV (which was greatly influenced by B) have followed the reading attested to by 𝔭75 et al.

▶ Luke 14:5

son or an ox 𝔭45 𝔭75 A B W: ASVmg RSV NASB NIV NEBmg TEV NJB.
donkey or an ox א L 33: ASV RSVmg NIVmg NJBmg.
sheep or an ox D: NEB.

The presence of "son" in the papyri certainly affected English translations published after the ASV (which but noted this reading, on the testimony of A and B). "Because the collocation of the two words [υἱὸς and βοῦς] appeared to be incongruous, copyists altered υἱὸς either to ὄνος [donkey] (cf. 13.15) or to πρόβατον [sheep] (cf. Mt 12.11)" (Metzger, *Textual Commentary*).

97

▶ Luke 15:21

omit **make me like one of your hired men** 𝔭75 A L W 𝔐: all the translations.

include ℵ B D 33: ASVmg RSVmg NIVmg NEBmg.

The omission of these words has early and diverse testimony. Furthermore, the testimony of 𝔭75 with A and W offsets that of B with ℵ and D. And it seems quite likely that the words were borrowed from Luke 15:19. Not one translation included the words; however, out of deference to the testimony of ℵ B D, several versions noted them.

▶ Luke 17:24

the Son of man in his day ℵ A L R W 𝔐: all the translations.
the Son of man 𝔭75 B D: ASVmg RSVmg NIVmg.

Although the phrase "in his day" appears in the text of UBS[3] and NA[26], it is bracketed to signal the editors' doubts about it being originally written by Luke. The editors had their doubts because the phrase is lacking in 𝔭75 B D—which represents early and diverse testimony (see Metzger). But it could be possible that the scribes of 𝔭75 B D dropped the phrase to make it conform to the Matthean parallel (Matt. 24:47). All of the translators must have favored this argument, for the phrase "in his day" is included in every version. However, the ASV and RSV translators, out of respect for the testimony of B, noted its omission; and the NIV translators, having respect especially to the testimony of 𝔭75, also noted its omission.

▶ Luke 17:36

omit verse 𝔭75 ℵ A B L W 33: all the translations.
include D and a few late MSS: the margin of all the translations.

This verse, absent from nearly all the early MSS, was not included in any modern version. Nonetheless, it is noted in the margin—in keeping with the practise of translators to make mention of every portion omitted from what was traditionally part of the text.

▶ Luke 18:11

the Pharisee standing by himself prayed these things A W 33[vid]: NEBmg TEV.

the Pharisee stood and prayed these things with [or, about] himself
𝔭75 ℵ² B L T: ASV RSV NASB NIV TEVmg NJB.
the Pharisee stood and prayed these things privately D: NEBmg.
the Pharisee stood and prayed these things ℵ*: NEB.

The editors of UBS³ and NA²⁶ adopted the first reading because in Greek it is the most difficult reading of all the variants, despite the fact that the second reading has the better attestation (see Metzger). Most of the translations followed the second reading because of the combined testimony of 𝔭75 with ℵ² B L T. Only the TEV followed the first reading.

▶ Luke 22:19b-20
include verses 𝔭75 ℵ A B C L T^vid W: ASV RSV NASB NIV NEBmg TEV NJB.
omit D and several Old Latin MSS: ASVmg RSVmg NASBmg NEB TEVmg.

All the early MSS except D testify to the presence of Luke 22:19b-20 in the account of the Last Supper. Perhaps the copyist of D omitted this portion in an attempt to conform Luke's account of the Last Supper to the other Gospels—not realizing that the cup mentioned in 22:17 was the cup of the Passover celebration or a kiddush cup (see 22:15-16), not the cup of the new covenant. Following the traditional Passover meal, Jesus instituted the supper first with the loaf (22:19) and then with the cup (22:20). (For a full discussion in defense of including Luke 22:19b-20 as part of Luke's original writing, see C. S. C. Williams's *Alterations to the Text of the Synoptic Gospels and Acts,* 47–51.)

All the translations except the NEB include this portion, though several provide a marginal note as to its omission. Tasker provides a lengthy discussion as to why the translators of the NEB did not include Luke 22:19b-20. Had 𝔭75 been available to the NEB translators, they may have thought twice about omitting this portion.

▶ Luke 22:43-44
include verses ℵ*,² D L 0171 𝔐: ASV NASB RSVmg NIV NEB TEV NJB.
omit 𝔭69^vid 𝔭75 ℵ¹ B N R T W: ASVmg RSV NIVmg NEBmg TEVmg NJBmg.

𝔓69[vid] is not cited in UBS[3] in support of the omission of Luke 22:43-44, but it is found in the apparatus of NA[26]. The editors, Lobel et al., were fairly confident that the only reason to account for the large lacuna in 𝔓69 (from Luke 22:41 to Luke 22:45) would be that the copyist's exemplar did not contain Luke 22:43-44, the passage about Jesus sweating drops of blood while in agony in Gethsemane and then being strengthened by angels. 𝔓69[vid] adds another early witness to the omission of this text; indeed, it is not found in 𝔓75 ℵ[1] B T W (also Marcion, Clement, and Origen). The earliest witness to the inclusion of this passage is 0170 (which actually shows only the last few words of Luke 22:44)—a D-type text dated around 300, followed by ℵ* (dated 350–375). Other early testimony comes from some early church fathers (Justin, Irenaeus, Hippolytus, Dionysius, Eusebius) who acknowledged this portion as part of Luke's Gospel.

The debate about the genuineness of this passage focused on whether or not Jesus needed to be strengthened by angels during his trial in the garden of Gethsemane. Some said that the passage was excised because certain Christians thought that "the account of Jesus overwhelmed with human weakness was incompatible with his sharing the divine omnipotence of the Father" (Metzger). But it is more likely that the passage was an early (second-century) interpolation, added from an oral tradition concerning the life of Jesus (so Westcott and Hort, 64-67).

Given the impressive documentary evidence in favor of the omission of this passage, it is unfortunate that only one version (RSV) omitted the passage from the text. And the RSV translators did so without the evidence of 𝔓69 and 𝔓75, which was not then available, while some of the more recent versions, having this evidence, did not follow it but maintained the tradition of keeping this passage in the text.

▶ Luke 22:62
include verse 𝔓75 ℵ A B D L T W: ASV RSV NASB NIV NEBmg TEV NJB.
omit 0171[vid] and several Old Latin MSS: NEB.

The NEB translators excised this verse from the text because they considered it to have been borrowed by scribes from Matt. 26:75 and/or Mark 14:72 (see Tasker). The earliest MS to support the decision of the NEB translators is 0170 (c. 300), but this MS is known for its affinities with D. The documentary evidence supporting the inclusion of the verse is both early and diverse. For this reason, all other translations include the verse and do not even provide a marginal note about its omission in various MSS.

▶ Luke 23:17

omit verse 𝔓75 A B L T: all the translations.
include ℵ (D after 23:19) W: margins of all the translations.

Since this verse is absent from several early MSS, its appearance in other MSS is very likely the result of scribal assimilation from Matt. 27:15 and/or Mark 15:6. Not one translation includes the verse.

▶ Luke 23:34

include **And Jesus said, "Father, forgive them, for they do not know what they are doing"** ℵ*,2 (A) C D² L 𝔐: all the translations.
omit 𝔓75 ℵ¹ᵛⁱᵈ B D* W 0124: margins of all the translations.

The omission of this text in early and diverse MSS (the earliest being 𝔓75) cannot be explained as a scribal blunder or as a purposeful scribal excision. Good reasons cannot be posited for either. Rather, it appears that this text was not a part of Luke's original writing, but was added later (as early as the second century—for it is attested to by Hegesippus, Marcion, the Diatessaron, and Justin) from an oral tradition. (This is the position expressed by Westcott and Hort, 67-69, and by Metzger.) The words appear in the text of UBS³ and NA²⁶ but are bracketed to signal the editors' hesitancy to include them as part of Luke's original writing and thereby demonstrate their respect for the testimony of 𝔓75 with ℵ¹ᵛⁱᵈ B D* W versus ℵ*,2 (A) C D² L 𝔐.

Though Jesus' first utterance during his crucifixion is not found in the earliest MSS, it has become so much a part of the traditional Gospel text that translators are not willing to excise this from their translations. Rather, all of the translations retain this portion as part of Luke's Gospel and provide a marginal note as to its absence in various ancient MSS.

▶ Luke 23:42

come into your kingdom 𝔓75 B L: ASVmg RSV NIV NEB NJB.
come in [or, with] your kingdom ℵ A C W 0124 33: ASV RSVmg NASB NEBmg TEV NJBmg.

There is a slight difference in meaning in the two readings. The first one, supported by 𝔓75 B L and followed by many of the versions, speaks of an imminent kingdom, a kingdom into which Jesus was about to enter—according to the perception of the believing thief. The second reading, having good support and some adherence by some of the versions, seems to refer to a coming, future kingdom.

▶ Luke 24:3

body of the Lord Jesus 𝔓75 ℵ A B C L W 33: ASV RSVmg NASB NIV TEV NJB.

body D and a few Old Latin MSS: ASVmg RSV NEB.

See comments on Luke 24:52.

▶ Luke 24:6

include **He is not here but is risen** 𝔓75 ℵ A B (C) L (W) 0124: ASV RSVmg NASB NIV NEBmg TEV NJB.

omit A and a few Old Latin MSS: ASVmg RSV NEB.

See comments on Luke 24:52 below.

▶ Luke 24:12

*include verse 𝔓75 ℵ A B L W 33 079 0124: ASV RSVmg NASB NIV NEBmg TEV NJB.

omit D and a few early versions: ASVmg RSV NASBmg NEB TEVmg NJBmg.

See comments on Luke 24:52 below.

▶ Luke 24:13

sixty stadia 𝔓75 A B D L W 0124 33^vid: all the translations.

one hundred and sixty stadia ℵ 079^vid: RSVmg NJBmg.

According to Metzger, the second reading "seems to have arisen in connection with patristic identification of Emmaus with 'Amwas (mod. Nicopolis), about twenty-two Roman miles (176 stadia) from Jerusalem." Of course, this distance would have been far too great for the two disciples to have re-traversed the same evening (see Luke 24:33).

▶ Luke 24:32

include **within us** ℵ A L W 33: ASV RSV NASB NIV TEV NJB.

omit 𝔓75 B D: RSVmg NEB.

The words "within us" are included in the text of UBS[3] and NA[26], but within brackets—out of respect to the testimony of 𝔓75 B D. All the translations except NEB include the phrase, but NEB's omission has nothing to do with the testimony of 𝔓75, which was not then available to the translators of the NEB.

▶ Luke 24:36

*include **and he said to them, "Peace be with you"** 𝔓75 ℵ A B L 33: ASV RSVmg NASBmg NIV NEBmg TEV NJB.

omit D and a few Old Latin MSS: ASVmg RSV NASB NEB TEVmg.

See comments on Luke 24:52 below.

▶ Luke 24:40

*include verse 𝔓75 ℵ A B L W 33: ASV RSVmg NASBmg NIV NEBmg TEV NJB.

omit D and some early versions: ASVmg RSV NASB NEB TEVmg NJBmg.

See comments on Luke 24:52 below.

▶ Luke 24:51

*include **and was carried up into heaven** 𝔓75 ℵc A B C L W 33: ASV RSV NASBmg NIV TEV NJB.

omit ℵ* D and some early versions: ASVmg RSVmg NASB NEB TEVmg NJBmg.

See comments on Luke 24:52 below.

▶ Luke 24:52

*include **they worshiped him** 𝔓75 ℵ A B C L W 33: ASV RSVmg NASBmg NIV NEBmg TEV NJB.

omit D and some early versions: ASVmg RSV NASB NEB NJBmg.

Westcott and Hort thought Codex Bezae (D) contained the original wording of Luke's Gospel in 24:3, 6, 12, 36, 40, 51, and 52. Calling the omissions in D "Western non-interpolations," they posited the theory that all the other MSS contain interpolations in these verses. This theory affected the Nestle text until its twenty-sixth edition, at which point this theory was abandoned—note the changes in Luke 24:12, 36, 40, 51, 52. This theory also affected several modern English versions—especially the RSV and NEB, which in nearly every instance followed the testimony of D against all other early MSS. The NASB was also affected by this theory, but not as much as the RSV and NEB. After all three of these translations were published, 𝔓75 was discovered. And in every instance, 𝔓75 attests to the longer reading. 𝔓75 influenced the Nestle text, which now in every verse noted above follows the testimony of 𝔓75 et al., and 𝔓75 affected the most recent versions (TEV, NIV, and NJB), which in every case followed its testimony to include those portions not included by previous translations.

John

Early manuscripts containing portions of John:

𝔓5: 1:23-31, 33-40; 16:14-30; 20:11-17, 19-20, 22-25
𝔓6: 10:1-2, 4-7, 9-10; 11:1-8, 45-52
𝔓22: 15:25–16:2, 21-32
𝔓28: 6:8-12, 17-22
𝔓39: 8:14-22
𝔓45: 10:7-25; 10:30–11:10, 18-36, 42-57
𝔓52: 18:31-34, 37-38
𝔓66: 1:1–6:11; 6:35–14:26, 29-30; 15:2-26; 16:2-4, 6-7; 16:10–20:20, 22-23; 20:25–21:9
𝔓75: 1:1–11:45, 48-57; 12:3–13:1, 8-9; 14:8-30; 15:7-8
𝔓80: 3:34
𝔓90: 18:36–19:7
𝔓95: 5:26-29, 36-38
0162: 2:11-22
0212: 19:38

▶ John 1:3-4

The last phrase of 1:3 (Greek: ὃ γέγονεν—"that which has been created") has been connected with 1:3 or with 1:4 by various ancient scribes and modern translators, by means of punctuation. The earliest manuscripts (𝔓66 𝔓75* ℵ* A B) do not have any punctuation in these verses. 𝔓66 does not contain the word ἐν after ὃ γέγονεν (due to haplography), suggesting that there was no break after γέγονεν (Schnackenburg). 𝔓75 was later emended, as was ℵ. In 𝔓75 a punctuation mark was placed before the phrase (as in #1 below); in ℵ, after it (as #2 below):

1. . . . and without him was not anything created. That which was created in him was life . . .
2. . . . and without him was not anything created that was created. In him was life . . .

The majority of the early church fathers exegeted John 1:3-4 according to the phrasing in #1. The passage was taken to mean that all created things were "life" by virtue of being in him. The statement was somehow supposed to affirm that the Word not only created the universe, he presently sustains it. Exegesis changed after some heretics used the passage to say that the Holy Spirit was a created thing. Then the fathers supported the reading as it is in #2. Most exegesis has followed this up to the present, although some scholars (e.g., Westcott) support the first reading. This is the reading adopted by the editors of NA26, although Metzger, one of the editors, disagreed—and not without good reason, for the passage hardly makes sense as punctuated in #1 (see *Textual Commentary*). According to John's Gospel, "life" was not created in Christ; "life" is the divine life, the eternal life, embodied in Christ. This life has always been in Christ, and now has become available to men through faith in Christ. Most modern translations (RSV, NASB, NIV, TEV) follow the punctuation as in #2; others (NEB, NJB) follow #1. (See Comfort's article, "An Analysis of Five Modern Translations of the Gospel of John" in *Notes on Translation*, Vol. 3, No. 3, 1989.)

▶ John 1:18
an only One, God [or, **God, the only begotten**—lit., "a unique God" but never translated as such] 𝔓66 𝔓75 ℵ B C L: ASVmg RSVmg NASB NIV(?—see explanation below) NEBmg TEV NJBmg.
the only begotten Son A C³ Wˢ 𝔐: ASV RSV NASBmg NIVmg NJB.

The manuscript evidence for the first reading (in Greek, μονογενὴς θεός) is superior to the evidence for the second reading (in Greek, ὁ μονογενὴς υἱός). The papyri (Ρ66 and Ρ75—which adds the article ὁ), the earliest uncials (א B C), and some early versions (Coptic and Syriac) support the first reading. Some of the earliest church fathers (Valentinus, Irenaeus, Clement, Origen, Eusebius, Serapion, Basil, Didymus, Gregory-Nyssa, and Epiphanius) knew of the first reading. Though later MSS support the second reading, it was known by many early church fathers (Irenaeus, Clement, Hippolytus, Alexander, Eusebius, Eastathius, Serapion, Julian, Basil, and Gregory-Nazianzus) and translated in some early versions (Old Latin and Syriac). Thus, both readings have early witness, but the first reading has earlier actual documentary testimony and is more likely the reading to have been changed.

In a volume called *Two Dissertations,* Hort argued extensively and convincingly for the reading μονογενὴς θεός. He argued that Gnostics (such as the Valentinians) did not invent this phrase; rather, they simply quoted it. And he argued that this phrase is very suitable for the closing verse of the prologue, in which Christ has been called "God" (in 1:1) and "an only One" (in 1:14), and finally, "an only One, God"—which combines the two titles into one. This is a masterful way of concluding the prologue; for 1:18 then mirrors 1:1. Both speak of Christ as (1) God's expression (the "Word" and "he has explained him"), (2) God, and (3) the one close to God ("the Word was face to face with God" [Williams' translation] and "in the bosom of the Father"). Thus, the unique yet perfectly acceptable reading μονογενὴς θεός was most likely changed to the more ordinary one, ὁ μονογενὴς υἱός, by later scribes.

The papyri made the difference in the way the English versions rendered John 1:18. All but one of the translations that had access to the testimony of Ρ66 and also Ρ75 (i.e., NASB, TEV, NIV—excepting NJB) adopted the superior reading. The NASB's literal translation ("the only begotten God"), however, could lead people to think that Christ is a begotten God. Most exegetes prefer to treat the word μονογενής as a substantive rather than as an adjective; thus, Christ is called both μονογενής and θεός. This is made clear in TEV's translation, "the only One, who is the same as God," or NIVmg, "God the only begotten." (Even though the NIV translators probably considered "only Son" to be a legitimate rendering of μονογενής, the reading "God the only Son" in

the NIV text appears as a conflation of the two readings noted above.)
See photo 2 for John 1:18 in 𝕻75.

▶ John 1:34

**the Son of God 𝕻66 𝕻75 A B C W 083: ASV RSV NASB NIV NEBmg
TEV NJBmg.**
the chosen One of God 𝕻5[vid] **ℵ*: NEB NJB.**

Even though the title "the Son of God" has superior external support,
several scholars have argued that it is more likely that the reading "the
chosen One of God" was changed to "the Son of God" than vice versa
because "chosen One of God" is the more unusual or difficult reading.
Furthermore, it has been urged by James Williams in an article, "Renderings from Some Johannine Passages" (*The Bible Translator*, 25,
3 [July, 1974], 352–353), that the title "chosen One" adds one more
messianic title to the chain of witnesses in John 1, while "Son" is
repetitive (see 1:14; 1:49). Christ as the Word is called God (1:1; 1:18—
in the earliest MSS; cf. Isa. 9:6); and Jesus is called the Christ or
Messiah (1:17, 41; cf. Ps. 2:2; Dan. 9:25), the Son of God (1:14, 34—in
some MSS, 49; cf. 2 Sam. 7:12-14; Ps. 2:7), the Lamb of God (1:29, 36;
cf. Isa. 53), the One predicted by Moses (1:45; cf. Deut. 18:16-18), the
King of Israel (1:49; cf. Ps. 2:6; Zeph. 3:15), and the Son of man (1:51;
cf. Dan. 7:13). If the title "the chosen One of God" also came from the
pen of John, there is yet another messianic witness—this one referring to
Isa. 42:1. (It should be noted that all the other Gospel accounts concerning Jesus' baptism by John contain a record of God's utterance from
heaven, "This is my beloved Son, in whom I am well pleased"—an
utterance echoing Isa. 42:1, "Behold, My Servant, whom I uphold; my
chosen one in whom My soul delights," NASB.)

Even though the reading "the chosen One of God" is attractive, most
textual critics and translators are reluctant to adopt this reading because
of the testimony of the other early papyri. But the testimony of 𝕻5 was
enough to persuade two groups of translators (NEB and NJB)—for it
would be hard to imagine that they would adopt this reading on the
testimony of ℵ alone. Even though the other translators adopted the
reading "the Son of God," they should at least include a marginal note
indicating that some early MSS read "the chosen One of God." And all
translators can make this note with confidence concerning 𝕻5, because,

even though it is marked with *vid*, the editors (Grenfell and Hunt) who produced the transcription of the text of 𝔭5 provided a very convincing argument for the reading being ὁ ἐκλεκτός ("the chosen One") versus ὁ υἱός ("the Son") (see *The Oxyrhynchus Papyri*, Vol. 2, 7).

▶ John 1:41

he [Andrew] **first finds his brother** 𝔭66 𝔭75 ℵ² A B 083: all the translations.
he [Andrew] **was the first to find his brother** ℵ* L Wˢ 𝔐: none.
early [in the morning] **he** [Andrew] **finds his brother** some Old Latin MSS: NEBmg NJBmg.

All the translations followed the first reading because of its superior testimony, especially from the papyri. The third reading, noted in NEB and NJB, represents an early interpretation found in a few Old Latin MSS.

▶ John 3:6

In English we can distinguish between the divine Spirit and the human spirit (or any other kind of spirit) by capitalizing the former. But in many Greek manuscripts there is no way to distinguish the divine Spirit from the human spirit because both were written with capital letters: ΠΝΕΥΜΑ. However, the copyist of 𝔭66 distinguished them by making the first word a *nomen sacrum* (ΠΝΑ) and by writing out the second (ΠΝΕΥΜΑ)—thereby indicating that the divine Spirit is that which generates and the human spirit is that which is generated (see photo 3). This sort of distinguishing of the divine Spirit from the human spirit was also done by the scribes of 𝔭13, 𝔭46, 𝔭75. (See Comfort's article, "Light from the New Testament Papyri Concerning the Translation of πνεῦμα" in *The Bible Translator*, Jan., 1984.)

▶ John 3:13

the Son of man 𝔭66 𝔭75 B L Wˢ 083 086: ASVmg RSV NASB NIV TEV NEBmg NJB.
the Son of man who is in heaven A* 𝔐: ASV RSVmg NIVmg NEB.

Though the last clause ("who is in heaven") is not found in the earliest MSS, it was known to many early church fathers (Hippolytus, Novatian,

Origen, Dionysius, Eustathius, Jacob-Nisibis, Aphraates, Hilary, Lucifer, Basil), included in the Diatessaron, and translated in some early versions (Old Latin, Syriac, and Coptic). Westcott and Hort argued that it was "a Western gloss, suggested perhaps by i.18: it may have been inserted to correct any misunderstanding arising out of the position of ἀναβέβηκεν, as coming before καταβάς" (75–76). But it could be that the statement was written by John and then excised by several early copyists because of its enigmatic meaning—i.e., how could the Son of man who was then and there on earth also be in heaven? Usually, scribes did not add text that created exegetical problems; rather, they are notorious for deleting text to alleviate perceived problems. However, all of the translations that had access to the papyri (i.e., NASB, NIV, TEV, and NJB) followed the testimony of $\mathfrak{P}$66 and $\mathfrak{P}$75, with B. Thus, the superior documentary evidence won out over against any argument of internal probability.

▶ John 3:25

a Jew $\mathfrak{P}$75 א[1] A B L W[s] 086 0193: ASV RSV NASB NIV TEV NJB.
Jews $\mathfrak{P}$66 א*: NEB TEVmg.

Both the singular and plural reading have ancient support, but it is far more likely that the singular was changed to a plural than vice versa. Thus, most of the translations followed the testimony of $\mathfrak{P}$75 et al. versus $\mathfrak{P}$66 א*. $\mathfrak{P}$66 may have influenced NEB (for this papyrus had been published before the NEB was), but Tasker never once mentioned $\mathfrak{P}$66 in his textual notes on John.

▶ John 3:31

include **is above all** $\mathfrak{P}$36[vid] $\mathfrak{P}$66 א[2] A B L W[s] 083 086 33 𝔐: ASV RSV NASB NIV NEBmg TEV NJBmg.
omit $\mathfrak{P}$75 א* D: ASVmg NEB NJB.

Good reasons could be given to defend the reason scribes would be tempted to add the words "is above all" (as a repeat from the first part of the verse) or delete the words because they seemed redundant. The early papyri, $\mathfrak{P}$66 and $\mathfrak{P}$75, are divided—as well as א and B, and thus they neutralize each other's testimony. Most translations retain the words in the text. (Note: NA[26] incorrectly cites $\mathfrak{P}$5[vid] as supporting the first

109

reading; 𝔓5 does not contain this portion of John. [When I pointed out this problem to Barabara Aland, she said it would be corrected in a future printing.])

▶ John 4:1

*Jesus knew ℵ D 086: NEB NJB TEV.
the Lord knew 𝔓66 𝔓75 A B C L Ws 083: ASV RSV NASB NIV.

The first reading is the more difficult one, and therefore the one adopted by UBS[3] and NA[26] (a change from previous editions of the Nestle text), in spite of the superior testimony of 𝔓66 𝔓75 with A B C, a testimony followed by NASB and NIV.

▶ John 4:9

include **For Jews do not associate with Samaritans** [or, **Jews do not use dishes Samaritans have used**—NIVmg TEV] 𝔓63 𝔓66 𝔓75 𝔓76 ℵ[1] A B C L Ws 33: all the translations.
omit ℵ* D: ASVmg NEBmg NJBmg.

The first reading has superior external support. Though some have thought the explanation ("For Jews do not associate with Gentiles") was a gloss that found its way into the text, it was customary for John to provide such explanations for his Gentile readers. All the versions included these words, while three of them noted its omission in some MSS.

▶ John 5:1

a feast of the Jews 𝔓66 𝔓75 A B D Ws 0125: all the translations.
the feast of the Jews ℵ C L 33: ASVmg NASBmg NEBmg NJBmg.

The first reading has the best attestation and is the one followed by all the translations. Undoubtedly, some scribes added the definite article before "feast" in an attempt to designate a specific feast (Tabernacles or Passover) and thus provide the narrative of John with a more specific chronology.

▶ John 5:2

Bethzatha ℵ (L) 33: ASVmg RSV NIVmg TEV NJBmg.
Bethsaida 𝔓66 𝔓75 B Ws 0125: ASVmg RSVmg NIVmg NJBmg.

Bethesda A C 078: ASV RSVmg NASB NIV NEB TEVmg NJB.
Belzetha D: NJBmg.

The second reading has the best documentary support ($\mathfrak{P}$66 $\mathfrak{P}$75 B), but it was rejected by the editors of UBS³ and NA²⁶ because they suspected assimilation to the name of the city on the Sea of Galilee. None of the versions adopted this reading. "Bethesda" (meaning "House of Mercy"), though popular among the translators, was rejected by the editors of the Greek text because it was also "suspect as a scribal alteration originally introduced because of its edifying etymology" (Metzger). The reading adopted by the editors, "Bethzatha," was followed by only two versions. However, most of the translators followed the third reading, and several noted the first and second—the latter out of respect to the earliest testimony found in $\mathfrak{P}$66 $\mathfrak{P}$75 B.

▶ John 5:3b-4
omit 5:3b $\mathfrak{P}$66 $\mathfrak{P}$75 $\aleph$ A* B C* L: all the translations.
include 5:3b A C³ D Wˢ 078: the margins of all the translations.
omit 5:4 $\mathfrak{P}$66 $\mathfrak{P}$75 $\aleph$ B C* D Wˢ: all the translations.
include 5:4 A C³ L 078 $\mathfrak{M}$: all the margins of the translations.

Following the best documentary evidence attesting to the omission of John 5:3b-4 (to which $\mathfrak{P}$66 and $\mathfrak{P}$75 provide the earliest testimony), all modern translations omit this portion from the text and relegate it to the margin. This portion is not found in the earliest MSS, and where it does occur in later MSS it is often marked with obeli or asterisks to signal probable spuriousness. Undoubtedly, the passage was a later addition— probably inserted to provide an explanation about the troubling of the water mentioned in John 5:7.

▶ John 5:44
glory from the only God $\mathfrak{P}$63ᵛⁱᵈ [not cited in UBS³] $\aleph$ A D L: all the translations.
glory from the only One [or, **unique One**] $\mathfrak{P}$66 $\mathfrak{P}$75 B W: ASVmg NIVmg NJBmg.

The second reading, supported by the earliest MSS ($\mathfrak{P}$66 $\mathfrak{P}$75 B) and also by several early versions (Old Latin and Coptic), was nevertheless rejected by the editors of UBS³ and NA²⁶ on the grounds that the word for

111

"God" (θεοῦ—abbreviated as $\overline{\Theta Y}$) probably dropped from the text due to homoeoteleuton: TOYMONOY$\overline{\Theta Y}$. Although this is a possibility, it seems much more likely that the word "God" was added by scribes to fill in what would otherwise seem incomplete. According to Edwin E. Abbott in his book *Johannine Grammar*, the expression τοῦ μόνου is a titular substantive, which could be written τοῦ Μόνου, translated as "the only One" or "the unique One." This reading suits the passage well. Since the Jews were seeking to receive glory from one another, they had neglected to seek the glory that comes from the unique One, the only One who gives glory (Comfort). Unfortuntately, not one of the translations adopted this reading supported by the two earliest papyri and B.

▶ John 6:23a

however, boats from Tiberias 𝔓75 (B): ASV RSV NASB NIV NEB.
but other boats from Tiberias A D L W 33: NEBmg TEV.

There are actually more variants for this part of John 6:23, but these are the two variants followed by the modern versions. The majority of editors of UBS[3] and NA[26] considered that 𝔓75 has "the reading that best explains the origin of the others" (Metzger). All of the translations except TEV (which normally follows the UBS text) adhered to the reading found in 𝔓75 (and basically in B).

▶ John 6:23b

include **after the Lord had given thanks** 𝔓75 ℵ A L W 33: ASV RSV NASB NIV NEB TEV NJBmg.
omit D 091 and some early versions: NEBmg NJB.

In view of the fact that John rarely referred to Christ as "the Lord" in his Gospel account and that this phrase is absent in several "Western" MSS, it is thought by some textual scholars (see Tasker and comments by Metzger) that the above phrase may not have been written by John, but was added later. This must have been the reasoning behind the NJB's omission and definitely the rationale for the NEB's marginal note. Nonetheless, the early and diverse documentary evidence attests to its early and widespread presence in the Gospel of John; and for this reason, nearly all the translations include the phrase "after the Lord had given thanks."

112

▶ John 6:36

you have both seen me and have not believed Ṗ66 Ṗ75ᵛⁱᵈ B D L (T) W: ASV RSV NASB NIV TEV NJB.

you have both seen and not believed ℵ A: NEB.

The inclusion of "me" has earlier and more diverse support than its omission. Accordingly, all the versions except the NEB adopted this reading.

▶ John 7:8

I am not going up to this feast ℵ D: ASV RSV NASB NIVmg NEB TEV NJB.

I am not yet going up to this feast Ṗ66 Ṗ75 B L T W: ASVmg RSVmg NIV NEBmg TEVmg NJBmg.

The editors of UBS³ and NA²⁶ selected the first reading on the basis of intrinsic probability versus documentary evidence that strongly favors the inclusion of "yet." Given the context of John 7, in which Jesus makes one of the above statements to his brothers and then later goes to the feast, it would make more sense if he said he was not *yet* going to the feast than he was simply not going to the feast. The latter statement is contradicted by his action—unless he meant "I am not *now* going to the feast " (see Morris). At any rate, the first reading is the harder one and therefore the one more likely to have been changed. Most of the translators preferred to follow this reading, but the NIV translators followed the reading found in the papyri (which is the reading that puts Christ in a better light)—and thus the reader of the NIV will not see any contradiction between what Jesus said and later did.

▶ John 7:39

the Spirit was not yet Ṗ66ᶜ Ṗ75 ℵ T: NJB.

the Holy Spirit was not yet Ṗ66* L W: none.

the Holy Spirit was not yet given B: none—but most translations follow in adding "given": "the Spirit was not yet given" (ASV RSV NASB NIV NEB TEV NJBmg).

The best-attested reading is the shortest one: "the Spirit was not yet"— supported by the papyri, Ṗ66ᶜ (see photo 4) and Ṗ75. Certain scribes could not resist the temptation to add the word "Holy" before "Spirit" (an addition that frequently happened throughout the course of the transmission of the NT text) and/or to add the verb "given." Most of the translators also felt compelled to add the word "given." But this addition slightly modifies the meaning as presented in 𝔭66ᶜ 𝔭75 ℵ.

In context, this statement was part of a parenthetical explanation provided by John, a statement providing the reader with the key to understanding Jesus' declaration in John 7:37-38. Jesus had just promised that anyone who believes in him could come to him and drink of him and thereby experience an inner flow of living water. John's parenthetical remark ("But this he spoke of the Spirit, which they that believe in him were about to receive, for the Spirit was not yet, because Jesus was not yet glorified") makes it clear that Jesus was promising the believer an experience of the Spirit that could not happen until after Jesus was glorified and the Spirit was made available. Thus, the availabilty of the Spirit is linked with the glorification of Jesus, for it was after Jesus' glorification via death and resurrection that the Spirit became available to the believers (see John 20:22).

According to 𝔭66ᶜ 𝔭75 ℵ, the best rendering would be, "there was no Spirit as yet" (NJB—see also NRSV) or—if a word must be added— "the Spirit was not yet *available*." But it is also possible that the Greek expression οὔπω γὰρ ἦν πνεῦμα could mean, "for he was not yet spirit"—that is, Christ had not yet become life-giving spirit through resurrection (see 1 Cor. 15:45; cf. 2 Cor. 3:17-18). Once he had become "spirit," he could be received as the living water.

▶ John 7:52
a prophet 𝔭66ᶜ ℵ A B 𝔐: all the translations.
the prophet 𝔭66* 𝔭75ᵛⁱᵈ?: NIVmg TEVmg.

Both the NIVmg and the TEVmg indicate a variant reading in John 7:52, "the prophet." The NIVmg simply reads, "Or *the Prophet*" (it is not entirely clear, however, if this is a note on a textual variant or simply an alternative rendering) and the TEVmg reads, *one manuscript has* "the Prophet will not come." The one MS that definitely reads "the Prophet" is 𝔭66*, which was then corrected to "prophet" (see photo 5). 𝔭75, however, may not read "the prophet." The editors of *Papyrus Bodmer XV* [𝔭75], Evangile de Jean chapters 1-15 (Victor Martin and Rudolfe

Kasser) wrote ὁ προφήτης in their transcription of the text, but the lacuna they filled could have been supplied with either ὁ προφήτης or προφήτης (see photo 6). Thus, as is stated in the TEVmg, there is only one MS that reads "the Prophet." Undoubtedly, the Pharisees had this particular prophet in mind in their retort to Nicodemus—unless their statement meant something like this: "If, according to the Scriptures, not even a prophet comes out of Galilee, how much less the Christ?" (Comfort). At any rate, all the versions followed the testimony of 𝔓66^c ℵ A B 𝔐.

► John 7:53–8:11
omit 𝔓66 𝔓75 ℵ A^vid B C^vid L T W and several ancient versions: ASVmg RSV (1st edition) NASBmg NIVmg NEBmg TEVmg NJBmg.
include D 𝔐: ASV (in brackets) RSVmg (1st edition) RSV (second edition) NASB (in brackets) NIV (marked off and noted in text) NEB (set in italics) TEV (in brackets) NJB.
This passage is included in the text of UBS³ and NA²⁶ but is set in double brackets to signify the editors' serious doubts about its place in the text.

The pericope about the adulteress woman (John 7:53–8:11) is not included in any of the earliest MSS (second–fourth century), including the two earliest, 𝔓66 and 𝔓75 (see photos 5 and 6). Its first appearance in a Greek MS is in D, but it is not contained in other Greek MSS until the ninth century. No Greek church father comments on the passage prior to the twelfth century—until Euthymius Zigabenus, who himself declares that the accurate copies do not contain it. When this story is inserted in later MSS, it appears in different places: after John 7:52, after Luke 21:38, at the end of John; and when it does appear it is often marked off by asterisks or obeli to signal its probable spuriousness. The story is part of an oral tradition that was included in the Syriac Peshitta, circulated in the Western church, eventually finding its way into the Latin Vulgate, and from there into later Greek MSS, the like of which were used in formulating the Textus Receptus (Metzger).

The external evidence against the Johannine authorship of the pericope about the adulteress is overwhelming. The internal evidence against Johannine authorship is also impressive. First of all, many scholars have pointed out that the vocabulary used in this pericope does not accord with the rest of John. Second, the insertion of the pericope at this point in John (after John 7:52 and before John 8:12) greatly disrupts the narrative flow. Westcott and Hort indicated that the setting of John 7 and 8 is at Jerusalem during the Feast of Tabernacles. During this feast, the Jews would customarily pour water over a rock (in commemoration of the water supply coming from the smitten rock in the wilderness) and light lamps (in commemoration of the pillar of light that accompanied the Israelites in their wilderness journey). With reference to these two ritualistic enactments, Jesus presented himself as the true source of living water (John 7:37-39) and as the true light to be followed (John 8:12). Westcott and Hort's argument is that the pericope about the adulteress disrupts the continuity between the events (87–88).

In addition to these arguments, it can also be said that the pericope concerning the adulteress interrupts the connection between John 7:40-52 and 8:12ff. John 8:12 contains a response—even though indirect—to John 7:52. In John 8:12ff. Jesus was speaking to the Pharisees who had boldly told Nicodemus that the Scriptures make no mention of even a prophet (much less the Christ) being raised up in Galilee. With respect to this assertion, Jesus made a declaration in which he implied that the Scriptures did speak of the Christ coming from Galilee. He said, "I am the light of the world; he who follows me will not walk in darkness, but will have the light of life." This statement was probably drawn from Isaiah 9:1-2, which contains images parallel to those in John 8:12. Both speak about the light, walking in darkness, and the shadow of death versus the light of life. Thus, John 8:12 parallels Isaiah 9:1-2 and thereby provides a reproof to the Pharisees' declaration in John 7:52. (For more on this, see Comfort's article, "The Pericope of the Adulteress (John 7:53–8:11)," in *The Bible Translator*, Jan., 1989.)

Having said all this, it is very disappointing to realize that most English readers of the NT will see none of the connections mentioned above because the pericope of the adultress is still printed in the text between John 7:52 and 8:12. True, the passage has been bracketed, or marked off with single lines (similar to the practice of marking obeli, employed by several ancient scribes to the same passage), or set in italics. But there it stands—an obstacle to reading the true narrative of John's Gospel. Even worse, its presence in the text misrepresents the testimony of the earliest MSS, especially the papyri.

▶ John 8:16

*the Father who sent me ℘39 ℘66 ℘75 ℵᶜ B L T W 0110: ASV RSVmg
NASBmg NIV TEV.
he who sent me ℵ* D: RSV NASB NEB NJB.

The second reading is the more difficult one in so far that it is easier to
imagine why scribes would change "he" to "Father" than vice versa. It
was for this reason, no doubt, that the second reading was the one
included in the Nestle text—until NA²⁶, when the first reading was
adopted on the basis of the testimony of the papyri (℘39, ℘66, and ℘75).
The translators of NIV and TEV, knowing of this testimony from all three
papyri, must have been influenced to include "the Father" in their translations.

▶ John 8:39

***(if you are Abraham's children,) you would be doing the works of
Abraham** ℘75 ℵ* B² D W: ASV RSV NIV NEB TEV NJBmg.
(if you are Abraham's children,) do the works of Abraham ℘66 B*:
ASVmg NASB NIVmg NEBmg TEVmg.

The earliest MSS (℘66 ℘75 ℵ B) support the first verb as being ἐστε (as
opposed to ἦτε found in later MSS), but other early MSS (as noted
above) are divided on the second verb. The editors of NA²⁶ chose the
reading of ℘75 et al. over ℘66 and B—a change from previous editions
of the Nestle text. According to these editors, the verse in the original
text reads, Εἰ τέκνα τοῦ Ἀβραάμ ἐστε τὰ ἔργα τοῦ
Ἀβραάμ ἐποιεῖτε—a mixed conditional sentence, with εἰ . . . ἐστε
in the protasis and ἐποιεῖτε in the apodosis (Metzger). Almost all of the
translations followed this text, though many noted the variant.

▶ John 8:57

you have seen Abraham ℘66 ℵᶜ A Bᶜ C D L: ASV RSV NASB NIV
NEB TEV NJB.
Abraham has seen you ℘75 ℵ*: RSVmg NEBmg TEVmg.

The second reading, though fairly well supported, appears to be an
assimilation to the preceding verse in which Jesus indicated that Abraham rejoiced to see his day. The first reading, being more difficult and

having better external attestation, is more likely the correct one. All the translations reflect this reading, and three of them have a marginal note on the variant because of the textimony of ℵ* (which would have affected RSV and NEB) and of 𝔓75 (which would have affected TEV).

▶ John 9:35

the Son of man 𝔓66 𝔓75 ℵ B D W: ASVmg RSV NASB NIV NEB TEV NJB.

the Son of God A 𝔐: ASV RSVmg NEBmg.

The first reading has superior documentary support; furthermore, it is far more likely that "Son of man" was changed to "Son of God" than vice versa. The title "Son of man" was a surrogate for "Messiah." Thus, Jesus was asking the blind man (now healed) if he believed in the Messiah.

Significantly, the papyri have shown their effect on the translations in this instance. The ASV reads "Son of God," and the RSV and NEB note "Son of God" in the margin. But all the translations that were published since the discoveries of 𝔓66 and 𝔓75 have adopted the reading "Son of man" and do not even mention the variant reading in a marginal note.

▶ John 10:16

*they shall become one flock, one shepherd 𝔓45 ℵ² B D L W 33: ASV TEV.

there shall be one flock, one shepherd 𝔓66 ℵ* A: ASVmg RSV NIV NEB TEVmg NJB.

The first reading, supported by 𝔓45 et al., is the more difficult yet better attested to—it thus caused a change in the Nestle text (which previously contained the second reading). Nevertheless, not all the translations followed this reading because the variant actually reads better—which is precisely why the scribes of 𝔓66 ℵ* and A emended the text.

▶ John 10:18

*no one takes 𝔓66 ℵ¹ A D L W: ASV RSV NASBmg TEV NIV NJB.

no one took 𝔓45 ℵ* B: ASVmg NASB NEB.

It is difficult to determine which verb tense was originally written by John. The present tense $\alpha \check{\iota} \rho \epsilon \iota$ was selected for the text of UBS³ and NA²⁶ (the previous editions of the Nestle text used to read $\mathring{\eta} \rho \epsilon \nu$); this tense accords with the other present-tense verbs in this sentence. However, John often used the proleptic aorist (in this verse ἦρεν) when Jesus spoke about certain future events, as in this case. The disparity among the translations demonstrates the difficulty of determining the original wording.

▶ John 10:29

that which my Father has given me is greater than all B*: ASVmg RSVmg NASBmg NIVmg NEBmg TEV NJBmg.
My Father who has given them to me is greater than all 𝔓66ᶜ 𝔓75ᵛⁱᵈ 𝔐: ASV RSV NASB NIV NEB TEVmg.
My Father, as to that which he has given me, is greater than all ℵ D L W: NJB.

These citations do not show all the variants of this text, only the primary ones. The first reading comes from a combination of ὅ and μεῖζον in the Greek; the second from ὅς and μείζων; the third from ὅ and μείζων. (Other variants have ὅς with μεῖζον.) 𝔓75 clearly reads ὅς (even with a rough breathing mark over the word), but deterioration has marred the word μεῖζον/μείζων. Perhaps this lack is why neither NA²⁶ or UBS³ cite 𝔓75 for this text. (In pointing out this lack to Barbara Aland, I was told that the testimony of 𝔓75 would be added to the apparatus of NA²⁶ in a future printing.) At any rate, both papyri support the second reading, followed by most of the translations. And it is no wonder, because out of all the readings this one makes the most sense and seems to be so characteristically Johannine (i.e., the Son often spoke of the Father as the One who had given various things to him—see John 5:26-27; 6:37, 39; 17:2). However, the simplicity of this reading (as compared to the others) has caused it to be suspect—for what scribe would have changed a simple, direct reading to a very difficult one? Thus, it is quite possible that John wrote this verse with the combination ὅ . . . μεῖζον. Elsewhere in his Gospel, John used the neuter singular to designate the corporate entity of believers (which encompasses all Christians as one unit) that was given to Jesus as a gift from the Father (see 6:37, 39; 17:2, 24). Given the context of John 10, Jesus would be saying that this one corporate entity (which could be called the church), which was given to the Son by the Father and was under the protective care of the Father's hand and the Son's hand, would be invincible to the attack of the enemy

119

(see 10:1, 5, 8, 10, 12) and therefore would be *greater than all* (i.e., greater than all the enemies mentioned in John 10).

Five of the translations (ASV, RSV, NASB, NIV, NEB) followed the more straightforward reading, the one supported by the papyri; and one (TEV) followed the first reading, the one found in NA[26] and UBS[3]—though almost every translation has a marginal note on this. The NJB followed the third reading noted above, which seems to make for impossible Greek, but some exegetes (such as Barrett—see his commentary, *The Gospel According to John*) and translators have made sense of it and render it, "My Father, as to that which he has given me, is greater than all."

▶ John 11:25

I am the resurrection and the life: 𝔓66 𝔓75 ℵ A B C D L W 33: ASV RSV NASB NIV NEB TEV NJBmg.

I am the resurrection: 𝔓45 and two old versions and Origen: RSVmg NEBmg NJB.

Without question, the translators of the RSV and NEB were affected by the testimony of 𝔓45 in this verse; otherwise, they would not have added a marginal note concerning the omission of "and the life" from certain manuscripts (actually only one Greek MS—𝔓45). The subsequent discoveries of 𝔓66 and 𝔓75 strengthen the case for the first reading. Besides, it is well known that the scribe of 𝔓45 had a proclivity for excision (see Colwell and comments above on the textual character of 𝔓45). What is amazing is that NJB adopted the shorter reading—and did so on the basis of one Greek MS known for excisions.

▶ John 11:45

*seeing the things he did 𝔓6 𝔓45 ℵ A W: ASVmg.

seeing whatever he did 𝔓66c: none.

seeing what [or, that which] he did 𝔓66* Ac B C* D: ASV RSV NASB NJB NIV NEB TEV.

The combined testimony of 𝔓6 and 𝔓45 was enough to convince the editors of NA[26] to adopt this first reading in the text and move the third reading to the critical apparatus. The first reading has other good manuscript support (ℵ A W) and is most likely the reading from which the others deviated. The scribes of 𝔓66 et al. probably changed the plural to the singular because the crowd saw Jesus perform only one sign—i.e., the raising of Lazarus.

Not one of the translations, however, follows the reading in 𝔭6 et al.—either because of the translators' preference for B or because they, like the scribes just mentioned, decided to use the reading that fit the overall context. Whatever the reasoning, the reading of 𝔭6 et al. should be noted in the margins—or better yet, incorporated into the texts of some of the modern versions.

▶ John 12:17

the crowd that had been with him when he called Lazarus out of the tomb and raised him from the dead was giving testimony ℵ A B W: ASV RSV NASB NIVmg NEB TEV NJB.

the crowd that had been with him was testifying that he called Lazarus out of the tomb and raised him from the dead 𝔭66 D L: NIV.

In the Greek, the difference between the above two readings is accounted for by a one-letter difference in various MSS: ὅτε ("when") versus ὅτι ("that"). The first reading has the best external support, and was followed by all the translations except NIV, which adhered to the witness of 𝔭66. The second reading probably arose as "an attempt to smooth out the difficulty concerning the mention of the various crowds in this narrative" (Newman and Nida, *A Translator's Handbook on the Gospel of John*).

▶ John 12:41

Isaiah said these things because he saw his glory 𝔭66 𝔭75 ℵ A B L: all the translations.

Isaiah said these things when he saw his glory D 𝔐: NEBmg NJBmg.

As in the previous instance (John 12:17), the difference between the above two readings in the Greek is accounted for by a one-letter difference in various MSS: ὅτι "(because)" versus ὅτε ("when"). The first reading has the best external support (including both papyri), and was followed by all the translations.

▶ John 13:2

during supper ℵ* B L W 0124: all the translations.

supper having ended [or, **supper having been served**] 𝔭66 ℵ² A D 𝔐: NJBmg.

121

The difference between the two variants noted above involves a single letter in the Greek text: δείπνου γινομένου (lit., "supper happening") versus δείπνου γενομένου (lit., "supper having happened"—or, taken as an ingressive aorist, "supper having been served"). If the second reading could not be understood as an ingressive aorist, the statement contradicts the context, which clearly indicates that the supper was in progress. But all the translators followed the first reading because it so readily suits the context. Nevertheless, the marginal note in the NJB reflects the influence of 𝔓66.

► John 13:10

he who has been bathed needs only to wash his feet (𝔓66) B C* (L) W: ASV RSV NASB NIV NEBmg TEV NJBmg.
he who has been bathed does not need to wash ℵ: ASVmg RSVmg NEB TEVmg NJB.

Arguments have been advanced for both the inclusion of εἰ μὴ τοὺς πόδας and its omission (see Beasley-Murray's summary of the arguments in his commentary on *John* in the Word Biblical Commentary series). 𝔓66, with B and C, attests to the reading followed by most of the modern versions.

► John 13:32

include **if God was glorified in him** ℵ² A C² 𝔐: RSV NASB NIV NEB TEV NJB.
omit 𝔓66 ℵ* B C D L W: ASV NIVmg NEBmg NJBmg.

Not one of the earliest MSS contains this first part of John 13:32. Nevertheless, many scholars think that it is an intrinsic part of John's original writing—and that it was omitted from many MSS because of homoeoteleuton or deliberate deletion of perceived redundancy (see John 13:31). On the other hand, it could be argued that the words were added to create a protasis. In either case, John 13:31-32 records Jesus' declaration (spoken proleptically) about his coming glorification. All the translators evidently sided with those scholars who considered this statement to be worthy of inclusion in the text, though a few noted its omission, based on the testimony of 𝔓66 et al.

▶ John 14:4

And where I go you know the way 𝔭66ᶜ ℵ B C* L W: all the translations.

And where I go you know and the way you know 𝔭66* A C³ D: ASVmg RSVmg NASBmg NIVmg NEBmg TEVmg.

The shorter text, having the best support among the MSS, is most likely the true reading, a reading followed by all the translations. The expanded reading, nevertheless, is noted in nearly every version. The copyist of 𝔭66 first wrote the longer reading and then corrected it to the shorter one.

▶ John 14:7

*If you have come to know me, you will know my Father also 𝔭66 ℵ D W: NIVmg NEBmg TEV NJB.

If you had known me, you would have known my Father also A B C L 𝔐: ASV RSV NASB NIV NEB TEVmg NJBmg.

The testimony of 𝔭66 with ℵ D W was apparently strong enough to offset the testimony of A B and C, for the editors of NA²⁶ chose the first reading over the second and thus adopted a reading not found in previous editions of the Nestle text. Two translations (NIV and NJB) adopted the reading of 𝔭66, and it is noted in two others. But the majority of translators followed the second reading, for it seems more appropriate to a context in which Jesus appears to be reproving his disciples for having not known the Father through him—rather than promising his disciples that they would attain a future knowledge of the Father. If he were making a promise, why would he have said in the very next sentence: "And from now on you know him and have seen him"?

▶ John 14:14

ask me anything 𝔭66 ℵ B W 33: ASVmg RSVmg NASB NIV NEBmg TEV NJB.

ask anything A D L Q: ASV RSV NEB TEVmg.

The first reading has the support of the earliest MSS (including 𝔭66); all of the translations since the NEB (1961) followed this reading. Quite significantly, 𝔭66 must have helped to create this change—for 𝔭66 was available to the translators of NASB, NIV, TEV, and NJB, but not ASV, RSV, and (probably) NEB.

▶ John 14:17

because he abides with you and will be in you 𝔓66c 𝔓75 ℵ A D L Q W:
ASV RSV NASB NIV NEBmg TEVmg NJBmg.
because he abides with you and is in you 𝔓66* B D* W: NIVmg NEB
TEV NJB.

The documentary evidence for both readings is impressive—with the
testimony of 𝔓66c 𝔓75 ℵ offsetting that of 𝔓66* B D*. Therefore, the
translators must have had difficulty in determining the most probable
reading. In context, Jesus was telling his disciples that he would send
them the Spirit as the παράκλητος (lit., "the Paraclete"—the Encour-
ager, the Comforter). Jesus added that they should know who "the
Paraclete" is because "he abides with you and will be [or, is] in you." If
the text originally had two present verbs, this statement could be understood to describe, proleptically, the twofold location of the Spirit in
relationship to the believer. In other words, the Spirit is viewed in its
future state as present *with* and *in* the believer. If the text originally had a
present-tense verb and a future-tense verb, then Jesus probably meant
that the Spirit as present with Jesus (then and there) was *with* the disciples, and in the future would be *in* the disciples.

▶ John 16:22a

you have sorrow 𝔓22 ℵ* B C Wc 054: ASV RSV NASB NIV TEV
NJB.
you will have sorrow 𝔓66 ℵ2 A D W*: NEB.

𝔓22 bolsters the testimony for the present-tense verb, a testimony followed by all the versions except the NEB. The future-tense verb appears
to be an assimilation to the future tense in John 16:20. (Note: the choice
of NEB to adopt the future tense was not necessarily influenced by 𝔓66,
for Tasker never once mentions 𝔓66 in all of his notes on John—even
though 𝔓66 had been published before the NEB was published.)

▶ John 16:22b

no one takes your joy from you 𝔓22 𝔓66vid ℵ A C: ASV NASB.
no one will take your joy from you 𝔓5 B D: RSV NIV NEB TEV NJB.

Since the evidence among the earliest MSS is divided, it is difficult to be
dogmatic about one reading or the other. The reading with the present

tense, however, is more characteristically Johannine. In the Gospel of John, Jesus frequently uses the present tense proleptically. Nonetheless, most of the translators must have been more impressed by the testimony of 𝔓5 with B D than that of 𝔓22 𝔓66ᵛⁱᵈ ℵ A C.

▶ John 16:23

*whatever you ask the Father in my name he will give it to you 𝔓22ᵛⁱᵈ A C3ᵛⁱᵈ D W: NIV NEB TEV.

whatever you ask the Father he will give it to you in my name 𝔓5ᵛⁱᵈ ℵ B C*: ASV RSV NASB NEBmg NJB.

The manuscript evidence for both readings is good—although the first reading has more diverse testimony, the second reading has earlier testimony. Nonetheless, the second reading is harder, internally speaking. Because the Lord usually spoke of making petition to the Father in his own name (see 14:13, 14; 15:16; 16:24, 26), it would have been quite natural for scribes to conform this clause to the more usual order. Conversely, it would be difficult to imagine why so many early scribes would have rearranged the syntax to the more difficult reading (Comfort, *Study Guide to Translating the Gospel of John,* 64). But both Metzger (on behalf of the UBS3 and NA26—in which the text was changed from previous editions) and Tasker (on behalf of the Greek text underlying the NEB) argue that the first reading is more suitable to this context that deals with praying in the Lord's name. The majority of translations follow the second reading.

Each reading, represented by one of the papyri (𝔓5 and 𝔓22), was followed by three modern English translations. 𝔓22ᵛⁱᵈ et al. was followed by NIV NEB and TEV; 𝔓5ᵛⁱᵈ et al. by RSV NASB and NJB.

▶ John 16:27

I came forth from God 𝔓5 𝔓66ᵛⁱᵈ ℵ*,2 A C3 W: NIV NEB TEV NJB.
I came forth from the Father ℵ1 B C D: ASV RSV NASB.

The reading with "God," supported by 𝔓5 et al., has earlier and more diverse support than the reading with "Father"—which was probably assimilated from the next verse (Comfort, *Study Guide to Translating the Gospel of John,* 65). Nevertheless, all the versions in the revised tradition (ASV, RSV, NASB) adhere to the reading with "Father," while the independent modern versions followed "God"—undoubtedly influenced by the combined testimony of 𝔭5 and 𝔭66[vid].

▶ John 17:11

keep them in your name which you have given me 𝔭60 (𝔭66[vid] ℵ) A B C (L W): ASV RSV NASB NEBmg TEV NJBmg.
keep in your name those whom you have given me D: NEB TEVmg NJB.

The first reading is the more difficult yet better attested one (so also in John 17:12—see below). Jesus was not asking that the Father keep the believers (whom he, the Son, had been given) in his name; rather, he was asking that the Father keep the believers in his own name, which he had given to his Son. Westcott said, "These passages [17:11-12] suggest the idea that the 'giving of the Father's name' to Christ expresses the fullness of his commission as the Incarnate Word to reveal God. . . . And all spiritual truth is gathered up in the 'name' of God, the perfect expression (for men) of what God is, which 'name' the Father gave to the Son to declare when he took man's nature upon him" (*Gospel According to St. John*).

Most of the translations followed the superior reading, but some (NEB NJB) chose to adopt the easier, smoother reading.

▶ John 17:12

I was keeping them in your name which you have given me 𝔭66[cvid] B C* L W: ASV RSV NASB NIV TEV NEBmg.
I was keeping in your name those whom you have given me A (C³) D 𝔐: NEB TEVmg NJB.

See comments on John 17:11 above.

▶ John 19:35; 20:31

In both these verses, 𝔭66[vid] (with ℵ* B) reads the present subjunctive πιστεύητε ("may continue to believe"). Other MSS (ℵ² A D L W) read the aorist, πιστεύσητε. The editors of UBS³ and NA²⁶ followed this reading, but signaled their doubt about the aorist verb by bracketing the sigma: πιστεύ[σ]ητε. Given John's tendency to use the present-tense verb when speaking about a continual believing, a believing that extends beyond the initial act of faith, it seems more likely that John here wrote the present subjunctive, not the aorist. In these verses John was certifying the trustworthiness of his testimony so that the readers (who were probably already believers) would continue to believe the veracity of the gospel. A few versions (see TEVmg for 19:35; NEB ["that you may hold to the faith"], NIVmg, and TEVmg for 20:31) made a point of using or noting the present-tense verb in these verses—influenced, no doubt, by the testimony of $\mathfrak{p}66^{vid}$ with ℵ* B.

Acts

Early manuscripts containing portions of Acts:

$\mathfrak{p}$8: 4:31-37; 5:2-9; 6:1-6, 8-15
$\mathfrak{p}$29: 26:7-8, 20
$\mathfrak{p}$38: 18:27–19:6, 12-16
$\mathfrak{p}$45: 4:27–17:17 (with many lacunae)
$\mathfrak{p}$48: 23:11-17, 23-29
$\mathfrak{p}$50: 8:26-32; 10:26-31
$\mathfrak{p}$53: 9:33–10:1
$\mathfrak{p}$91: 2:30-37, 46–3:2
0189: 5:3-21

▶ Acts 2:47
See comments on this verse in the description of $\mathfrak{p}$91 (Section 2).

▶ Acts 4:33
the resurrection of the Lord Jesus $\mathfrak{p}$8 B: all the translations.
the resurrection of the Lord Jesus Christ ℵ A D: ASVmg NASBmg.

Scribes were known for expanding divine titles. The shorter, superior reading is found in $\mathfrak{p}$8 and B—followed by all the translations.

▶ Acts 5:3
See comments on this verse in the description of 0189 (Section 2).

▶ Acts 6:3

the Spirit 𝔓8 𝔓74 ℵ A B C² D: ASV RSV NASB NIV NEB NJB.
the Holy Spirit C* E 𝔐: TEV.

Very often scribes added the word "Holy" to the word "Spirit" in an attempt to clarify the identity of the Spirit. The translators of the TEV, although committed to follow UBS³, deviated from their text probably for the same reason—i.e., they wanted to make it clear which Spirit filled Stephen.

▶ Acts 8:18

Spirit ℵ B: ASVmg RSV NASB NIV NEB TEV NJB.
Holy Spirit 𝔓45 𝔓74 A C D E 33 1739: ASV.

Since scribes had the tendency to add the word "Holy" before the word "Spirit," the editors of UBS³ and NA²⁶ deemed it more appropriate to print τὸ πνεῦμα in the text. All the translators, except those of the ASV, followed this reading. It is surprising that the ASV did not follow ℵ and B, and that none of the translations followed the testimony of the papyri—or even noted their testimony in the margin.

▶ Acts 8:37

omit verse 𝔓45 𝔓74 ℵ A B C: all the translations.
include verse E and later MSS: the margins of all the translations.

The verse is an obvious later addition. The only reason it is printed in the margins of all the versions is that translations invariably inform the reader about omissions of text.

▶ Acts 10:30

praying 𝔓74 ℵ A* B C 1739: all the translations.
praying and fasting 𝔓50 A² D E 049 056 0142: NJBmg.

This is the only instance in which 𝔓50 is cited in UBS³. Unfortunately, it is here given an unrepresentative showing (see description above under "textual character") because in this case it aligns with D and other Western MSS against B and other Alexandrian MSS. In all likelihood, the addition of "and fasting" is a pietistic expansion (as in Mark 9:29 and 1 Cor. 7:5). None of the modern translations adopted the longer reading, and only the NJB, which is known for its attentiveness to the Western text, noted the variant in 𝔓50 et al.

▶ Acts 11:11

the house where we were 𝔓74 ℵ A B D: ASV RSV NASB NEBmg TEVmg NJB.

the house where I was 𝔓45 E 33: NEB NIV TEV.

The NEB translators considered the first reading to be secondary to the one supported by 𝔓45 E 33. The NIV and TEV translators must have also been influenced by the testimony of 𝔓45 to have selected a reading against one supported by ℵ A B D.

▶ Acts 11:12

making no distinction [between Gentiles and Jews] (𝔓74) ℵ A B E 33: ASV RSV NEBmg.

without doubting [or, **with no hesitation**] later MSS: NASB NIV NEBmg TEV NJB.

omit 𝔓45ᵛⁱᵈ D: NEB.

The translators of the NEB thought that the first and second readings noted above were additions (echoing Acts 10:20) to the original text. The testimony of 𝔓45ᵛⁱᵈ bolstered their opinion (see Tasker). However, other textual critics and translators thought the testimony for the first reading was ample proof that Luke probably wrote these words, while other translators followed the testimony of later MSS. (It should also be remembered that the copyist of 𝔓45 was given to excision.)

▶ Acts 13:33

second psalm 𝔓74 ℵ A B C E 33: ASV RSV NASB NIV NEB TEV NJBmg.

first psalm D and some Old Latin MSS: NEBmg NJBmg.

psalms 𝔓45: NJB.

The first and second psalms (as we know them in our English Bibles) were often put together as one psalm in the Hebrew text. Metzger provides a lengthy discussion concerning the textual problem here. Good reasons are advanced for each of the readings, but in the final analysis the editors of UBS³ and NA²⁶ (as well as almost all the translators) preferred the testimony of the four great uncials over against D or 𝔓45. Nevertheless, the translators of the NJB preferred the testimony of 𝔓45 against all the other MSS because it is the oldest extant MS containing this portion of the NT.

▶ Acts 13:48
word of the Lord 𝔓45 𝔓74 ℵ A C 33: ASVmg NASB NIV NEB TEV NJB.
word of God B D: ASV RSV NJBmg.

Since the ASV was so strongly influenced by the testimony of B and the papyri had not yet been discovered by the turn of the century, it is no wonder that the ASV favored the reading "word of God." But one would think the RSV would have followed the testimony of 𝔓45 et al.

▶ Acts 15:20a
include **and from fornication** 𝔓74 ℵ A B C D E: all the translations.
omit 𝔓45: NEBmg.

See comments below.

▶ Acts 15:20b
include **and from what is strangled** 𝔓45 𝔓74 ℵ A B C E 33: all the translations.
omit D and some Latin fathers: RSVmg NEBmg NJBmg.

See comments below.

▶ Acts 15:20c
from blood 𝔓45 𝔓74 A B C E 33: all the translations.
from blood and from doing to others what they would not like done to themselves D: NEBmg NJBmg.

In each of the three variation units in Acts 15:20, the first reading cited above has the best testimony, and was followed by all the versions.

▶ Acts 16:32
*****word of the Lord** 𝔓45 𝔓74 ℵ¹ A C D E 33: all the translations.
word of God ℵ* B: ASVmg NEBmg NJBmg.

In deference to the testimony of ℵ and B, some translations provide a marginal note on the second reading. Nevertheless, the testimony of 𝔓45 et al. was adopted for the text of NA²⁶ (a change from previous editions of the Nestle text) and all the translations. The testimony of 𝔓45 helped to offset that of ℵ* and B.

▶ Acts 16:36
include **in peace** 𝔓45ᵛⁱᵈ 𝔓74 ℵ A B C E 33: ASV RSV NASB NIV NEB TEV NJBmg.
omit D and two Old Latin MSS: NEBmg NJB.

Those favoring the second reading argue that scribes would be more likely to add such words of farewell than delete them. But it is hard to argue against the preponderance of testimony in favor of their inclusion.

▶ Acts 19:2
See comments on this verse in the description of 𝔓38 (Section 2).

▶ Acts 23:12
the Jews banded together 𝔓74 ℵ A B C E 33: ASV RSV NASB NIV NEB NJB.
some Jews banded together 𝔓48 P 049 056 0142: TEV.

The TEV follows the reading in 𝔓48 et al., which has the word "some" before "Jews"; thus, the reading harmonizes with Acts 23:13, which speaks of forty Jews who had banded together in a plot against Paul.

▶ Acts 23:29
The NJB provides a marginal note on this verse, saying that the Western text adds "of Moses, and a man called Jesus" after the statement "I found that the accusation concerned disputed points of their law." Thus, in the Western text the entire statement reads, "I found that the accusation concerned disputed points of the Law of Moses and of a man [lit., 'a certain one'] called Jesus." In NA²⁶ the variant is cited with the following MSS in support of it: 614, 2147, Old Latin Gigas, and Syriac Harclean mg. To this should be added 𝔓48ᵛⁱᵈ. According to the transcription provided by Vitelli and Mercati, the last three lines of the 𝔓48 text read as follows:

[γνωναι την αιτ]ιαν ην εκαλουν αυτω κατη-
[γαγον αυτον εις το] συνεδριον· ουδεν πλειον ευ-
[ρον ----- ----- ----- -----]ω**εωσκαι

According to Clark (see bibliography on 𝔓48 in Section 2), Mercati later filled out the last line:

[ρον ενκαλουμενον η περι του νομου μ]ω[υσ]εως και

This restoration thus indicates that 𝔓48 must have also included the addition "of Moses, and [a certain one called Jesus]."

Romans

Early manuscripts containing portions of Romans:

𝔓10: 1:1-7
𝔓27: 8:12-22, 24-27; 8:33–9:3, 5-9
𝔓40: 1:24-27, 31–2:3; 3:21–4:8; 6:4-5; 9:17, 27
𝔓46: 5:17–6:14; 8:15–15:9; 15:11–16:27
0220: 4:23–5:3, 8-13

▶ Romans 1:1
Christ Jesus 𝔓10 B: NASB NIV TEV NEB NJB.
Jesus Christ 𝔓26 ℵ A 𝔐: ASV RSV.

Evidently, the most recent translations decided to follow the testimony of the two earliest MSS (𝔓10 and B) against the testimony of almost all the other MSS.

▶ Romans 3:22
See comments on this verse in the description of 𝔓40 (Section 2).

▶ Romans 5:1
we have peace ℵ¹ B² 0220ᵛⁱᵈ: ASV RSV NASB NIV NEBmg TEV NJB.
let us have peace ℵ* A B* C D: ASVmg RSVmg NASBmg NIVmg NEB TEVmg NJBmg.

There is but a one-letter difference between the two readings: o/ω—ἔχομεν ("we have") versus ἔχωμεν ("let us have"); the first reading contains a present indicative and the second, a present subjunctive. The first reading, which has the support of the earliest MS (0220vid), was adopted by NA26 and UBS3 and followed by all the translations except NEB. Tasker, arguing for the rendering in the NEB, considered that the first reading was weakly attested (had he overlooked the testimony of 0220vid?) and that the second reading, with the support of ℵ* A B* C D, was harmonious with the series of subjunctives in Rom. 5:2-3.

▶ Romans 8:21

*in hope that the creation 𝔓46 A B C D2: ASV NASB NIV NEBmg TEV.

in hope; because the creation ℵ D: ASVmg RSV NASBmg NEB NJB.

It is difficult to determine which of the two readings affected which translations because both readings in the Greek (ὅτι, the first reading, and διότι, the second) can be translated "because." But only ὅτι can be rendered "that"—which permits the first rendering, a rendering that connects together the last two words of Rom. 8:20 with the beginning of 8:21 ("in hope that the creation itself will be freed from the bondage of corruption"). At any rate, the testimony of 𝔓46 with A B C (the oldest and best witnesses) caused the editors of NA26 to adopt the first reading over the second—a change from previous editions of the Nestle text. Several of the translations (NASB NIV TEV) also followed the reading of 𝔓46 et al., but not the RSV, which set out to adopt the testimony of 𝔓46 but did not always do so.

▶ Romans 8:23

include **sonship** [or, **adoption as sons**] ℵ A B C 33 1739: ASV RSV NASB NIV NEB TEV NJBmg.

omit 𝔓46vid D: NEBmg TEVmg NJB.

The omission of "sonship" (Greek, υἱοθεσίαν) in 𝔓46vid D (and other Western MSS) is best explained as a scribal effort to eliminate a seeming contradiction between Paul's statement here about sonship and the statement he made in Rom. 8:15. In Rom. 8:15, Paul spoke about the believers' initial reception of the Spirit of sonship; in 8:23 he was

speaking about the ultimate appropriation of each son's inheritance—
i.e., the possession of a glorified body (see NJBmg). Thus, there is not
really a contradiction; but certain scribes may have thought there was, so
they eliminated the word. Nonetheless, the testimony of $\mathfrak{P}$46[vid] with D
and other witnesses was followed by NJB and noted in NEBmg (see
Tasker's reason) and TEVmg.

▶ Romans 8:24
Although there are several variant readings in this verse, they basically
yield one of two statements. Some MSS ($\mathfrak{P}$46 B* 1739mg) read "who,"
while others (א[2] B[2] A C) read "why"; and some MSS ($\mathfrak{P}$46 א[2] B C D)
read "hopes," while others (א* A 1739mg) read "waits." Thus, the text
could read "who hopes for what he sees" (as in ASV RSV NASBmg
NIV NEB TEV NJB) or "why wait for what he sees" (as in ASVmg
NASB NEBmg). The first reading was adopted by the editors of UBS[3]
and NA[26] because of the weight of $\mathfrak{P}$46 with B, and was, therefore,
followed by most of the modern versions.

▶ Romans 8:28
*everything works together for good [or, he works together every-
thing for good] א C D 33 1739: ASV RSVmg NASBmg NEB TEVmg
NJBmg.
God works all things together for good $\mathfrak{P}$46 A B: ASVmg RSV NASB
NIV NEBmg TEV NJB.

Quite possibly the scribes of $\mathfrak{P}$46, A, and B added "God" to the existing
text in order to clarify an ambiguous text, which is reflected in the first
reading above; i.e., the subject could be "everything" or "he." In the
context of Romans 8, it would seem that the subject is "God" or "the
Spirit" (both mentioned in Rom. 8:27). God or the Spirit is the One who
works all things together for good. However, most of the translators
adhered to the reading with "God." Note again the change from the ASV
to the RSV; $\mathfrak{P}$46 was definitely influential in the decision (see Grant).

▶ Romans 8:34
whom he raised $\mathfrak{P}$27[vid] $\mathfrak{P}$46 א[2] B D: NASB NIV TEV.
whom he raised from the dead: א* A C: ASV RSV NASBmg NEB
NJB.

The first reading has strong external and internal support. The three earliest witnesses contain the shorter reading. (Though there is a lacuna in 𝔭27, there is not enough space to have fit ἐκ νεκρῶν—"from the dead".) Later scribes would have easily been tempted to add the words "from the dead." Why did not all the translators follow the superior reading?—especially the RSV translators, who had the testimony of 𝔭27ᵛⁱᵈ and 𝔭46 available at that time and usually revised the ASV when presented with earlier (and reliable) evidence. Perhaps the translators of ASV, RSV, etc. went beyond the text at this point and they—as with so many scribes—thought it necessary to fill out the expression "whom he raised" with the usual formula "from the dead."

▶ Romans 9:4
the covenants ℵ C 33: all the translations.
the covenant 𝔭46 B D: TEVmg.

Textual scholars would observe here that it is much more likely that the scribes changed the plural reading to a singular than vice versa because the plural reading is seemingly more difficult. The natural tendency is to think that God enacted only one covenant with Israel—that which came to be known in NT times as the old covenant. Actually, God initiated covenants with Abraham, with the nation of Israel at Sinai, and with David. Or the plural "covenants" could refer to the one covenant made with Abraham (Gen. 15), then renewed with Isaac (Gen. 17), and then Jacob (Gen. 28). Everett F. Harrison said, "There is rather good manuscript evidence for 'covenant' rather than 'covenants,' but this reading can hardly be original, for it would most naturally suggest the Mosaic covenant (2 Cor. 3:6, 14), which would render the next item [in Paul's list], the reception of the law, quite unnecessary" ("Romans," in *Expositor's Bible Commentary*). Accordingly, none of the translations followed the plural reading; only TEV noted the variant in the margin—in deference to combined testimony of 𝔭46 B D.

▶ Romans 11:17
of the root of the fatness ℵ* B C: ASV RSVmg NIV NASB NJB.
of the root and of the fatness ℵ² A D² 33 1739 𝔐: ASVmg NEB.
of the fatness 𝔭46 D*: RSV.

135

Quite manifestly, the rendering in the RSV displays the effect of 𝔓46. Translations since the RSV have, for the most part, adhered to the first reading.

▶ Romans 11:31
they may now receive mercy ℵ B D*: ASV NASB NIV TEV NEB.
they may receive mercy 𝔓46[vid] A D²: RSV TEVmg NJB.

The Greek word for "now" (νῦν) is bracketed in the NA²⁶ and UBS³ Greek texts, reflecting the balanced testimony of the MSS. The RSV, again, shows the influence of 𝔓46, while most of the versions since the RSV have followed ℵ B D*.

▶ Romans 12:11
serving the Lord 𝔓46 ℵ A B D²: all the translations.
serving the time [or, **meeting the demands of the hour**] D* F G: ASVmg NEBmg NJBmg.

In the Greek, the words for "time" (καιρῷ) and "Lord" (κυρίῳ) could easily be mistaken for each other by a scribe—even when both words were abbreviated (see Metzger). In this case, it was more likely that κυρίῳ was changed to καιρῷ. All the translations adhered to the first reading supported by 𝔓46 et al., and a few noted the variant.

▶ Romans 12:14
***persecute you** ℵ A D 𝔐: all the translations.
persecute 𝔓46 B 1739: NASBmg.

The Greek word for "you" (ὑμᾶς) has been bracketed in NA²⁶ and UBS³ to reflect the editors' indecision about its inclusion (the word was not included in previous editions of the Nestle text). Nonetheless, all the translations followed the first reading, and only the NASB, perhaps influenced by the testimony of 𝔓46, noted the second.

▶ Romans 15:19
***the Spirit of God** 𝔓46 ℵ D¹ 𝔐: ASVmg TEV NJB.
the Spirit B: ASVmg NASB NIV.
the Holy Spirit A D* 33: ASV RSV NEB.

Given the fact that scribes were known to expand titles of the divine Spirit, the reading in B could very well be original. The translators of the NASB and NIV must have thought so. And the editors of NA²⁶ and UBS³ must have been inclined to this view because they bracketed θεοῦ ("of God") after πνεύματος ("Spirit"). They included θεοῦ, however, in deference to the testimony of 𝔭46 with ℵ and D versus B—a change from previous editions of the Nestle text which followed B. Thus, those translations that follow the first reading are reflecting a well-attested text. But one wonders why any translations would have adopted the third reading, for it has inferior external support and, as was just mentioned, it was most likely the work of scribes who had a proclivity for expanding the bare title "the Spirit" to "the Holy Spirit" and/or changing less usual titles of the Spirit to the more usual one, "the Holy Spirit."

▶ Romans 15:33

At the end of this verse, 𝔭46 alone has the doxology usually placed at Rom. 16:25-27. No translation follows this, but it is noted in RSVmg, NEBmg, and NJBmg. See comments on Rom. 16:25-27 and see photo 7.

▶ Romans 16:7

Junias ℵ A B C D: all the translations.
Julia 𝔭46 and some Old Latin MSS: NEBmg TEVmg.

Most likely, the second reading came as a result of a transcriptional error—the Greek *nu* was made a *lambda*. The reverse error happened in 16:15 in a few MSS (C* G), where the name "Julia" appears (Metzger). The marginal notes in NEB and TEV undoubtedly reflect the influence of 𝔭46.

▶ Romans 16:20

include **the grace of our Lord Jesus be with you** 𝔭46 ℵ B (add **Christ** after **Jesus** A C 33 𝔐): all the translations.
omit D F G: ASVmg RSVmg NEBmg TEVmg.

The scribes of D F and G added these words after 16:23 (comprising a whole new verse in KJV—16:24); therefore, they excluded them here. The omission is noted in the margins of several translations in connection with textual variation in 16:24.

► Romans 16:24

omit verse 𝔓46 𝔓61^{vid} א (A) B C 1739: all the translations.
include verse D P 33 𝔐: the margins of all the translations.

The omission of this verse is strongly supported by all the earliest MSS. All the translations, following this testimony, did not include the verse. At the same time, all the translations provide a textual note concerning this verse because of its place in traditional English translations.

► Romans 16:25-27

The doxology to the book of Romans has been put in various places in different MSS, as follows: after 16:23 (𝔓61$^{vid?}$ א B C D 1739); after 14:23 and 16:23 (A 33); after 14:23 (L Ψ 0209^{vid}); after 15:33 (𝔓46—see photo 7). All the translations kept the doxology at the end of chapter 16 and provided various kinds of textual notes explaining some of the different transpositions. Metzger provides a thorough discussion concerning the textual and critical issues which arise from the various transpositions of the doxology. Most of these issues extend beyond the field of textual criticism into literary criticism and thus are not pertinent to this study.

1 Corinthians

Early manuscripts containing portions of 1 Corinthians:

𝔓15: 7:18–8:4
𝔓46: 1:1–16:22 (all of the epistle)

► 1 Corinthians 1:13

has Christ been divided? א A B C D 33 1739: ASV RSV NASB NIV TEV NJB.
Christ can not be divided, can he? 𝔓46^{vid} and some later MSS: NEB TEVmg.

According to 𝔓46^{vid} (which adds μή at the beginning of the sentence), Paul asked a question expecting a negative answer. The NEB chose this reading, and TEV noted it. But since all the other MSS support the first reading, all the other translations adhered to their testimony.

► 1 Corinthians 1:28

the despised things, [even] **the things that are not** 𝔭46 א* A C* D* 0129 33 1739: ASV RSV NASB NEB TEV NJB.

the despised things, and the things that are not $א^2$ B C^3 D^2 𝔐: ASVmg NIV.

According to 𝔭46 et al., the expression "the things that are not" is in apposition to "the despised things." This is the best-attested reading (note the corrections in א C D). Thus, one wonders why the NIV did not follow it.

► 1 Corinthians 2:1

the mystery of God $𝔭46^{vid}$ א* A C: ASVmg RSVmg NASBmg NIVmg NEBmg TEV NJB.

the testimony of God $א^2$ B D 33 1739: ASV RSV NASB NIV NEB TEVmg NJBmg.

UBS^3 cites $𝔭46^{vid?}$ in support of the first reading. The question mark follows *vid* because the editors were not sure that 𝔭46 contains the word μυστήριον ("mystery"). I examined the facsimile of the papyrus containing this verse at the University of Michigan's library. Though there is a lacuna in 1 Cor. 2:1, I can affirm that the reading is μυστήριον ("mystery"), not μαρτύριον ("testimony"). I can affirm this because the Greek letter *eta* (H), though partially broken, is visible before the final four letters—also visible (PION). (See photo 8.) The one letter makes all the difference in determining whether the Greek word is MAPTYP-ION ("testimony") or MYΣTHPION ("mystery") because the first four letters of either word were missing and the last four letters of both words are the same (Comfort).

Given that 𝔭46 supports the first reading, this reading has better testimony than the second. However, most of the translations followed the second reading and noted the first in the margin. If these translators knew of the certainty of the reading in 𝔭46, they would perhaps reverse this.

▶ 1 Corinthians 5:5
Lord 𝔓46 B 1739: ASVmg RSVmg NASBmg NIV NEB TEV NJB.
Lord Jesus ℵ and some later MSS: ASV RSV NASB.
Lord Jesus Christ D 𝔐: none.
omit A 33: none.

The most modern translations (NIV NEB TEV NJB) have followed the
testimony of 𝔓46 and B, but the RSV and NASB did not alter the ASV.

▶ 1 Corinthians 7:15
called you ℵ* A C: ASVmg NASBmg RSVmg TEV NJB.
called us 𝔓46 ℵ² B D 33 1739 𝔐: ASV RSV NASB NIV NJBmg.

Most of the translators did not choose the text later approved by the
editors of UBS³ and NA²⁶; instead, they followed the reading in 𝔓46 et
al. While the ASV had the testimony of B, the translators of the RSV,
NASB, and NIV had the added witness of 𝔓46.

▶ 1 Corinthians 7:33-34
**But a married man is concerned about the affairs of this world—
how he can please his wife—and his interests are divided. An unmarried woman or virgin is concerned about the Lord's affairs**
(taken from NIV) 𝔓15 B—and 𝔓46 ℵ A 33 1739, which add "unmarried" before "virgin": all the translations.
**But a married man is concerned about the affairs of this world—
how he can please his wife. And there is a difference between the
wife and the virgin; she that is unmarried is concerned about the
Lord's affairs** some early versions and later Greek MSS: ASVmg
NASBmg NEBmg NJBmg.

In the critical apparatuses of UBS³ and NA²⁶ there are listed many more
variants than those noted above. Of all the readings, the one represented
by 𝔓15 and B best accounts for the origin of all the others.

▶ 1 Corinthians 7:40
𝔓15 with 33 contains the reading "the Spirit of Christ," whereas all the
other MSS have the reading "the Spirit of God." Given the good textual
character of 𝔓15 (and 33), should not this reading be given some consideration? The title "Spirit of Christ" is far less common than "the Spirit of

God"; the former appears only in Rom. 8:9 and 1 Pet. 1:11, the latter in many NT verses. It would be much more likely that scribes changed "the Spirit of Christ" to "the Spirit of God" than vice versa. In this chapter Paul has made the point of separating his advice from the Lord's directives (see 7:10, 25). Nonetheless, he claims that his advice concerning virgins and the unmarried is to be heeded because he has the Spirit of God/of Christ. Having made the Lord (i.e., the Lord Jesus Christ) the source of reference throughout this chapter, Paul would have found it natural to conclude with an affirmation of his possession of "the Spirit of Christ" rather than "the Spirit of God." But all these arguments, it must be admitted, cannot completely outweigh the fact that all the other MSS read "the Spirit of God." Nevertheless, some modern versions would do well to list this reading in the margin.

▶ 1 Corinthians 8:3a

if a man loves God 𝔓15 ℵ A B D: ASV RSV NASB NIV TEV NJB NEBmg.

if a man loves 𝔓46: NEB.

See comments below.

▶ 1 Corinthians 8:3b

he is recognized [or, **known**] **by him** 𝔓15^vid ℵ^c A B D: all the translations.

he is recognized [or, **known**] 𝔓46 ℵ* 33: NEBmg.

The testimony of 𝔓15 with ℵ A B D was followed by all the translations because it is such a strong witness. But a majority of the NEB translators preferred the reading of 𝔓46 (in the first part of the verse) because they thought the context calls for a statement about loving one's fellow Christians, not loving God (Tasker).

▶ 1 Corinthians 8:12

their conscience when it is weak ℵ A B D 33 1739 𝔐: ASV RSV NASB NIV NEBmg TEV NJB.

their conscience 𝔓46 and Clement: NEB.

Tasker argued for the reading in the NEB (supported by 𝔓46) by saying that the longer reading "was considered an addition to the text, natural in

141

view of the general context, but less effective at this point, where to wound a brother's conscience seems to be regarded as a sin against Christ, whether that conscience is 'weak' or not." The editors of NA[26] and UBS[3] thought that the scribe of 𝔭46 either made a mistake of omission or modified the text—perhaps for the very reason Tasker gave.

▶ 1 Corinthians 10:2

were baptized ℵ A C D 33: ASV RSV NASB NIV TEV NJB.
received baptism 𝔭46ᶜ B 1739: NASBmg NEB.

The first reading is a passive-voice verb, ἐβαπτίσθησαν; the second, a middle-voice, ἐβαπτίσαντο. The first reading was adopted by the majority of UBS[3] and NA[26] editors, with Bruce Metzger and Allen Wikgren voicing the minority view (see Metzger). According to Metzger and Wikgren, the reading in 𝔭46ᶜ B and 1739 is more likely Pauline because the Jews baptized themselves (conveyed by the middle voice), whereas Christians were baptized by others (conveyed by the passive voice)—and Christian scribes would be more likely to change the middle voice to the passive than vice versa. Undoubtedly, the NEB translators must have been convinced by similar arguments and followed the testimony of 𝔭46ᶜ with B, while the NASB translators noted the reading in deference to 𝔭46ᶜ with B.

▶ 1 Corinthians 10:9

*Christ 𝔭46 D 1739 𝔐: ASVmg RSVmg NEBmg TEVmg NJBmg—now included in NRSV.
Lord ℵ B C 33: all the translations.
God A: none.

It is far more likely that "Christ" was changed to "Lord" (or, "God") than vice versa. Given the context of 1 Cor. 10, it would not be inappropriate for Paul to talk about Christ being tempted by the Israelites, for he had just previously mentioned that Christ was the spiritual rock that accompanied the Israelites in their wilderness wanderings (10:4). Thus, Paul twice spoke of Christ with respect to his preincarnate presence with the Israelites. But some scribes from the fourth century onward must have had a theological problem with the reading "Christ," and thus tried to neutralize it by changing it to "Lord" or "God." I say fourth-century scribes because not one witness prior to the fourth century attests to the reading "Lord" or "God." The earliest MS, 𝔓46, and several early church fathers (Irenaeus, Clement, Origen—as well as Marcion) attest to the reading "Christ." Later MSS and later church fathers attest mainly to the reading "Lord." However, a majority of the MSS persisted in keeping the reading "Christ." (Note, the KJV reads "Christ" because the KJV followed the majority text.) Textual critics and translators alike have been reluctant to include the reading "Christ" in their texts. Prior to NA[26] and UBS[3], the reading in the Nestle text was κύριον ("Lord"). Now that has been changed to Χριστόν ("Christ"). We await this change in more modern English translations and revisions. For the present, most translators place the reading "Christ" in a marginal note because they could not ignore the testimony of the earliest MS, 𝔓46. The NRSV is the first modern translation to contain the reading "Christ." (For a full discussion of this textual problem, see "The Text of 1 Corinthians 10:9" by Carroll D. Osburn in *New Testament Textual Criticism: Its Significance for Exegesis.*)

▶ 1 Corinthians 11:24
my body which is for you 𝔓46 ℵ* A B C* 1739: all the translations.
my body which is broken for you ℵ² C³ D² 𝔐: ASVmg RSVmg NASBmg NJBmg.
my body which is given for you some early versions: NJBmg.

𝔓46 adds more weight to a very substantial witness to the first reading. The second reading, supported by a number of corrected MSS, is obviously a scribal attempt to conform Paul's words about the Lord's supper to Jesus' words (see Matt. 26:26-28; Mark 14:22-24; Luke 22:19-20). The second and third readings, therefore, are hardly worth being put in a marginal note.

▶ 1 Corinthians 13:3
***if I give my body that I may boast** 𝔓46 ℵ A B 048 33 1739: the margins of all the translations (except NRSV).
if I give my body to be burned C D L (𝔐): all the translations.

In Greek, there is but a one-letter difference between the first reading and the second (χ/θ): καυχήσωμαι ("I may boast") and καυθήσωμαι ("I may be burned"). Therefore, either word could have been mistaken for the other. Nevertheless, it is evident that the first reading has, by far, the superior testimony; in fact, the witness of 𝔓46 with ℵ A B was enough to convince the editors of the Nestle text to adopt this reading for NA²⁶ and relegate the other one to the margin.

Christian martyrdom by burning was a phenomenon yet unknown to the original readers of this epistle, so Paul could not have been alluding to this. It is possible, however, that he was referring to the incident in Dan. 3, where Shadrach, Meshach, and Abednego were cast into the fiery furnace. Thus, Paul could have written καυθήσωμαι. But if he did not, as the better evidence suggests, what did he mean by giving his body that he might boast about it? Gordon Fee has pointed out that in Clement of Rome's epistle to the church in Corinth (c. 96), Clement spoke of those who delivered themselves to bondage in order to ransom others (*First Corinthians* in the *New International Commentary on the New Testament*). Thus, it is quite possible that Paul was speaking about giving one's body for the sake of others.

Remarkably, not one of the translations prior to the NRSV has the superior reading!—either because it was too difficult to break with the traditional rendering or because the translators thought the second reading to be the *lectio facilior*.

▶ 1 Corinthians 14:38

if anyone ignores [or, does not recognize] this, he himself is ignored [or, not recognized] ℵ* A*ᵛⁱᵈ 048 33 1739: ASVmg RSV NASB NIV NEB TEV NJB.

if anyone ignores this, let him ignore this [or, if he is ignorant, let him be ignorant] 𝔓46 ℵ² Aᶜ B D² 𝔐: ASV NASBmg NIVmg NEBmg NJBmg.

The first reading, though slightly more difficult than the second, does not necessarily have better external support. It is no wonder that the ASV followed the testimony of B, which was later bolstered by 𝔓46. But no other translation followed suit; rather, some have provided a marginal note concerning the variant.

▶ 1 Corinthians 15:49

we shall also bear the image B I: all the translations.
let us also bear the image 𝔭46 א A C D 33 1739 𝔐: ASVmg RSVmg NASBmg NIVmg TEVmg NJBmg.

Despite the slender support, the first reading has been taken by most scholars to be the one that best suits the context—which is didactic, not hortatory (Metzger). Evidently, all the translators thought the same and therefore rejected the reading with the superior attestation. Nonetheless, out of deference to the testimony of 𝔭46 et al., most of the versions show the second reading in the margin.

▶ 1 Corinthians 15:54

when the perishable has been clothed with the imperishable, and the mortal with immortality א² B C²ᵛⁱᵈ D (33) 1739mg: ASV RSV NASB NIV NEBmg.
when the mortal has been clothed with immortality 𝔭46 א* 1739* 088: ASVmg NEB TEV NJBmg.

Some textual scholars would argue that the reading in 𝔭46 et al. was the result of homoeoarcton (so Metzger); others would argue that the first reading is an expansion contrived by scribes attempting to make 15:54 parallel in structure with 15:53 (so Tasker and the NEB). Thus, the translators of NEB (and TEV) followed the testimony of 𝔭46 with א*.

2 Corinthians

Early manuscripts containing portions of 2 Corinthians:

𝔭46: 1:1–13:13 (all of the epistle)

▶ 2 Corinthians 1:10a

so great a death א A B C D 33 1739* Clement: ASV RSV NASB NIV NEB NJB.
so great deaths 𝔭46 1739c Origen: TEV.

Zuntz argued for the reading in 𝔭46, which is plural; he translated the phrase "out of such tremendous, mortal dangers" (*The Text of the*

Epistles, 104). Bratcher, who translated the TEV, also supported the plural, rendering the phrase "such terrible dangers of death" (*Translator's Guide to 2 Corinthians,* 11). This shows the influence of 𝔓46, at least upon TEV. The other translations followed the reading with greater support. Those who favor this reading argue that Paul was probably speaking of a particular encounter with death (as recorded in Acts 19:23-41)—especially in view of the phrase "in Asia" (2 Cor. 1:8), which adds specificity to his statement.

▶ 2 Corinthians 1:10b
he will deliver 𝔓46 א B C 33: all the translations.
he delivers D² 1739: NEBmg NJBmg.

𝔓46 adds weight to the excellent testimony of א B C, the witness followed by all the translations.

▶ 2 Corinthians 1:11
prayer on our behalf 𝔓46ᶜ א A C D*: all the translations.
prayer on your behalf 𝔓46* B D²: NIVmg NJBmg.

The first reading has excellent support and is best suited for the context; all the translations, accordingly, reflect this reading. But NIV and NJB noted the variant, probably out of respect for the combined testimony of 𝔓46* and B.

▶ 2 Corinthians 1:12
*simplicity [or, **sincerity**] א² D 𝔐: NEBmg TEV NJBmg.
holiness 𝔓46 א* A B C 33 1739: ASV RSV NASB NIV NEB TEVmg NJB.

In Greek, one word could have easily been confused for the other because the two words differ in only two letters (πλ/γι): ἁπλότητι ("simplicity") and ἁγιότητι ("holiness"). The manuscript evidence (𝔓46 et al.) favors the second reading, and that is the reading followed by all the translations but one—TEV. The first reading, adopted for the text of NA²⁶ (a change from previous editions of the Nestle text) and UBS³, was selected because the context seems to call for a word that describes Paul's forthrightness in handling the contribution from the Gentile churches to the saints in Jerusalem (see 1:11). (See Ralph Martin's arguments on behalf of ἁπλότητι in *2 Corinthians* in the *Word Biblical Commentary* and Margaret Thrall's argument for ἁγιότητι in *Studies in New Testament Language and Text*, 366-372.)

▶ 2 Corinthians 2:1

*For I decided 𝔓46 B 0223 33: ASVmg RSV NIV NEB TEV.
But I decided ℵ A C D¹ 𝔐: ASV NASB.

According to the context, the reading with "for" (γάρ) must connect with 1:23 ("to spare you, I did not come to Corinth . . . for I determined that I would not come again to you in heaviness"), 1:24 being parenthetical. The reading with "but" (δέ) would mark a change of direction from the preceding discourse. The first reading, having the earliest support, was the one followed by most of the translators. Note again the effect of 𝔓46 on the RSV as compared to the ASV.

▶ 2 Corinthians 2:17

the many ℵ A B C 𝔐: all the translations.
the rest 𝔓46 D L: NJBmg.

The editors of UBS³ rejected the second reading as being too offensive for Paul to have written—how could Paul say that all the rest of the (so-called) Christian workers hawk the word of God? Evidently, all the translators concurred; but the NJB translators gave the variant supported by 𝔓46 et al. in the margin.

▶ 2 Corinthians 3:2

you are our epistle written on our hearts 𝔓46 A B C D 33 1739: ASV RSVmg NASB NIV NEB TEV NJB.
you are our epistle written on your hearts ℵ 33: RSV NJBmg.

The first reading has by far the best external support and is therefore the reading adhered to by almost all the translations. The translators of the RSV, contrary to their usual practice of following 𝔓46 with other good testimony (especially B), followed the second reading probably on exegetical grounds. The RSV translators could argue that it was more natural for Paul to say that the Corinthians were "written upon" than that he and his co-workers were "written upon." Actually, both readings can be argued for on the basis of 3:1, for Paul makes reference to epistles "to us" (which would correspond to "epistles written on our hearts") and epistles "from us" (which would correspond to "epistles written on your hearts").

▶ 2 Corinthians 3:9

For if there was glory in [or, accompanying—NEB] the ministry of condemnation [or, For if the ministry of condemnation has glory— NASB] 𝔓46 ℵ A C D 33 1739: ASV RSV NASB NEB.

For if the ministry of condemnation was glory B D² 𝔐: ASVmg NIV TEV NJB.

The difference between the first reading and the second in the Greek is that the first is a dative, $\tau\hat{\eta}$ διακονίᾳ, and the second a nominative, ἡ διακονία. The second reading, though lacking in early support, is the bolder of the two readings. For this reason, several modern translations reflect this reading. But the first reading makes perfectly good sense, has the best external testimony, and therefore was adopted for several modern translations. But the testimony of 𝔓46 offsets that of B. Indeed, 𝔓46 must have been responsible for the change in the Nestle text, as well as in the RSV and NASB (compared to the ASV, which followed B) and NEB.

▶ 2 Corinthians 8:7

our love for you 𝔓46 B 1739: NASB NIVmg NEBmg.

your love for us ℵ C D 33 𝔐: ASV RSV NASBmg NIV TEV NEB NJB.

The first reading has the earliest support and is the more difficult of the two; and if Paul wrote it, he probably meant to say, "the love we have for you" or "the love which we have kindled in your hearts" (see NEBmg). But the second reading, superficially more natural in context, was the one followed by most of the translators. However, the testimony of 𝔓46 (with B) must have caused the change from the ASV to the NASB and motivated the NIV and NEB translators to put this reading in a marginal note. (See comments by Martin, op. cit., who supports the first reading.)

▶ 2 Corinthians 11:3
include **and pure devotion** 𝔭46 ℵ* B D* 33: ASV RSV NASB NIV NEBmg (TEV) NJB.
omit ℵ² D² H 1739 𝔐: NEB NJB.

The omission of the Greek words καὶ τῆς ἁγνότητος is very likely the result of homoeteleuton—the word before καὶ, ἁπλότητος, has the same ending. Therefore, the words were most likely written by Paul and then later deleted accidentally. Some scholars, however, have thought that they were a later addition influenced by the word "pure" in 11:2 (see Tasker, for example). But most of the translations include the words supported by 𝔭46 et al.

Galatians

Early manuscripts containing portions of Galatians:

𝔭46: 1:1–6:18 (all of the epistle)
𝔭51: 1:2-10, 13, 16-20

▶ Galatians 1:3
God our Father and Lord Jesus Christ ℵ A 33: ASVmg NASB NIV NEBmg TEV.
God the Father and our Lord Jesus Christ 𝔭46 𝔭51ᵛⁱᵈ B D 1739: ASV RSV NEB NJB.

The editors of UBS³ and NA²⁶ adopted the first reading because it accords with Paul's usual style (cf. Rom. 1:7; 1 Cor. 1:3; 2 Cor. 1:2; Eph. 1:2; Phil. 1:2). But the papyri and B evidence another reading, which could very well have been changed by scribes to accord with Paul's usual formula. The translations are split—but notice again the influence of B on the ASV and the papyri on the RSV.

▶ Galatians 1:6
grace of Christ 𝔭46ᵛⁱᵈ? (see comment below) 𝔭51 (see comment below) ℵ A B 33: ASV RSV NASB NIV NEBmg TEV NJB.
grace 𝔭46ᵛⁱᵈ? (see comment below) Hᵛⁱᵈ and some early patristic citations: NEB TEVmg.

𝔓46 could have very well read "grace of Christ" or simply "grace," even though it is listed in critical texts as supporting the shorter reading. When I examined this papyrus in the University of Michigan library, it was evident to me that there was enough space in the lacuna (as consistent with the line lengths of other unfragmented lines on the same sheet) to fit the two more letters required to designate the words "of Christ" ($\overline{XY}$, the abbreviation for Χριστοῦ). It should also be noted that UBS³ incorrectly cites 𝔓51[vid], when it should be 𝔓51 (as in NA²⁶). This being said, we can readily believe that the best-attested reading is the first one, which every version followed except NEB (see Tasker's reasons).

▶ Galatians 1:8

preach to you a gospel 𝔓51[vid] ℵ² A B H: ASV RSV NASB TEV NJB.
preach a gospel ℵ* G Ψ: ASVmg NIV NEB.

The above citation shows only the textual difference concerning the inclusion or exclusion of the Greek word ὑμῖν ("to you"), which has been included in the texts of UBS³ and NA²⁶ but within brackets. There are also several variations of the tense of the verb εὐαγγελίζω ("to preach the gospel"), but the best-attested reading is a third-person singular present subjunctive—followed by all the translations. The inclusion of ὑμῖν is not certain because in some MSS it appears before the verb and in other MSS after the verb. Nevertheless, it was kept in the text because 𝔓51[vid] with B offsets the testimony of ℵ. Most of the modern translations followed this reading.

▶ Galatians 1:15

*God was pleased ℵ A D 33 1739: ASV NIV NEB TEV NJB.
he was pleased 𝔓46 B: RSV NASB.

The title ὁ θεός ("God") is bracketed in UBS³ and NA²⁶ to signal the editors' doubts about its inclusion in the text—the title was not present in the previous editions of the Nestle text. They were influenced by the testimony of 𝔓46 and B, whose text does not specify the subject as "God." Note again how the RSV followed 𝔓46.

▶ Galatians 2:5

to whom we did not yield for a moment 𝔓46 ℵ A B C Dc 1739: all the translations.

to whom we did yield for a moment D* a few Old Latin MSS and patristic citations: NEBmg NJBmg.

The second reading is an obvious emendation, which in context indicates that Paul, on account of the false brothers there, did yield for a moment. But this runs contrary to Paul's entire argument—that he would not yield to the demands of the "false brothers" (and have Titus circumcised), so that he might defend the truth of the gospel of liberty. This variant, however, is placed in the margin of the NEB (see Tasker's comments) and NJB (which says that the Beatty Papyrus [i.e., $\mathfrak{P}$46] reads "yield" rather than "defer"—actually, all the early MSS have "yield"). All the other versions, nevertheless, followed the best-attested reading.

▶ Galatians 2:12

The NEBmg notes a variant reading here, saying that "some witnesses read *a certain person*." Actually, only one Greek MS, $\mathfrak{P}$46, reads this way. Other MSS ($\aleph$ B D* 33), with $\mathfrak{P}$46[vid], later in the verse read "he came." All the translations, however, follow the plural reading in both instances.

▶ Galatians 4:25

Hagar is Mount Sinai in Arabia A B D 062[vid] 33: ASV RSV NASB NIV TEV NJBmg.
Sinai is a mountain in Arabia $\mathfrak{P}$46 $\aleph$ C 1739: ASVmg RSVmg TEVmg NEB NJB.

The first reading is the more difficult one, which led to several kinds of variations (see the critical apparatus of UBS³); the most notable one mentioned is the second reading above. A few translators preferred this variant on the basis of the testimony of $\mathfrak{P}$46 with $\aleph$ C versus A B D—and probably for the same reason, several thought it wise to note it in the margin.

▶ Galatians 4:28

you are $\mathfrak{P}$46 B D* 33 1739: ASVmg RSVmg NASB NIV NEB TEV NJB.
we are $\aleph$ A C D² 062 $\mathfrak{M}$: ASV RSV.

151

The two pronouns in Greek were often mistaken for one another (see comments on Eph. 4:32). Nonetheless, the testimony of 𝔓46 B D* is sufficiently weighty to have convinced most translators to follow the first reading—except those of the RSV, who deviated from their intended purpose of following the testimony of 𝔓46 and instead retained the reading of the ASV. Most likely, the RSV translators kept the reading with "we" in order to keep continuity with the pronoun "we" in Gal. 4:31.

▶ Galatians 6:2

you will fulfill (𝔓46— ἀποπληρώσετε) B G several early versions: NIV NEB TEV NJB.

fulfill (an imperative) ℵ A C D 0122 33 1739 𝔐: ASV RSV NASB TEVmg NJBmg.

The editors of UBS³ and NA²⁶ preferred the first reading because it was more likely that scribes changed a future-tense verb to an imperative than vice versa because the preceeding verse has two imperative verbs (Metzger). Furthermore, the evidence of 𝔓46 with B strengthens the case for adopting the first reading.

▶ Galatians 6:13

are being circumcised ℵ A C D 33 1739: all the translations.

have been circumcised 𝔓46 B: ASVmg NASBmg.

The first reading has the most diverse support and therefore was followed by all the translations. But in deference to B, ASV added the variant in a marginal note, and NASB also added a note—probably following ASV and influenced by 𝔓46.

Ephesians

Early manuscripts containing portions of Ephesians:

𝔓46: 1:1–6:24 (all of the epistle)
𝔓49: 4:16-29; 4:31–5:13
𝔓92: 1:11-13, 19-21

▶ Ephesians 1:1

include **in Ephesus** ℵ² A B² D 33 𝔐: ASV RSVmg NASB NIV NEB TEV NJBmg.

omit 𝔓46 ℵ* B* 1739: ASVmg RSV NASBmg NIVmg NEBmg TEVmg NJB.

In the Greek texts of UBS³ and NA²⁶, the words ἐν Ἐφέσῳ ("in Ephesus") have been bracketed to show that the editors had good reason to doubt that the words were written by Paul. Indeed, the three earliest MSS (𝔓46 [see photo 9] ℵ B) do not have this phrase, which when translated becomes "to the saints who are faithful in Christ Jesus" (see RSV). If this is the way it originally read, Paul could very well have intended this epistle to be a general encyclical sent to the churches in Asia, of which Ephesus was one of the leading churches. No doubt the epistle would have gone to Ephesus (perhaps first) and then on to other churches. Each time the epistle went to another church, the name of the locality would be supplied after the expression "to the saints [in _____]." Zuntz indicated that this procedure also occurred with some multiple copies of royal letters during the Hellenistic period; the master copy would have a blank for the addressee and would be filled in for each copy. Thus, Zuntz considered the blank space in the address to the Ephesians as going back to the original (*The Text of the Epistles,* 228). The very content of this epistle affirms its general nature, for it lacks the usual references to local situations and persons (as found in Paul's other epistles).

But whatever the arguments concerning the intrinsic nature of this textual variant, the documentary evidence points to the absence of the phrase "in Ephesus." The three earliest MSS did not have the phrase, and later scribes added the phrase to ℵ and B. Given this evidence, the words should not have been included in UBS³ or NA²⁶ (even bracketed) or incorporated in the text of any translation. The words should be included, however, in a marginal note (as in NJBmg). The RSV translators, influenced by the evidence of 𝔓46 with ℵ B (see Grant), omitted the phrase from their text.

▶ Ephesians 1:14

*the Spirit, which is the earnest 𝔓46 A B 1739: ASV RSV.

the Spirit, who is the earnest ℵ D 33: NASB NIV NJB.

With few exceptions, the Greek pronominal reference to the Spirit in the Greek NT is in the neuter case because the Greek word for "Spirit" ($\pi\nu\epsilon\hat{\upsilon}\mu\alpha$) is neuter. Two reasons can be given for the variation in Eph. 1:14: (1) Paul originally wrote the masculine pronoun, which was changed to the more common neuter, or (2) Paul originally wrote the neuter pronoun, which was later changed to the masculine by scribes who wanted to personalize the Spirit. The manuscript evidence seems to favor the second view, for the earliest MSS (𝔓46 B) contain the neuter and later MSS have the masculine. The textual evidence of 𝔓46 with B influenced the editors of NA[26] to make a change from previous editions of the Nestle text.

Translators also tend to personalize the Spirit, referring to the Spirit as "him" or "who" rather than "it" or "which." Thus, one cannot always be sure whether or not the translators strictly adhered to one variant reading over the other (as with TEV and NJB), but it is clear that ASV (based on A and B) and RSV (based on 𝔓46 with A and B) rendered the neuter pronoun.

▶ Ephesians 1:15
include **your love** ℵ² D² 𝔐: all the translations.
omit 𝔓46 ℵ* A B 33 1739: ASVmg RSVmg NASBmg NJBmg.

Even though the omission of "your love" has such good manuscript support, it is quite likely that the words were dropped due to homoeoarcton—the eye of the scribe passing from $\tau\dot{\eta}\nu$ to $\tau\dot{\eta}\nu$. Thus, all the translations retain these words, and some (influenced by the testimony of 𝔓46 with ℵ* A B) provide a marginal note about the omission, which produces the rendering "having heard of your trust in the Lord Jesus and in all the saints."

▶ Ephesians 2:5
made us alive together with Christ ℵ A^vid D 1739: all the translations.
made us alive together in the Christ 𝔓46 B 33: ASVmg NASBmg NJBmg.

Metzger thinks the second reading was the result of accidental dittography or deliberate assimilation to Eph. 2:6, $\dot{\epsilon}\nu$ Χριστῷ Ἰησοῦ ("in Christ Jesus"). Evidently, all the translators must have also considered the second reading to be an aberration—though three versions, in deference to the antiquity of 𝔓46 and B, noted it as an optional reading.

▶ Ephesians 3:9
*to enlighten all men 𝔓46 ℵ² B C D 33 𝔐: ASV RSV NIV TEV.
to bring to light ℵ* A 1739: ASVmg NASB NEB NJB.

The difference between the two readings in Greek concerns the inclusion of the word πάντας ("all men"). The first reading includes the word; the second does not. Arguments can be offered for both readings, and thus the translations are divided. However, it should be noted that the Nestle text was changed to include the reading found in 𝔓46, which, with B C D, offsets the weight of ℵ and A. And for similar reasons, the RSV translators (and probably the others) were probably influenced by the testimony of 𝔓46 et al.

▶ Ephesians 4:8
he led captivity captive, he gave gifts 𝔓46 ℵ* A C² D* 33: NEB TEV NJB.
he led captivity captive, and he gave gifts ℵ² B C*,³ D² 𝔐: ASV RSV NASB NIV.

The reading with "and" is quite obviously a later addition, intended to relieve an awkward (incomplete) expression. The translators of ASV etc. reproduced the second reading, whether consciously or unconsciously, for the same reason.

▶ Ephesians 4:9
descended 𝔓46 ℵ* A C* D I^vid 33 1739: ASV RSV NASB NIV NEB NJB.
first descended ℵ² B C³ 𝔐: ASVmg TEV.

The second reading, containing the addition of "first," has inferior external support. G. B. Caird said, "This reading would exclude a descent at Pentecost after the Ascension, but it is a late gloss, not supported by the best manuscripts" (*Paul's Letters from Prison*, 75). However, the translators of ASV noted it in deference to B, and the translators of TEV followed it. But all the other translations reflect the superior testimony of 𝔓46 et al.

▶ Ephesians 4:28

working with his own hands ℵ* A D: NASB NIV NEB NJB.
working with his hands 𝔓46 𝔓49vid ℵ2 B: ASV RSV.

The Greek word ἰδίας ("own") has been bracketed in UBS³ and NA²⁶ to show the editors' doubts about its right to be in the text. Surely the manuscript evidence is against it, but the editors included it on the grounds that it represents Koine usage (Metzger). The ASV, however, remained faithful to B, and the RSV to 𝔓46. (𝔓49 was not available to the translators of the RSV—see comments under 𝔓49.)

▶ Ephesians 4:32

forgiven you 𝔓46 ℵ A: all the translations.
forgiven us 𝔓49vid B D 33 1739: ASVmg NASBmg NJBmg.

The Greek word for "you" (ὑμῖν) is required because earlier in the sentence Paul uses ὑμῶν. The two pronouns (ὑμῖν and ἡμῖν) were often confused for one another because *upsilon* and *eta* in Greek sound very similar. This probably accounts for the variant reading in 𝔓49 et al. All the versions followed the first reading.

▶ Ephesians 5:2

loved us 𝔓46 ℵ2 D 𝔐: ASVmg RSV NASBmg NIV TEV.
loved you ℵ* A B: ASV NASB NEB NJB.

Both readings have good, early support—and the pronouns "us" and "you" in Greek were often confounded by scribes (see explanation on Eph. 4:32 above). The translations display this duality. Note, however, ASV's allegiance to B and RSV's allegiance to 𝔓46.

▶ Ephesians 5:5

one who is covetous, which is idolatry 𝔓46 𝔓49vid ℵ B: NEB TEV NJB.
one who is covetous, who is an idolater A D 𝔐: ASV RSV NASB NIV.

The first reading is the more difficult reading and has the best textual support—two papyri (𝔓46 𝔓49vid) and the two earliest uncials (ℵ B). The second reading, clearly inferior and almost certainly an emendation, is the easier reading and the one followed by several translations. But there is a way to render the passage and still remain faithful to the superior text (see TEV—"for greediness is a form of idolatry" and NJB—"greed—which is worshiping a false god").

▶ Ephesians 5:9
fruit of the light 𝔓49 ℵ A B D*: all the translations.
fruit of the Spirit 𝔓46 D² 𝔐: TEVmg.

Here is an instance in which the testimony of one papyrus MS, 𝔓49, is a great help to offset the testimony of another, 𝔓46, which in this verse contains an emendation. Quite obviously, the scribe of 𝔓46 (and other, later scribes) harmonized this verse with Gal. 5:22, which has the phrase "the fruit of the Spirit" (which, incidentally, is the reading in the KJV). All of the translations followed the superior reading, and only one version, TEV, noted the variant—probably out of deference to 𝔓46.

▶ Ephesians 6:1
include in the Lord 𝔓46 ℵ A D¹ I^vid 𝔐: ASV RSV NASB NIV TEV NJB.
omit B D*: NEB TEVmg NJBmg.

The phrase "in the Lord" is bracketed in UBS³ and NA²⁶ to signify that the editors had doubts about its authenticity (see Metzger). Nevertheless, most of the translations included the phrase out of respect to the testimony of ℵ A I^vid, bolstered by 𝔓46.

Philippians

Early manuscripts containing portions of Philippians:

𝔓16: 3:10-17; 4:2-8
𝔓46: 1:1–4:23 (all of the epistle)

▶ Philippians 1:14
*to speak the word 𝔓46 D² 1739 𝔐: TEV NJB.
to speak the word of God ℵ A B D* 33: ASV RSV NASB NIV NEB TEVmg.
to speak the word of the Lord F G: NJBmg.

157

Most of the translators were impressed with testimony of ℵ A B D* in support of the second reading. But the editors of UBS³ and NA²⁶ considered the second and third readings noted above to be expansions of the first. They, therefore, chose the reading supported by 𝔭46—causing a change in the Nestle text, which prior to NA²⁶ included τοῦ θεοῦ ("of God"). TEV and NJB also followed the witness of 𝔭46 versus ℵ A B D*.

▶ Philippians 2:30

the work of Christ 𝔭46 B D 𝔐: all the translations.
the work of the Lord ℵ A: ASVmg NJBmg.
the work C: NJBmg.

Nowhere else does Paul use the term "the work of Christ," but he does use the phrase "the work of the Lord" in 1 Cor. 15:58; 16:10. Therefore, it is quite likely that the reading "work of the Lord" is an assimilation (Hawthorne, *Philippians* in the *Word Biblical Commentary*). All the translations followed the best-attested reading, the one found in 𝔭46 et al.

▶ Philippians 3:3

who worship by [or, **in**] **the Spirit of God** ℵ* A B C D² 33 1739 𝔐: ASV RSVmg NIV NEBmg TEV NJB.
who worship God in spirit ℵ² D*: RSV NEBmg NJB.
who worship in spirit 𝔭46: NEB.

According to Greek grammar, the first reading (οἱ πνεύματι θεοῦ λατρεύοντες) can be rendered, "the ones worshiping by the Spirit of God" or "the ones worshiping the Spirit of God." In Greek, the verb λατρεύω ("worship") is normally followed by the dative (in this verse, πνεύματι—"Spirit"); hence, the Spirit becomes the recipient of the worship. Since the grammar allows a rendering that might be offensive to those who do not think the Spirit should be worshiped, some scribes added another object in the dative case, θεῷ ("God")—hence, the second reading noted above. But it should be understood that Lightfoot demonstrated that the verb λατρεύω had acquired a technical sense referring to the worship of God, and therefore one does not have to understand the phrase "the Spirit of God" as the object of the worship (see Lightfoot, *St. Paul's Epistle to the Philippians*, and Kent, "Philippians" in *The Exposi-*

tor's Bible Commentary). Thus, many commentators and translators understand the phrase to function as a dative. The earliest MS, 𝔓46, does not have any object after the participle, but Hawthorne (op. cit.) argues that the expression in context of necessity means "to worship God." If the translators of the RSV and NJB had the same understanding, they may have been following 𝔓46. At any rate, the NEB, influenced by the witness of 𝔓46, produced a rendering in which there is no direct object after "worship."

▶ Philippians 3:13
*I count not myself to have laid hold 𝔓46 B D²: ASVmg RSV NEB TEV NJB.
I count not myself yet to have laid hold 𝔓16ᵛⁱᵈ 𝔓61ᵛⁱᵈ ℵ A D*: ASV NASB NIV.

Since the papyri and other early uncials (ℵ A B) are divided on this reading, textual critics and translators alike are hard pressed to pick one reading against the other. Nevertheless, the first reading is a slightly better candidate because of the 𝔓46 B D combination supporting that reading and because scribes tended to add words like "yet" rather than delete them. For these reasons, the Nestle text was changed in the twenty-sixth edition; the word οὔπω was deleted from the text and placed in the apparatus.

▶ Philippians 4:3
they have labored side by side with me in the gospel together with Clement and the rest of my co-workers, whose names are in the book of life 𝔓46 ℵ¹ A B D Iᵛⁱᵈ: all the translations.
they have labored side by side with me in the gospel together with Clement and my co-workers and the rest whose names are written in the book of life 𝔓16ᵛⁱᵈ ℵ*: NEBmg.

The textual variant in 𝔓16ᵛⁱᵈ and ℵ* should not be taken seriously (and certainly not added to the margin of any English version) because it is clearly the result of scribal inadvertence—in which the scribes wrote καὶ τῶν συνεργῶν μου καὶ τῶν λοιπῶν instead of καὶ τῶν λοιπῶν συνεργῶν μου.

▶ Philippians 4:16
you sent to my need ℵ B 𝔐: ASV RSV (NASB).
you sent money to me 𝔓46 A: RSVmg NIV TEV.
you contributed to my needs D² P: NEB.

The first reading in the Greek has no object after "sent." The second reading, in 𝔓46 and A, has no preposition, so as to create a direct object. The third reading changed μοι ("to me") to μου ("my"). The most literal translations followed the first, preferred reading; other, less literal versions, followed those copyists who added an object to complete the sense. (The NASB puts the object in italics, "you sent *a gift*," to show that the words have been added.) The RSV translators preferred to retain the wording of the ASV as opposed to following 𝔓46, though they noted its wording in the margin.

Colossians

Early manuscripts containing portions of Colossians:

𝔓46: 1:1–4:18 (all of the epistle)

▶ Colossians 1:7
on your behalf ℵ² C D2 33 1739 𝔐: the margins of all the translations.
on our behalf 𝔓46 ℵ* A B D*: all the translations.

Not one translation followed the text of UBS³ and NA²⁶—and rightly so, for the second reading has the better testimony. (But see Metzger's argument.)

▶ Colossians 2:2
the mystery of God, Christ 𝔓46 B: ASV RSV NASB NIV NEB TEV.
the mystery of God, which is Christ D: ASVmg.
the mystery of God, the Father of Christ ℵ* A C 048: TEVmg NJBmg.
the mystery of God and of the Father and of Christ ℵ² D² 𝔐: NIVmg TEVmg NJBmg.
the mystery of God H P: TEVmg NJB.
the mystery of Christ 1739 and a few other late MSS: NJBmg.

The reading in 𝔓46 and B is very likely the reading from which all the other readings deviated—either by expansion (readings 2–4) or abbreviation (readings 5 and 6). According to the Greek, the first reading (τοῦ μυστηρίου τοῦ θεοῦ, Χριστοῦ) could mean "the mystery of God, which mystery is Christ" or "the mystery of God, who is Christ" because Χριστοῦ can stand in apposition to the whole phrase or just to θεοῦ. Most of the translations followed the best reading—the ASV on the basis of B alone; the others having the added testimony of 𝔓46 (see photo 10). At the same time, many of the translations provided footnotes on some of the variants.

▶ Colossians 2:18
things which he has seen 𝔓46 ℵ* A B D* I 33 1739: all the translations.
things which he has not seen ℵ² C D² 𝔐: ASVmg NJBmg.

The best MSS support the first reading, which all the translations follow. Paul was arguing against those who based their religion on visions they had seen.

▶ Colossians 3:4
your life 𝔓46 ℵ C D: ASVmg NIV TEV NJB.
our life B D¹ 𝔐: ASV RSV NASB NEB NJBmg.

The two Greek pronouns (ὑμῶν and ἡμῶν) were often confused one for the other because of their similarity in pronunciation. The editors of UBS³ and NA²⁶ adopted the reading supported by 𝔓46 et al. (causing a change from previous editions of the Nestle text), but most of the translators went with the second reading—probably because it is the more difficult of the two in context.

▶ Colossians 3:6
*include **upon the sons of disobedience** ℵ A C D^vid I 𝔐: ASV RSVmg NASBmg NIVmg TEV NJB.
omit 𝔓46 B: ASVmg RSV NASB NIV NEB TEVmg NJBmg.

This phrase was included in UBS³ and NA²⁶ (a change from previous editions of the Nestle text) but set within brackets to show the editors' doubts about its authenticity because this phrase is not present in 𝔓46 and B and because it has every appearance of having been assimilated from Eph. 5:6. Nevertheless, the words were retained because of their presence in so many witnesses. Accordingly, several translations do not contain this phrase as part of the text, or they provide a marginal note concerning its omission in some ancient MSS.

▶ Colossians 3:16

word of Christ 𝔓46 ℵ2 B C2 D 𝔐: all the translations.
word of God A C*: ASVmg NASBmg NJBmg
word of the Lord ℵ* I: ASVmg NASBmg NJBmg.

Since the first reading has the best attestation (supported by 𝔓46 et al.), this is the one that all the translations followed. In the margin of NJB, the translators conjectured that "possibly the text read simply 'the word'"; but there is no textual evidence for this shortened reading.

1 Thessalonians

Early manuscripts containing portions of 1 Thessalonians:

𝔓30: 4:12-13, 16-17; 5:3, 8-10, 12-18, 25-28
𝔓46: 1:1; 1:9–2:3; 5:5-9, 23-28
𝔓65: 1:3-10; 2:1, 6-13

▶ 1 Thessalonians 2:7

we were babes among you 𝔓65 ℵ B C* D* I: ASVmg RSVmg NASBmg TEVmg.
we were gentle among you ℵc A C2 D2 33 1739 𝔐: all the translations.

There is a one-letter difference between the words "babes" and "gentle" in Greek: $\nu\acute{\eta}\pi\iota o\iota$ ("babes"); $\acute{\eta}\pi\iota o\iota$ ("gentle"). It is difficult to know which reading produced the other. With respect to transcriptional errors, the first word ($\nu\acute{\eta}\pi\iota o\iota$) could have been created by dittography—the preceding word ($\acute{\epsilon}\gamma\epsilon\nu\acute{\eta}\theta\eta\mu\epsilon\nu$) ends in ν; or the second word ($\acute{\eta}\pi\iota o\iota$) could have been created by haplography—also influenced by the preceding word. Several of the MSS (ℵ C D) originally had the first reading, but then were later corrected. The second reading is the most natural in context—especially in connection with the following metaphor: "we were gentle in your midst, like a nursing mother caring for her children."

The first reading creates a very contorted metaphor: "we were babes in your midst, like a nursing mother caring for her children." Nevertheless, the majority of editors of UBS³ and NA²⁶ decided to adopt the word νήπιοι because it has the earliest support (𝔭65 providing the earliest witness) and because it is the more difficult reading. As such, the Nestle text was changed to read νήπιοι. But two of the editors, Metzger and Wikgren, did not agree with the choice. However, they suggested that if the reading νήπιοι must be in the text, the punctuation must be changed (see Metzger). Perhaps a change in punctuation could justify the following kind of translation of 2:6b-8: "[6]. . . when we could have become burdensome to you as apostles of Christ. [7] But we were babes in your midst; we were as a nursing mother who cares for her children—[8] being so affectionately desirous of you, we were willing to impart to you not the gospel of God only, but also our own souls, because you became dear to us." In this way, the two tropes of 2:7 are separated, and the last one of 2:7 is connected with 2:8.

Not one of the English translations followed the reading in UBS³ and NA²⁶; very likely, the translators considered the contorted metaphor too strange to incorporate into a translation. Some of the translations, however, provide a marginal note citing the reading "babes" out of deference to its presence in all the earliest MSS—𝔭65 being the most ancient.

▶ 1 Thessalonians 5:9
𝔭30, B, and a few early versions read "salvation through our Lord Jesus"—versus all the other MSS, which read "salvation through our Lord Jesus Christ." The NA²⁶ and UBS³ Greek texts adhere to the second reading—as do all the versions. But given the fact that scribes tended to add names to divine titles and that the two earliest MSS do not contain the word "Christ," is it not possible that 𝔭30 and B contain the original reading? If the translators will not adopt this reading, should they not at least note it in the margin?

▶ 1 Thessalonians 5:25
pray ℵ A Dᶜ: ASV RSV NASB NIV NJB.
pray also 𝔭30 B D* 33: ASVmg NASBmg NEB TEV.

Since scribes would be more inclined to add "also" than drop it, the decision to leave it out of a translation is a good one. Nevertheless, the testimony of the two earliest MSS (𝔓30 and B) cannot be totally neglected; therefore, it is wise to note this reading in the margin (as did ASV and NASB).

Titus

Early manuscripts containing portions of Titus:

𝔓32: 1:11-15; 2:3-8

▶ Titus 2:7

See comments on this verse in the description of 𝔓32 (Section 2).

Philemon

Early manuscripts containing portions of Philemon:

𝔓87: vv. 13-15, 24-25

▶ Philemon 25

omit **Amen** 𝔓87 A D* 048: ASVmg RSV NASB NIV NEB TEV NJB.
include ℵ C D² 𝔐: ASV NASBmg NJBmg.

It is well known that scribes were fond of adding "Amen" to the end of various epistles. However, prior to the discovery of 𝔓87, two of the earliest MSS containing Philemon (ℵ C) ended the epistle with "Amen." 𝔓87 now provides the earliest testimony to the absence of "Amen" at the end of Philemon and therefore should be added to the critical apparatus of NA[26]. None of the versions since the ASV conclude this epistle with "Amen." Thus, 𝔓87 lends added support to this omission.

Hebrews

Early manuscripts containing portions of Hebrews:

𝔓12: 1:1
𝔓13: 2:14–5:5; 10:8-22; 10:29–11:13; 11:28–12:7

𝔭17: 9:12-19
𝔭46: 1:1–13:25 (all of the epistle)
𝔭89: 6:7-9, 15-17

▶ Hebrews 1:1
the fathers: ℵ A B C: ASV NASB.
our fathers 𝔭12 𝔭46: RSV NIV NEB TEV NJB.

Several of the most recent versions followed the reading in 𝔭12 and
𝔭46—unless, of course, the translators understood the article τοῖς to
function as a possessive.

▶ Hebrews 1:8
your kingdom A D 33 1739 𝔐: ASV RSV NASBmg NIV TEV NJB.
his kingdom 𝔭46 ℵ B: ASVmg RSVmg NASB NEB TEVmg NJBmg.

The second reading affects how the entire verse must be read because a
text with αὐτοῦ (instead of σου) means that the verse cannot be taken in
the form of direct address. Thus, the entire statement would have to read,
"God is your throne [or, your throne is God] for ever and ever, and the
scepter of uprightness is the scepter of his [i.e., God's] kingdom"
(Metzger). But most commentators prefer the first reading because it
allows for the form of direct address throughout. As such, God is
addressing his Son and calling him "God": Ὁ θρόνος σου, ὁ θεός
("your throne, O God"). Accordingly, the second part of this verse
is also a direct address: ἡ ῥάβδος τῆς εὐθύτητος ῥάβδος τῆς
βασιλείας σου ("the scepter of uprightness is the scepter of your
kingdom"). As such, the verse perfectly follows Ps. 2:6 in the LXX. The
second reading, though supported by the earliest MSS, deviates from the
LXX. For this very reason, some have argued that later scribes made the
earliest reading conform to the Septuagint reading. Given that the second
reading has the support of 𝔭46 with ℵ and B, and that it is the more
difficult reading, some translations (NASB, which still has the vocative
in the first part of the quote; and NEB) reflect the second reading.

▶ Hebrews 1:12
include **like a garment** 𝔭46 ℵ A B D 1739: ASV RSVmg NASB NIV
NEB TEV NJB.
omit D² 33 𝔐: RSV.

We can safely assume that the words "like a garment" were deleted in later MSS because these words are not included in the scripture the author of Hebrews is quoting—namely, Ps. 102:26 LXX. But one wonders why the RSV, which usually followed the testimony of 𝔭46 et al., has the inferior reading.

▶ Hebrews 2:7
omit **and did set him over the works of your hands** 𝔭46 B D² 𝔐: ASVmg RSV NASBmg NIV NEB TEV NJB.
include ℵ A C D*: ASV RSVmg NASB TEVmg.

Prior to the discovery of 𝔭46, the external testimony for this portion of Hebrews was fairly balanced—especially since ℵ and B stood on opposite sides. The testimony of 𝔭46, however, tipped the scales. Most likely, the words were added by later scribes in order to make the verse conform to Ps. 8:7 LXX. Note how all the translations since the ASV (except the NASB) followed the reading of 𝔭46 et al.

▶ Hebrews 2:9
by the grace of God he should taste death for every man 𝔭46 ℵ A B C D: all the translations.
apart from God he should taste death for every man 1739 a few ancient versions and several patristic citations: NEBmg NJBmg.

Most likely, some scribe mistook χάριτι θεοῦ ("grace of God") for χωρὶς θεοῦ ("apart from God"), and this mistake found its way into certain MSS—known to church fathers like Origen, Eusebius, and Ambrosiaster. According to Tasker, the Nestorians favored the second reading—no doubt because they emphasized Jesus' humanity as distinct from his divinity and thus would use the variant reading to show that Jesus died on the cross apart from God. But the best MSS support the first reading, and this is the one followed by all the translations. The variant reading should not be included in any margin of an English translation without an explanation. The NEB has no such explanation, while the NJB does.

▶ Hebrews 3:2
in all his house ℵ A C D: ASV RSVmg NASB NIV TEV NJB.
in his house 𝔭13 𝔭46 B: RSV NEB.

The first reading exactly follows Num. 12:7 in the LXX and perfectly accords with Heb. 3:5. These two facts, however, can be used to defend the second reading—for one can argue that the scribes of ℵ A C D conformed the text to Num. 12:7 LXX and/or to Heb. 3:5.

In keeping with their goal to incorporate the new manuscript evidence in their revision, the RSV translators favored the second reading supported by the two early papyri and B (see Grant)—as did the NEB translators.

▶ Hebrews 3:6

omit **firm to the end** 𝔓13 𝔓46 B: RSV NIV NEB TEV NJB.
include ℵ A C D 33: ASV RSVmg NASB NJBmg.

The three earliest MSS do not contain the phrase "firm to the end." Most likely, the phrase was borrowed from Heb. 3:14 and inserted here.

The weight of 𝔓13 with 𝔓46 and B was enough to convince the RSV translators to change the ASV text (see Grant), but not the NASB translators, who had a tendency to retain many ASV readings. All the other modern versions also followed 𝔓13 et al.

▶ Hebrews 4:2

they were not united in faith with those who heard 𝔓13vid 𝔓46 A B C D: ASVmg RSVmg NASBmg NIVmg NJB—also NRSV.
those who heard did not combine it [the word] **with faith** ℵ and some early versions: ASV RSV NASB NIV NEB TEV NJBmg.

The first reading is most likely original because it has better external attestation and it is more difficult. According to 𝔓13, 46 et al., the Greek word for "united" or "combined" (συγκεκερασμένους) agrees grammatically with "those who heard" (τῆς ἀκοῆς ἐκείνους). (Both UBS³ and NA²⁶ cite 𝔓13vid, as opposed to simply 𝔓13, as supporting the reading συγκεκερασμένους because the last three letters of this word are not very visible. When I examined a microfiche of this portion of 𝔓13 at the Ancient Biblical Manuscript Center for Preservation and Research in Claremont, California, I could discern that three letters followed ΣΥΓΚΕΚΕΡΑΣΜΕΝ—namely, ΟΥΣ—thus confirming that 𝔓13 reads συγκεκερασμένους.) The second reading (συγκεκερασμένος) agrees with "the word" (ὁ λόγος). (See photo 11.) According to the best MSS, this verse is not talking about combining faith with the word, but about the fact that the majority of Israelites were not united in faith with those men who heard the good news about the promised land (i.e., Moses, Joshua, and Caleb)—"the original and immediate hearers . . . through whom the Divine word was conveyed to those who were hearers in the second degree" (Westcott and Hort, 130). Moses, Joshua, and Caleb truly heard the word concerning the promise of entering Canaan, and they believed it. But the Israelites, who heard the word through these men, did not share their faith.

Of all the modern versions, however, only the NJB (and now the NRSV) followed the superior reading supported by the papyri, 𝔓13 and 𝔓46, with A B C D. All of the other versions followed the easier (and inferior) reading—although some of them noted the superior reading in the margin.

► Hebrews 6:1-2

not laying again a foundation of repentance from dead works and of faith toward God, of instruction about baptisms . . . ℵ A C D I 33 1739: ASV RSVmg NASB NEB TEV.

not laying again a foundation of repentance from dead works and of faith toward God, with [or, even] instruction about baptisms . . . 𝔓46 B: RSV NIV NEBmg NJB.

The difference in the English translations is based on a variant of the Greek word for "instruction"; it is either διδαχῆς (a genitive, translated as in first citation above) or διδαχήν (an accusative in apposition to "foundation," translated as in the second citation). According to the second reading, the foundation is the instruction; according to the first reading, the instruction about baptisms is but one element of the foundation. It is difficult to determine which word the writer of Hebrews wrote. The earliest testimony, that of 𝔓46 and B, favors the second reading; but the first reading has good and diverse testimony. This division of testimony is reflected in the translations. Nonetheless, the effect of 𝔓46 is seen in the RSV (see Grant), NIV, and NJB.

► Hebrews 9:11

of the good things that have come 𝔓46 B D* 1739: ASVmg RSV NIV NASBmg NEB TEV NJBmg.

of the good things that are about to come ℵ A D² Iᵛⁱᵈ 33: ASV RSVmg NASB NIVmg NEBmg TEVmg NJB.

The second reading, manifesting the influence of Heb. 10:1, is probably an emendation. Note the change from the ASV to the RSV, showing the impact of 𝔓46 (see Grant). But the NASB did not follow suit.

▶ Hebrews 9:14
See comments on this verse in the description of 𝔓17 (Section 2).

▶ Hebrews 10:1
𝔓46 (the one witness alluded to in NEBmg) offers a very interesting variant here (καί for οὐκ αὐτήν), which produces the following translation: "the law contains but a shadow and likeness of the good things to come" (see Tasker).

▶ Hebrews 10:38
my righteous one will live by faith 𝔓46 ℵ A H* 33ᵛⁱᵈ: ASV RSV NASB NEB TEV NJB.
the righteous one will live by faith 𝔓13 Dᶜ Hᶜ: ASVmg NIVmg.

The difference in the readings concerns the inclusion or omission of the Greek word μου. "Influenced by the citation of the same Old Testament quotation in Ro 1.17 and Ga 3.11, where Paul omits the personal pronoun μου, 𝔓13 and the majority of later witnesses . . . followed by the Textus Receptus, omit the word here. But it undoubtedly belongs in the text, being strongly supported by early and reliable witnesses" (Metzger).

All the versions follow the preferred reading, while the secondary reading is noted in the margins of ASV and NIV. The NIVmg indicates that one early manuscript reads "the righteous one." That MS is 𝔓13.

▶ Hebrews 11:4
offered to God ℵ A D 33: ASV RSV NASB NIV TEV NJB.
offered 𝔓13: NEB.

Usually the writer of Hebrews did not add the words "to God" after using the verb "offer." For this reason, some scholars think 𝔓13 displays the original reading. (Obviously, this was the thinking of the NEB translators.)

Nevertheless, it cannot be readily explained why the scribes of ℵ et al. would have added the words "to God," unless they were influenced by the one place in Hebrews that has this phrase—namely, 9:14.

▶ Hebrews 11:11

by faith, even though Sarah was barren, he [Abraham] received power to beget 𝔓46 D: NIV TEV.
by faith Sarah herself received power to conceive 𝔓13ᵛⁱᵈ ℵ A Dᶜ: ASV NASB RSV NIVmg NEB TEVmg NJB.

The first reading could also be rendered "by faith Abraham, even though he was past age—and Sarah herself was barren—was enabled to beget" (see NIV and F. F. Bruce, *The Epistle to the Hebrews*). The second reading differs in that the Greek word στεῖρα ("barren") is absent. This, of course, makes for an easier reading, which was followed by most of the translators. However, the first reading (supported by 𝔓46) is to be preferred because it is more difficult. The Nestle text now has the first reading—reflecting the impact of 𝔓46, and two of the most recent versions (NIV and TEV) follow the testimony of 𝔓46.

▶ Hebrews 11:37

The textual variants in this verse are numerous. The Greek word ἐπειράσθησαν ("they were tested") (1) appears in 𝔓13ᵛⁱᵈ A Dᶜ 1739 after ἐπρίσθησαν ("they were sawn in two")—see RSVmg, (2) is not in 𝔓46, (3) is included in ℵ 048 33 after ἐλιθάσθησαν ("they were stoned")—see NIVmg and NEBmg. The evidence of 𝔓46 was adhered to by UBS³ and NA²⁶ (see Metzger) and by RSV, NASBmg, NIV, NEB, NJB, and TEV. Two translations (ASV and NASB) followed the first reading noted above, and three translations note this reading in the margin. Because this reading is supported by 𝔓13, the NIVmg can correctly say, "Some early MSS add *they were put to the test*."

▶ Hebrews 12:1

clinging sin 𝔓13 ℵ A D: all the translations.
distracting sin 𝔓46: NEBmg.

In deference to the antiquity of 𝔓46, the NEB translators added a marginal note that says, "one witness reads *the sin which too easily distracts us*."

► Hebrews 12:3

against himself A Dᶜ 1739ᶜ: all the versions.
against them[selves] 𝕻13 𝕻46 ℵ D* 048 33 1739: ASVmg NJBmg.

The second reading, though not included in the text of NA[26] nor adopted by any of the modern versions, is definitely the earlier and harder reading—and therefore is to be preferred. (See comments by Leon Morris on this verse in his commentary on "Hebrews" in the *Expositor's Bible Commentary*.)

► Hebrews 13:21a

every good thing 𝕻46 ℵ D*: ASV RSV NASB NIV NEB TEV.
every good work C D² 33 1739 𝔐: ASVmg NJB.

All the translations except the NJB followed the best-attested reading.

► Hebrews 13:21b

in us 𝕻46 ℵ A D 33 1739: ASV RSVmg NASB NIV NEB TEV NJB.
in you C and later MSS: ASVmg RSV.

Since the pronoun in the preceding clause is "you," copyists would be inclined to make the next pronoun the same. But the two clauses can be separated by means of punctuation (see NIV and TEV). The RSV translators diverted from their usual course of following the reading in 𝕻46 and/or the earliest reading. Perhaps they did this for stylistic reasons—to keep the pronouns in the successive clauses the same.

James

Early manuscripts containing portions of James:

𝕻20: 2:19–3:9
𝕻23: 1:10-12, 15-18

► James 1:12

he promised 𝕻23 ℵ A B: ASV (*Lord* in italics) NASB (*Lord* in italics) NEB NJBmg.
the Lord promised C L: NJB.
God promised 33ᵛⁱᵈ 1739: RSV NIV TEV.

According to the best testimony, the subject is left unspecified. Copyists and translators alike took it upon themselves to supply a subject. Some chose "the Lord" and some "God."

▶ James 1:17

the Father of lights with whom there is no variation or shadow of turning ℵ² A C 1739: ASV RSV NASB NEBmg TEV.
the Father of lights with whom there is no variation which consists in the turning of the shadow ℵ* B: RSVmg NIV NEB NJB.
the Father of lights with whom there is no variation or turning of the shadow 𝔓23: none.

Due to the complexity of the metaphor, different scribes attempted to clarify the sense, and it is not easy to determine which scribe emended what. The image seems to portray God as an unchanging orb of light— quite unlike the natural sun, which from our perspective shifts and thus causes shadows. The image also indicates that God, who has sovereignty over the luminaries, is unlike them because they are always moving, while he never changes in himself or in his dealings with his people (Martin, *James* in the *Word Biblical Commentary*, 39). The reading in 𝔓23 could possibly allude to the image of an ancient sundial (which told time by the movement [turning] of the shadow). If so, James would be indicating that God is changeless *and* timeless. But the context appears to deal only with God's unchanging, steadfast nature (Comfort). (See photo 12.)

The modern translations are divided on this verse, and only two of them (RSV and NEB) give an alternate reading in the margin. Given the general reliability of 𝔓23, one would think that one of the translations that occasionally note singular readings of the earliest papyri (for examples, see John 7:52 in NIV and TEV with respect to 𝔓66, and Heb. 10:1 in NEB with respect to 𝔓46) would have done so in this case as well.

1 Peter

Early manuscripts containing portions of 1 Peter:

𝔓72: 1:1–5:14 (all of the epistle)
𝔓81: 2:20–3:1, 4-12

► 1 Peter 1:22

pure heart 𝔭72 ℵ C P 33 𝔐: ASVmg NASBmg NIVmg TEVmg NJBmg.

heart A B: all the translations.

The majority of editors of UBS³ and NA²⁶ adopted the first reading for the text because they were influenced, according to Metzger, by the testimony of 𝔭72 ℵ* et al. (This necessitated a change from previous editions of the Nestle text.) But in deference to the minority of the editors who thought καθαρᾶς ("pure") was an addition, the words are bracketed in the text. Evidently, the translators were of the same opinion as the minority of editors, for not one translation includes the word "pure"—though it is noted in several.

► 1 Peter 2:21

suffered 𝔭72 A B C 33 1739 𝔐: all the translations.

died 𝔭81 ℵ: NEBmg NJBmg.

As in 1 Pet. 3:18 (see comments below), there is a textual variation in this verse as to whether Christ "suffered" for sins or "died" for sins. In 1 Pet. 2:21, 𝔭81 adds another early witness for the reading "died"—against the evidence of the early papyrus, 𝔭72. This creates the situation where 𝔭72 and B versus 𝔭81 and ℵ produces a virtual standoff. Thus, future translators will have to determine which reading most likely created the other and then be obliged to note the other in the margin—as did a most recent version, the NJB.

► 1 Peter 2:25

for you were going astray [or, **wandering**] **as sheep** ℵ A B: ASV RSV NASB NIV NEB NJB.

for you were as wandering sheep 𝔭72 C P 𝔐: TEV NJBmg.

The difference in meaning between the two readings is very slight: the first reading compares the people's wandering with that done by sheep, while the second compares the people themselves with wandering sheep. Thus, the translators may not have been conscious that they were following one reading as against the other.

173

▶ 1 Peter 3:7

𝔭81 supports 𝔭72 ℵ² B in reading the dative, συγκληρονόμοις, instead of the nominative, συγκληρονόμοι (in A C 𝔐). The dative indicates that the wives are the co-heirs; the nominative, the husbands. Most of the more recent translations follow the dative, for it is more likely to have been the reading that was changed, and it has the support of the papyri, 𝔭72 and 𝔭81, with B.

▶ 1 Peter 3:18

suffered B P 𝔐: ASV RSVmg NEBmg TEVmg.
died 𝔭72 ℵ A Cᵛⁱᵈ 33 1739: ASVmg RSV NASB NIV NEB TEV NJB.

Like 1 Pet. 2:21, in which the context seems to favor the reading "suffered" instead of "died" (see comments on this verse above), it would *seem* natural for Peter (again speaking about suffering—see 3:14-18) to say that Christ "suffered for sins" rather than "died for sins." But the evidence of 𝔭72 with ℵ A C offsets the testimony of B. Furthermore, the second reading in this context is the more difficult reading and therefore the one more likely to have been changed. All the translators since the ASV preferred the reading "died" over "suffered."

▶ 1 Peter 4:14

the Spirit of glory and of God 𝔭72 B L: all the translations.
the Spirit of glory and of power and of God ℵ A P 33 1739: RSVmg NJBmg.

If the extra phrase "and of power" had been original, there is no good reason to explain why it would not be in the two earliest MSS, 𝔭72 and B. Thus, the second reading appears to contain a scribal addition. Not one version contains this addition, though it is noted in RSVmg and NJBmg.

▶ 1 Peter 5:2a

*include **overseeing** [or, **exercising the oversight**] 𝔭72 ℵ² A P 33 𝔐: ASV RSVmg NIV NJB.
omit ℵ* B: ASVmg RSV NASB NEB TEV NJBmg.

The documentary evidence supporting the inclusion of "overseeing" is both early and diversified. Actually, ℵ* and B are the only two Greek

MSS that lack the word (and the word was inserted by a corrector of ℵ). Perhaps, the scribes of ℵ* and B omitted the word ἐπισκοποῦντες ("overseeing") because they had the misconception that the elders (*presbytery*—1 Pet. 5:1) could not function as overseers (see Alford's *Greek Testament*). At that time in church history (fourth century), the offices of elder and overseer (i.e., bishop) were differentiated. The overseer or bishop had been elevated to a rank above an elder—though this deviates from the situation in the NT, in which the overseers and elders were two functions of the same individuals (see Tit. 1:5, 7). For example, Paul told the elders at Ephesus that the Holy Spirit had made them overseers (bishops) of the flock (Acts 20:17, 28). And so also here in 1 Peter 5:1-2, Peter was charging the elders that they should shepherd the church of God by overseeing it (i.e., by functioning as bishops).

However, most of the versions followed the combined testimony of ℵ* and B in not adding the participle "overseeing" to 1 Peter 5:2. But here again we see the influence of 𝔓72 on NA26 (for the Nestle text previously excluded the word ἐπισκοποῦντες), on the NIV, and on the NJB—for these translations included the word.

▶ 1 Peter 5:2b
include **according to God's will** [lit., "according to God"] 𝔓72 ℵ A 33 1739: ASV RSVmg NASB NIV NEB TEV NJB.
omit B L: ASVmg RSV NJBmg.

Since most of the ancient MSS include the words κατὰ θεόν ("according to God") and since it is easier to explain why scribes would delete the words (being deemed unnecessary or unclear) than add them, it is very likely that the first reading contains the original text. All of the modern translations except the RSV (probably influenced by B) followed the reading of 𝔓72 et al.

▶ 1 Peter 5:10
perfect, confirm, strengthen, establish you ℵ 33vid 1739: ASVmg RSVmg NASB NIV NJB.
perfect, confirm, strengthen you A B 0206: ASV RSV NASBmg NEB TEV.
perfect, confirm, establish you 𝔓72: none.

175

It could be argued that the shorter readings came as the result of homoioteleuton—four words in a row end with σ(ξ)ει: καταρτίσει, στηρίξει, σθενώσει, θεμελιώσει; thus, it would be easy for a scribe to miss one. Or it could be argued that the longer reading is an expansion. The translations (some with marginal notes) reflect the uncertainty. However, not one translation even noted the shorter reading of 𝔓72.

▶ 1 Peter 5:13

she that is at Babylon 𝔓72 A B C: all the translations.
the church that is at Babylon ℵ and a few ancient versions: NASBmg TEV.

Without a doubt, the second reading is an attempt by the scribe of ℵ (and a few ancient translators) to specifically identify the one Peter calls συνεκλεκτὴ (lit., "the co-chosen one," in the feminine gender). "Church" is a good conjecture as to this one's identity, but it is nothing more than a conjecture. Thus, it seems odd that the NASBmg would cite this as a variant reading. And the TEV translators did exactly what a few other ancient translators did; they gave an interpretative rendering: "Your sister church in Babylon, also chosen by God, sends you greetings, and so does my son Mark."

2 Peter

Early manuscripts containing portions of 2 Peter:

𝔓72: 1:1–3:18 (all of the epistle)

▶ 2 Peter 1:1

Simeon ℵ A 1739: ASVmg RSV NASBmg NEB TEV NJB.
Simon 𝔓72 B: ASV RSVmg NASB NIV.

The UBS[3] and NA[26] editors considered that it was more likely that "Simeon" was changed to "Simon" than vice versa. Two of the more recent versions (NASB and NIV), however, adopted the second reading. (This perhaps shows the influence of 𝔓72 on the NIV.)

► 2 Peter 1:3

called us by [or, **to**] **his own glory and virtue** ℵ A C 33 1739: all the translations.

called us through his glory and virtue 𝔓72 B: ASVmg TEVmg.

The difference in the two readings is very slight in the Greek; in fact, there is only a one-letter difference: ἰδίᾳ ("to his own") versus διὰ ("through"). Both readings have good support and are suitable to the context—for God did call the believers to participate in his own glory and virtue and/or he did so by means of expressing his glory and virtue though his Son. However, not one version followed the second reading—though it is noted in ASVmg (in respect to the testimony of B) and TEVmg (in respect to the testimony 𝔓72, especially, and B).

► 2 Peter 2:4

***chains** 𝔓72 33 1739: ASVmg NIVmg NEBmg TEV (NJB).

pits ℵ A B C: ASV RSV NASB NIV NEB TEVmg.

The two Greek words are very similar to one another—σειραῖς ("chains") and σιροῖς ("pits")—and therefore could have been confounded one for the other. The editors of UBS[3] and NA[26] adopted the reading "chains" on the basis that 𝔓72 provides the earliest reading. This caused a change in the Nestle text, which previously followed the testimony of ℵ A B C. But most of the translators preferred "pits," while a few translators (i.e., those of the TEV and NJB) adopted "chains," having its earliest attestation from 𝔓72.

► 2 Peter 2:13

deceits (or, **dissipation**) 𝔓72 ℵ A* C 33: ASV RSV NASB NIV NEB (TEV) NJBmg.

lovefeasts A[c] B: ASVmg RSVmg NASBmg NIVmg NEBmg (TEV) NJB.

The two words could have been easily confused in textual transmission: ἀπάταις ("deceits") and ἀγάπαις ("love feasts"). The first reading has better documentary support (𝔓72 with ℵ A* C is stronger testimony than A[c] B), and it is quite possible that the second reading was taken from the parallel passage in Jude 12. Almost all the translations followed the first reading, except NJB and TEV (which seem to have incorporated both readings in their text).

▶ 2 Peter 2:20

*our Lord and Savior, Jesus Christ 𝔭72 ℵ A C P 048[vid]: ASVmg RSV NIV NEB TEV NJB.

the Lord and Savior, Jesus Christ B 𝔐: ASV NASB.

The testimony of 𝔭72 et al. is stronger than that of B, which was the testimony adhered to in previous editions of the Nestle text. All the versions except ASV and NASB reflect the first reading. The ASV translators showed their usual preference for B, and the NASB translators made no change from the ASV—despite the better evidence for the other reading.

▶ 2 Peter 3:10

the earth and the works that are upon it will be exposed [or, **found out** or, **laid bare**] ℵ B 1739txt: ASVmg NASBmg NIV NEB TEV NJBmg.

the earth and the works that are upon it will be burned up A 048 33 1739mg: ASV RSV NASB NIVmg NEBmg TEVmg NJB.

the earth and the works that are upon it will be found dissolved 𝔭72: TEVmg.

The above readings represent only some of the variants found in this verse—that is, only those followed or noted by the translations. Many textual scholars think there is a primitive error in the text which led to all kinds of textual variations, which in turn has led to the proposal of several different kinds of conjectural emendations (see Metzger for a list of these). Given the textual evidence that is available, translators have had to decide which reading best represents what Peter originally wrote. Many have chosen to follow the first reading, for it is the more difficult reading and the one with the best attestation. 𝔭72, whose singular reading is noted in TEVmg, also supports the reading with εὑρεθήσεται ("will be found")—to which the scribe added λυόμενα ("dissolved" or "destroyed").

Jude

Early manuscripts containing portions of Jude:

𝔓72: vv. 1-25 (all of the epistle)
𝔓78: vv. 4-5, 7-8

▶ Jude 4

See comments on this in the description of 𝔓78 (Section 2).

▶ Jude 5

the Lord delivered his people out of Egypt ℵ C* L: ASV RSVmg
NASB NIV NEB TEV NJB.
Jesus delivered his people out of Egypt A B 33 1739: the margin of all
the translations.
God, the Messiah, delivered his people out of Egypt 𝔓72: none.
God delivered his people out of Egypt C²: RSVmg.

Among all the readings cited above, the second reading is the most
remarkable, for it says that "Jesus delivered his people out of Egypt."
This reading is found in A, B, 33, 1739, early Coptic MSS, Origen, and
Bede. 𝔓72 is possibly an indirect witness to the reading with "Jesus"
because it shows that the scribe had before him (in his exemplar) a
messianic title—"Messiah" or "Christ." At any rate, it is easier to argue
(from a textual perspective) that the reading with "Jesus" is the one from
which all the others deviated than to argue that the reading with "Lord"
(or "God") was changed to "Jesus." Scribes were not known for fabricat-
ing difficult readings.

Perhaps Jude wrote Ἰησοῦς in Jude 5 intending to mean "Joshua"
(e.g., see NEBmg), as in Heb. 4:8, but this is very unlikely. Joshua led
the Israelites into the good land but not out of Egypt, and Joshua certainly did not destroy those who did not believe (Jude 5b). Given the fact that
Jude was writing from a NT perspective, a perspective that viewed Jesus
as being Yahweh the Savior, it is not difficult to imagine that Jude would
say that Jesus delivered the Israelites out of Egypt (cf. 1 Cor. 10:4, 9 and
see discussion on 1 Cor. 10:9). Thus, several scholars are convinced that
Jude wrote "Jesus." (For example, see Henry Alford's *Greek Testament*
on this verse; Eberhard Nestle's *Introduction to the Textual Criticism of
the New Testament*, 328–329; F. F. Bruce, *This is That*, 35–36; Allen

Wikgren, "Some Problems in Jude 5" in *Studies in the History and Text of the New Testament in Honor of Kenneth W. Clark*, 147–152.)

Though the reading with "Jesus" seems to be the one Jude wrote, not one translation has adopted this reading for the text. Rather, it has been universally relegated to the margin. The first edition of the UBS *Greek New Testament* contained the reading "Jesus" in the text. But this changed in the third edition when a slim majority of the editors voted to put the reading with "Lord" in the text and the one with "Jesus" in the margin. (Metzger and Wikgren voted against this decision and stated their reasons for doing so in the *Textual Commentary*.) All the versions, however, note this reading in the margin; but not one version indicates the variant, "God, the Messiah" as found in 𝔓72.

▶ Jude 22-23

This text appears in a variety of forms in various MSS.

Some MSS indicate three classes of people, as follows:

*and show mercy to some who have doubts [or, **who dispute**]; **and save some, snatching them from fire; and to some show mercy with fear** ℵ: ASV NASB NIV NEBmg TEV NJB.

and reprove some who have doubts [or, **who dispute**]; **and save some, snatching them from fire; and to some show mercy with fear** A: RSV.

Some MSS indicate two classes of people, as follows:

and show mercy to some who have doubts—save them by snatching them from fire; and to some show mercy with fear B: NEB NJBmg.

and reprove some who have doubts [or, **who dispute**], **and in fear save some from fire** C*: none.

and some snatch from fire, and show mercy with fear to others who have doubts 𝔓72: none.

The textual problems in this passage are extremely complicated and require great effort to unravel. Sakae Kubo has done this unraveling in a chapter called "Jude 22-3: Two-division Form or Three?" in *New Testament Textual Criticism: Its Significance for Exegesis* (239–253). In his work called 𝔓72 *and Codex Vaticanus* (*Studies and Documents* 27, 1965), Kubo had previously argued for the two-division form as found in 𝔓72 or B (as did J. N. Birdsall in "The Text of Jude in 𝔓72" in *Journal of Theological Studies* 14 [1963], 396–399). But then Kubo changed his mind and presented a new argument for the threefold division as found in א. Evidently, most translators also favor this form of text, for all but the RSV (which followed a similar text in A) and NEB (which was the only version to adopt the two-division form) followed the reading of א. Unfortunately, not one version noted the variation in 𝔓72, which indirectly supports the form of B.

Revelation

Early manuscripts containing portions of Revelation:

𝔓18: 1:4-7
𝔓24: 5:5-8; 6:5-8
𝔓47: 9:10–17:2
𝔓85: 9:19–10:1, 5-9

▶ Revelation 1:5
loosed [or, freed] us from our sins 𝔓18 א A C: ASV RSV NASB NIV NEB TEV NJBmg.
washed us from our sins P 046 𝔐: NJB ASVmg.

In the Greek there is only a one-letter difference between the two readings. The first reading contains the Greek participle λύσαντι ("loosing" or "freeing"); the second reading contains the Greek participle λούσαντι ("washing"). The earliest and best witnesses attest to the first, more difficult reading. Uncomfortable with this wording, later scribes changed the word by adding an *omicron*. Nevertheless, all the versions except NJB followed the superior reading.

▶ Revelation 5:6
the seven Spirits of God 𝔓24 א: all the translations.
the Spirits of God A P[vid]: ASVmg.

The word "seven" (ἑπτά) has been bracketed in UBS[3] and NA[26] because the editors could not determine if certain copyists borrowed the word from 1:4; 3:1; and/or 4:5, or if other copyists accidentally dropped the word ἑπτά ("seven") after having just written the same word twice. All the translators, nevertheless, followed the reading found in 𝔓24 et al.

I examined this MS at the Franklin Trask Library of Andover Newton Theological School and noticed how the scribe of 𝔓24 wrote out the Greek expression for "the seven Spirits of God." The scribe wrote TA Z̄ Π̄N̄A TOY Θ̄Ȳ (see photo 13). By writing the entire title as a *nomen sacrum*, the scribe of 𝔓24 was indicating that he considered the words "the seven" to be part of the title for the divine Spirit. Many translators have been hesitant to identify τὰ ἑπτὰ πνεύματα here with the divine Spirit. This is reflected in translations that render the word πνεύματα in the lower case: "the seven spirits" (see RSV, NIV, NEB, TEV). But how could τὰ ἑπτὰ πνεύματα ("the seven Spirits"), listed with the Father and the Son in 1:4-5 and identified with the Lord Jesus in 3:1 and 4:5, be anything other than the divine Holy Spirit of God? Evidently, the scribe of 𝔓24 thought this, or he would not have written the entire expression as a *nomen sacrum*. (Some early scribes did in fact distinguish between the divine Spirit and other spirits by writing the former as a *nomen sacrum* and writing out the latter—see Comfort's article "Light from the New Testament Papyri concerning the Translation of πνεῦμα" in *The Bible Translator*, Jan., 1984.)

Other translators (see ASV NASB NJB) considered the title to be a description of the divine Spirit and therefore rendered it with a capital letter: "the seven Spirits." The most ingenious—and perhaps most accurate—way of rendering this title is found in TLB: "the sevenfold Spirit of God" (also noted in NIVmg). Many scholars would affirm that this is what the title means—God's one divine Spirit is called "seven" (a number symbolizing fullness) to express its full supply to the seven churches.

▶ Revelation 10:7
See comments on this verse in the description of 𝔓85 (Section 2).

▶ Revelation 11:12
they heard ℵ* A C P: ASV RSV NASB NIV NEB TEV NJBmg.
I heard 𝔓47 ℵ^c 𝔐: NJB.

The NJB was the only translation influenced by the testimony of 𝔭47 et al. As such, the NJB text has John hearing the voice from heaven saying, "Come up here." The other versions follow the excellent testimony of ℵ* A C and thereby produce a translation that seems to be more suitable to the context—for the next part of the verse says that "they [the two witnesses] ascended up into heaven."

▶ Revelation 12:18/13:1

And he stood on the sand of the sea 𝔭47 ℵ A C: ASV RSV NASB NIV NEB TEV NJBmg.

And I stood on the sand of the sea P 𝔐: ASVmg RSVmg NASBmg NIVmg NEBmg TEVmg NJB.

The first reading, having the best support (𝔭47 with ℵ A C), necessitates that the arrangement of the traditional English text (as in KJV) be adjusted. In the Greek, the editors of UBS[3] and NA[26] added a new verse (12:18), but most translations join this clause to 12:17—the pronoun "he," therefore, referring to its antecedent, "the dragon." In the KJV and NJB, which follow the second reading, the clause goes with 13:1—and the pronoun "I," therefore, refers to the writer of the Revelation. All the versions have a note on this textual variation primarily because of its effect on the rearrangement of the traditional format for the end of Rev. 12 and the beginning of Rev. 13.

▶ Revelation 13:6

blaspheming his name and his dwelling place, that is, those who dwell in heaven ℵ* A C: ASV RSV NASB NEBmg.

blaspheming his name and those who dwell in heaven ℵ2 P 𝔐: NIV TEV NJB.

blaspheming his name and his dwelling place in heaven 𝔭47: NEB.

The NEB translators considered the text of 𝔭47 to contain the original wording (see Tasker's explanation). However, the first reading has better external support (especially the combined testimony of A and C with ℵ), is seemingly the most difficult reading, and is most likely the reading from which the others deviated. According to the syntax of this verse in Greek, the phrase "those who dwell [lit., 'tabernacle'] in heaven" is in direct apposition to "his dwelling place [lit., 'tabernacle']." Thus, those who dwell in heaven are God's tabernacle in heaven; the people in heaven and the heavenly place are not two separate entities (Comfort). This is made clear in versions like ASV, RSV, and NASB.

▶ Revelation 13:7

include **And it was allowed to make war on the saints and to conquer them** ℵ and many later MSS: all the translations.
omit 𝔭47 A C: ASVmg RSVmg NEBmg.

The absence of this clause in several MSS is probably the result of an early scribal mistake—the eye of the scribe passing over the first occurrence of καὶ ἐδόθη αὐτῷ to the second. Accordingly, none of the translations followed the reading of 𝔭46 A C, even though this combined testimony would normally certify a genuine reading. The marginal notes in ASV, RSV, and NEB must have been written in deference to this early testimony.

▶ Revelation 13:18

666 𝔭47 ℵ A P 𝔐: all the translations.
616 C and a few versions: ASVmg RSVmg NASBmg NJBmg.

𝔭47 adds weight to the testimony of A (reading "666") versus C (reading "616"), the two best witnesses to Revelation, here divided in their testimony. Irenaeus supported the reading "666," but indicated that he knew of several MSS that read "616" (*Contra Haereses* 5.30). Most likely the variant "616" was created by some scribe who intentionally changed the Greek number χξϛ (equivalent to the Greek name "Neron Caesar" written in Hebrew) to χιϛ (equivalent to the Latin name "Nero Caesar" written in Hebrew).

▶ Revelation 14:3

*they sing, as it were, a new song A C 𝔐: ASV.
they sing a new song 𝔭47 ℵ: RSV NASB NIV NEB TEV NJB.

The Greek word for "as it were" (ὡς) has been bracketed in UBS[3] and NA[26] (it was not included in previous editions of the Nestle text); no doubt the word was included because of its presence in A and C but bracketed because of its absence in 𝔭47 and ℵ. The ASV translators, who did not have the testimony of 𝔭47, followed A and C. All the other translations followed 𝔭47 and ℵ.

► Revelation 15:3

King of the nations ℵ¹ A P 𝔐: ASVmg RSVmg NASB NEBmg TEV NJB.

King of the ages 𝔭47 ℵ*,2 C: ASV RSV NASBmg NIV NEB TEVmg.

Those translators who chose the first reading could argue that the second reading had been adopted from 1 Tim. 1:17, whereas the first reading is a unique expression in the NT. But it can also be argued that the words "the nations" in the next verse caused the scribes to change "ages" to "nations" (see Tasker). Thus, arguments pertaining to internal considerations are offsetting. With respect to the documentary evidence, the testimony of 𝔭47 with ℵ* and C demonstrates weightier external support than does ℵ¹ and A. The ASV had the support of ℵ* and C, while the RSV, NIV, and NEB had the added testimony of 𝔭47.

► Revelation 15:6

linen 𝔭47 ℵ P: ASVmg RSV NASB NIV NEB TEV NJB.

stone A C: ASV NASBmg.

The two words in Greek are very similar: λίνον ("linen") and λίθον ("stone"); they could have easily been mistaken for one another. However, it is much more likely that "linen" was changed to "stone" (either accidentally or under the influence of Ezek. 28:13) than vice versa. The ASV translators followed the best testimony available to them at the time—namely, A and C. But the subsequent discovery of 𝔭47 and its reading in this verse (concurring with ℵ) offset the weight of A and C. Hence, all translations since the ASV have followed the reading in 𝔭47 and ℵ.

► Revelation 16:4

it became blood ℵ C P: ASV NASBmg.

they became blood 𝔭47 A: ASVmg RSV NASB NIV NEB TEV NJB.

The first reading is the more difficult one because "it" does not agree grammatically with the preceding nouns ("rivers" and "fountains"). Thus, scribes would be prone to fix the grammar; and translators, desiring a polished rendering, would adhere to the grammatically correct variant. Thus, it is not likely that 𝔭47 had much effect on those translations which reflect the variant reading.

SECTION FOUR

Concluding Observations

As was stated in the introduction, one of the purposes of this book has been to examine how the papyri effected (and affected) changes in successive editions of English versions of the NT. The ASV is a good starting point, for it reflects the text current at the beginning of this century (a text heavily influenced by B and ℵ) and serves as a good comparison for later, twentieth-century translations. Two versions then came forth as revisions of the ASV—namely, the RSV and NASB. These versions should have shown the impact of the papyri. The most influential (and popular) English version to have been published since the RSV and NASB is the NIV. Thus, in this conclusion I will examine how these three versions (RSV, NASB, NIV) have been affected by the papyri, and I will note some comparisons of the NEB with the RSV, as well as TEV and NJB with the NIV.

FROM THE AMERICAN STANDARD VERSION
TO THE REVISED STANDARD VERSION
The RSV translators basically followed the seventeenth edition of the Nestle text (1941)—adopting (for the most part) the reading in the text, or selecting a reading from the apparatus. At the time of translation, only some of the already published papyri had been incorporated into this edition of the Nestle text—namely, 𝔭1, 8, 10, 13, 15, 22, 23, 28, 37, 38, 45, 46, 47, 48, 50, 52, and 53. Other early papyri were available at that time (such

as 𝔓4, 5, 6, 9, 12, 16, 17, 18, 24, 29, 30, 32, 35, 39, 40); but since these papyri were not included in the seventeenth edition of the Nestle text, it is rather doubtful that the RSV translators consulted these specific MSS—at least they made no mention of doing so. As was stated earlier, the translators did state that they gave special attention to the Chester Beatty Papyri (𝔓45, 46, 47) in their work.

One of the objectives of this study was to determine how the documentary evidence in these papyri affected the RSV—especially by comparison to its predecessor, the ASV. The following data will demonstrate how the RSV was affected by the papyri in one of four ways: (1) the RSV followed a reading in a particular papyrus MS, affirming the same reading followed by the ASV; (2) the RSV followed a reading in a particular papyrus MS, demonstrating a change from the ASV; (3) the RSV did not choose a reading in a particular papyrus MS, and thus adopted a reading usually found in the ASV or ASVmg; or (4) the RSV did not follow a reading in a particular papyrus MS but noted it in the margin.

1. In certain portions, the RSV translators followed a reading in a papyrus MS (or MSS) which supported the same reading previously adopted by the ASV. This is the case in forty-six occurrences:

𝔓1 Matt. 1:18
𝔓8 Acts 4:33; 6:3
𝔓15 1 Cor. 7:33-34; 8:3a, 3b
𝔓22 John 16:27
𝔓37 Matt. 26:28
𝔓45 Mark 7:4; 9:24; Luke 9:35; 9:54; 9:55b-56a om.; 10:38; 10:42
𝔓46 Rom. 12:11; 12:14; 15:29; 1 Cor. 1:28; 7:15; 7:33-34; 2 Cor. 1:11; 11:3; Gal. 1:3; 1:6; 2:5; 6:13; Eph. 1:14; 3:9; 4:9; 4:28; 4:32; 6:1; Phil. 2:30; 4:3; Col. 1:7; 2:2; 2:18; 3:16; Heb. 10:11; 10:34; 10:38; 13:21a;
𝔓47 Rev. 12:18–13:1; 13:18; 15:3

2. In other portions, the RSV translators followed a reading supported by a papyrus MS (or MSS) which caused the RSV to have a different text from the ASV. This is true for the following:

𝔓13 with 𝔓46
Heb. 3:2—"in all his house" vs. "in his house"
Heb. 3:6—om. "firm to the end"

𝔭45

Luke 11:11—om. "if his son asks for bread will he give him a stone?"

Luke 14:5—"son or an ox" vs. "donkey or an ox"

𝔭46

Rom. 8:28—"God works all things together for good" vs. "everything works together for good"

Rom. 11:17—"of the fatness" vs. "of the root of the fatness"

Rom. 11:31—om. "now" from the phrase "they may now receive mercy"

2 Cor. 2:1—"for I decided" vs. "but I decided"

2 Cor. 3:9—"if there was glory in the ministry of condemnation" vs. "if the ministry of condemnation was glory"

Gal. 1:15—"he was pleased" vs. "God was pleased"

Eph. 1:1—om. "in Ephesus"

Eph. 5:2—"loved us" vs. "loved you"

Col. 3:6—om. "upon the sons of disobedience"

𝔭47

Heb. 2:7—om. "and did set him over the works of his hands"

Heb. 6:1-2—"with instruction about baptisms" vs. "of instruction about baptisms"

Heb. 9:11—"of the good things that have come" vs. "of the good things that are come"

Heb. 11:37—om. "they were put to the test"

Rev. 14:3—om. "as it were" from the phrase "they sing, as it were, a new song"

Rev. 15:6—"linen" vs. "stone"

Rev. 16:4—"they became blood" vs. "it became blood"

This accounts for only twenty changes—a suprisingly low figure, especially since the RSV translators proclaimed that they had undertaken a new translation (in part) because of the evidence in the papyri.

3. In many more portions where there are variant readings supported by the early papyri, the RSV translators did not follow a reading in a particular papyrus MS (or MSS)—but instead adopted a reading usually reflected in the ASV or ASVmg. This is true for the following:

𝔓13 Heb. 11:4; 12:3

𝔓37 Matt. 26:27

𝔓45 Matt. 26:20; Mark 6:23; 6:44; 7:28; 8:38a, 38b; Luke 11:33; John
    10:16; 10:18; Acts 11:11; 11:12; 13:33; 13:48

𝔓46 Rom. 8:21; 8:23; 9:4; 15:19; 16:7; 1 Cor. 1:13; 10:2; 14:38; 15:49;
    2 Cor. 1:10a; 2:17; 3:2; 8:7; Eph. 2:5; 4:8; 5:5; 5:9; Gal. 6:2; Phil. 1:14;
    3:3; Col. 3:4; Heb. 13:21b

𝔓47 Rev. 11:12; 13:6

𝔓48 Acts 23:12

𝔓50 Acts 10:30

In every passage noted here, at least one of the English translations adopted
the reading supported by a papyrus MS (or MSS). But the RSV translators
chose not to do so in the above forty-two occurrences—and yet it must be
said that they made several such decisions with perspicuity. In most instances (thirty-two), the RSV translators followed the reading in the Nestle
text (seventeenth edition, 1941). In ten occurrences, they adopted readings
from the apparatus not supported by the early papyri.

4. The lack of adherence to the early papyri (just mentioned) is somewhat
   compensated for by the fact that the RSV translators provided several
   marginal notes on variant readings which are often supported by the
   early papyri. This is the case for the following:

𝔓13 with 𝔓46

Heb. 4:2—"they were united in faith with those who heard"

𝔓37

Matt. 26:20—"the twelve disciples"

𝔓45

Mark 8:15—"Herodians"

Mark 9:29—"prayer and fasting"

Mark 10:17—"seventy-two disciples"

John 11:25—om. "and the life" from the phrase "the resurrection and the
   life"

𝔓46

1 Cor. 2:1—"mystery of God"

1 Cor. 5:5—"Lord"

1 Cor. 10:9—"let us not tempt Christ"

1 Cor. 13:3—"if I give my body that I may boast"

1 Cor. 15:49—"let us also bear the image of the heavenly man"

Eph. 1:15—om. "your love"

Eph. 4:28—"working with his hands"

Phil. 4:16—"you sent to my need"

𝔓47

Heb. 1:8—"his kingdom"

Rev. 13:7—om. "and it was allowed to make war on the saints and to conquer them"

Of all the NT portions in which the papyri (available to the RSV translators) contained significant variant readings, the RSV followed twenty readings that caused it to be different from the ASV and noted an additional sixteen readings in the margin. This does not amount to a very substantial change over the ASV—though, of course, it must be kept in mind that the papyri readings often substantiated the readings followed by the ASV. By way of comparison, the NEB translators adopted several more readings from the papyri and noted far more readings found in the papyri than did the RSV. But it must be kept in mind that the NEB translators also adopted many other readings not supported by the papyri or other early uncials and appended many notes concerning variant readings from a variety of sources other than the papyri—including readings in D, Old Latin MSS, patristic citations, and late miniscules. Thus, the NEB does not necessarily reflect a text more in tune with the early papyri than the RSV does.

FROM THE REVISED STANDARD VERSION
TO THE NEW AMERICAN STANDARD BIBLE

The translators of the NASB basically followed the twenty-third edition of the Nestle text (1957)—adopting for the most part the reading in the text or selecting a reading from the apparatus. Several more early papyri had been discovered and published since the time of the seventeenth edition of the Nestle text (1941), but not all of these had been included in this Nestle text. By the time of the twenty-third edition, thirteen more papyri had been added to the Nestle text: 𝔓16, 18, 20, 25, 27, 30, 40, 41, 49, 51, 64, 65, and 66—all of which, except 𝔓41, are early papyri. It is again assumed that the NASB translators did not consult any other papyri for variant readings outside those listed in the twenty-third edition of the Nestle text.

One of the goals of this study was to determine how the documentary evidence in these papyri affected the NASB—especially by comparison to the RSV, for both the RSV and the NASB basically were revisions of the ASV. From a textual point of view, the NASB had the advantage over the RSV because there was more evidence from the papyri available to the NASB revisers than to the RSV revisers. For example, the NASB revisers had access to the first major Bodmer papyrus, 𝔭66. The following data will demonstrate how the NASB was affected by the papyri in one of four ways: (1) the NASB followed a reading in a particular papyrus MS, affirming the same reading followed by the RSV; (2) the NASB followed a reading in a particular papyrus MS, demonstrating a change from the RSV; (3) the NASB did not follow a reading in a particular papyrus MS and thus adopted a reading usually found in the ASV or ASVmg (for the NASB is a revision of the ASV); or (4) the NASB did not follow a reading in a particular papyrus MS but noted it in the margin.

1. For the most part, the translators of the NASB chose a reading supported by one of the papyri (mentioned above) that affirmed the text of the
   RSV. This is true in twenty-seven occurrences:

𝔭18 Rev. 1:5
𝔭25 Matt. 19:3
𝔭40 Rom. 3:22
𝔭49 Eph. 5:9
𝔭51 Gal. 1:6; 1:8
𝔭66 John 1:34; 1:41; 3:13; 4:1; 4:9; 5:1; 5:3b-4; 6:36; 7:52; 7:53–8:11;
     8:39; 8:57; 9:35; 10:29; 11:25; 12:41; 13:10; 14:4; 14:17; 17:11; 17:12

2. Very rarely did the NASB translators adopt a reading in the papyri
   (mentioned above) which caused their text to be different from the RSV.
   Such a change happened only five times, in the following instances:

𝔭16
Phil. 3:13—add "yet" to the sentence "I count not myself to have laid hold"

𝔭27
Rom. 8:34—"whom he raised" vs. "whom he raised from the dead"

𝕻66

John 1:18—"only begotten God" vs. "only begotten Son"

John 14:14—"ask me anything" vs. "ask me"

John 16:22—"no one will take away your joy" vs. "no one takes away your joy"

3. The NASB translators were conservative in their evaluation of the new evidence in the papyri. Quite often, they followed the textual basis behind the ASV or ASVmg as over against the new evidence in the papyri. This is true for the following sixteen portions:

𝕻16 Phil. 4:3

𝕻49 Eph. 4:32

𝕻51 Gal. 1:3

𝕻66 John 3:25; 5:2; 5:44; 7:8; 7:39; 12:17; 13:2; 13:32; 14:4; 14:7; 16:27; 19:35; 20:31

4. Also the NASB translators provided only five marginal notes on readings found in these papyri. This is true for the following:

𝕻25

Matt. 19:9—add "marries a divorced woman"

𝕻30

1 Thess. 5:25—"pray also"

𝕻49

Eph. 4:32—"forgiven us"

𝕻65

1 Thess. 2:7—"babes"

𝕻66

John 8:16—"the Father who sent me"

Although the NASB translators had claimed that "consideration was given to the latest available manuscripts with a view to determining the best Greek text" (cited by Kubo and Specht in *So Many Versions?*, 173), the evidence does not bear this out. On the contrary, the NASB does not reflect the impact of the latest available manuscripts. On the whole, the NASB translators tended to be more conservative than the RSV translators in following the fresh evidence.

FROM THE NEW AMERICAN STANDARD BIBLE
TO THE NEW INTERNATIONAL VERSION

When the translators of the NIV were working on the NT, they had access to the twenty-fifth edition of Nestle's text (1963) and the first edition of the United Bible Societies' *Greek New Testament* (1966). But it must be kept in mind that their approach to these texts was eclectic—choosing (most often) from the text and (occasionally) from the apparatus.

One of the objectives of this study was to determine how the documentary evidence in these papyri affected the NIV—especially by comparison with the NASB. From a textual point of view, the NIV translators had the advantage over the NASB because there was more evidence from the papyri available to the NIV translators than to the NASB translators. The NASB translators had only one Bodmer papyrus ($\mathfrak{P}$66) to use; the NIV translators had the other two Bodmer papyri ($\mathfrak{P}$72 and $\mathfrak{P}$75), plus $\mathfrak{P}$4, 5, 6, 21, 24, 39, 67, 69, 70, and 71. The following data will demonstrate how the NIV was affected by the papyri in one of four ways: (1) the NIV followed a reading in a particular papyrus MS, reflecting the same reading followed by the NASB; (2) the NIV followed a reading in a particular papyrus MS, demonstrating a change from the NASB; (3) the NIV did not follow a reading in a particular papyrus MS, and thus adopted a reading usually found in the NASB or NASBmg; (4) the NIV did not follow a reading in a particular papyrus MS but noted it in the margin.

1. The NIV translators selected many readings that are found in one of the newly available papyri (mentioned above) and that, at the same time, affirm the same readings adopted by the NASB translators. This is true for the following portions, which total seventy:

$\mathfrak{P}$4 Luke 1:66; 1:78
$\mathfrak{P}$24 Rev. 5:6
$\mathfrak{P}$67 Matt. 5:22
$\mathfrak{P}$72 1 Peter 2:21; 3:7b; 3:18; 4:14; 5:2b; 5:13; 2 Peter 1:1; 1:21; 3:13; 3:9; Jude 1; 4

𝔭75 Luke 4:44; 6:48; 7:11; 8:26; 8:43; 9:26; 9:35; 9:54; 9:55b-56a; 9:62; 10:21; 10:22; 11:2a; 11:2b; 11:2c; 11:4; 11:11; 11:23; 11:33; 11:42; 12:21; 12:27; 12:39; 14:5; 15:21; 17:36; 18:11; 22:19b-20; 22:62; 23:17; 24:3; 24:6; 24:12; 24:13; 24:32; John 1:18; 1:28; 1:34; 3:13; 3:25; 4:1; 4:9; 5:1; 5:3b-4; 6:23a; 6:23b; 6:36; 7:53–8:11; 9:35; 10:29; 11:25; 12:8; 12:41; 14:17

One of the main reasons the NIV affirms the NASB so often is that the readings in 𝔭75 often concur with those in 𝔭45 and with 𝔭66—two papyri that were available to the NASB translators.

2. The NIV translators followed some readings in the newly available papyri, which caused the NIV text to differ from the NASB. This is true in the following:

𝔭5
John 16:22—"no one will take away your joy" vs. "no one takes away your joy"
John 16:27—"I came forth from God" vs. "I came forth from the Father"

𝔭39 with 𝔭75
John 8:16—"the Father who sent me" vs. "he who sent me"

𝔭72
1 Peter 5:2a—incl. "overseeing"
2 Peter 2:20—"our Lord and Savior, Jesus Christ" vs. "the Lord and Savior, Jesus Christ"

𝔭75
Luke 10:1 and 10:17—"seventy-two disciples" vs. "seventy disciples"
Luke 10:42—"but one thing is needful" vs. "but few things are needful, or only one"
Luke 24:36—incl. "and he said, 'Peace be with you'"
Luke 24:40—incl. verse
Luke 24:51—incl. "and was carried up into heaven"
Luke 24:52—incl. "they worshiped and returned to Jerusalem"
John 7:8—"I am not yet going up to this feast" vs. "I am not going up to this feast"

This accounts for little change from the NASB to the NIV—only fourteen such changes. The most noticeable change occurs in Luke 24, where 𝔭75 affirms the inclusion of text (in 24:36, 40, 51, 52) found in the major Alexandrian MSS—as opposed to the D-text, which excludes portions from each of these verses. The NASB translators had followed the Nestle text (twenty-third edition) in excluding what Westcott and Hort had called Western non-interpolations. The NIV translators followed the testimony of 𝔭75 ℵ B and the text of UBS[1] in including these portions. (Later, the NA[26] was conformed to the UBS text in retaining these portions as part of Luke's Gospel.)

3. Quite often the NIV translators did not follow a reading in a papyrus and so usually reflected the NASB. This is so with the following eighteen portions:

𝔭4 Luke 1:68; 3:22; 6:1
𝔭5 John 1:34
𝔭6 John 11:45
𝔭21 Matt. 12:25
𝔭69 Luke 22:43-44
𝔭72 1 Peter 2:25; 5:10; 2 Peter 1:3; 2:15; 2:20; Jude 22-23
𝔭75 Luke 6:1; 10:38; John 5:2; 7:39; 8:57

4. On a few other occasions, the NIV translators added a marginal note concerning a reading found in one of the newly available papyri when they decided not to adopt that reading for the NIV text. This is so with the following:

𝔭4
Luke 3:32-33—"Sala" and "the son of Amminadab, the son of Admin, the son of Arni"

𝔭69 with 𝔭75
om. Luke 22:43-44

𝔭72
1 Peter 1:22—"pure heart"
2 Peter 2:4—"chains of darkness"

$\mathfrak{p}$75

Luke 17:24—om. "in his day" in the expression "the Son of man in his day"

Luke 23:34—om. "Father, forgive them, for they do not know what they are doing"

John 5:44—"glory of the only One"

John 7:52—"the prophet"

Again, one would think they could have provided more notes concerning variant readings found in some very early and important papyri. By comparison, the NJB (one of the most recently published English versions—1986) shows a tendency to add several notes on variant readings supported by the papyri, even though the translators chose not to follow the papyri-supported reading.

The text of TEV, with respect to the portions cited above, is nearly identical to that of NIV. Of course, this should not surprise us because both translations were primarily based on the UBS[1]. Where they differ, it is usually because the NIV translators selected a reading supported by one of the above-mentioned papyri. This is the case for the following: $\mathfrak{p}$72 (1 Pet. 3:18b; 5:2a; 2 Pet. 1:1) and $\mathfrak{p}$75 (Luke 8:43; 18:11; 23:42; John 4:1; 6:23a; 7:8; 10:29).

RECENTLY PUBLISHED PAPYRI AND MODERN ENGLISH TRANSLATIONS

In 1990, Tyndale House Publishers (in cooperation with the United Bible Societies) is publishing an interlinear English translation of the UBS[4] text (which has the same text as UBS[3]—with a revised critical apparatus). Also in 1990, the New Revised Standard Version Bible will be published; the NT portion of this version closely follows UBS[3] and therefore is very reflective of the evidence of the early papyri. But UBS[3] does not reflect the evidence of the most recently published papyri. (See the Introduction to UBS[3], which gives a listing of papyri up to $\mathfrak{p}$76; and even this listing does not include several of the papyri between $\mathfrak{p}$1 and $\mathfrak{p}$76.)

The NA[26] has some papyrus MSS that were all published before 1945 but were not included in any previous edition of the Nestle text—namely, $\mathfrak{p}$9, 12, 17, 29, 32, 35, 62. These papyri were not included because they offer very little to the textual apparatus or to translators. The only papyrus among these with significance for translators is 𝔭12, which (with 𝔭46) reads "our fathers" in Heb. 1:1 (followed by RSV, NIV, NEB, TEV, NJB), as opposed to the reading "the fathers," supported by א A B C (followed by ASV, NASB).

NA²⁶ also included several other recently published early papyri— namely, 𝔭77, 78, 80, 81, 82, 85, 86, 87, 88, 89, 92 (the last two being included in the seventh printing, 1983). Some of these papyri are very fragmentary; they offer very little to the textual apparatus or to translators. This is basically true for 𝔭80, 82, 85, 86, 89, and 92. The other MSS offer new (though limited) resource for translators.

In Matt. 23:38, 𝔭77ᵛⁱᵈ (with א C D W) supports the reading "your house is left to you desolate" (followed by all the translations except NEB), as opposed to the reading (found in B L) that omits "desolate." In Jude 4, 𝔭78 (with 𝔭72 א A B C) has the reading "our only Lord and Master, Jesus Christ" (followed by all the translations), as opposed to the reading in the Majority Text, "our only Lord God and our Lord Jesus Christ" (KJV, NEBmg).

𝔭81 offers some fresh, early evidence for a few readings in 1 Peter. In 1 Peter 2:21, 𝔭81 supports א in reading "Christ died for you" (noted only in NEBmg and NJBmg), as opposed to the reading followed by all the translations, "Christ suffered for you" (𝔭72 A B C P 33 1739 𝔐). Translators should take note of this early, divided support—𝔭81 and א versus 𝔭72 and B. 𝔭81 supports 𝔭72 א² B in reading the dative, συγκληρονόμοις, instead of the nominative, συγκληρονόμοι (in A C P 𝔐), in 1 Peter 3:7; the dative indicates that the wives are the co-heirs; the nominative, the husbands. Most of the more recent translations follow the dative. And all the modern translations follow the reading "the grace of life" (supported by 𝔭81ᵛⁱᵈ with 𝔭72 B C*), as opposed to the expanded reading "the manifold grace of life" (noted in NJBmg).

In Philemon 25, 𝔭87 (with A D* 048) does not include the final "Amen." All modern translations since the ASV have followed suit—though the inclusion of "Amen" (supported by א C D² 𝔐) has been noted in NASBmg and NJBmg. 𝔭87 provides the earliest testimony to the absence of this "Amen."

𝔭88 offers some new, early evidence for a few important variation units in Mark 2. In Mark 2:24, 𝔭88 (with א B L 33) reads "they could not bring him" (followed by NASB, NIV, TEV, NJB), as opposed to "they could not bring him near"—supported by A C D 090 (followed by ASV, RSV, NEB).

In Mark 2:10, 𝔭88 (with ℵ C D L 090) reads "the Son of man has authority on earth to forgive sins" (followed by all the translations except NJB), as opposed to the reading in B, "the authority the Son of man has to forgive sins on earth." In Mark 2:16a, 𝔭88 (with ℵ B L W 33) attests to the superior reading, followed by all the translations, "the scribes of the Pharisees," as opposed to the reading "the scribes and the Pharisees" (found in A C D 𝔐, noted in ASVmg and RSVmg). Yet in the same verse, 𝔭88 has the expanded text, "why does he eat and drink with tax collectors and sinners?" (also supported by A 33 and followed by ASV and NASB), as opposed to the shorter reading that leaves out the words "and drink" (according to B D W; followed by RSV, NEB, TEV, NJB).

LOOKING TO THE FUTURE:
NEW TESTAMENT TRANSLATIONS REFLECTING
THE EVIDENCE OF EARLY PAPYRUS MANUSCRIPTS

Imagine having a NT based solely on the early papyrus MSS. Of course, such a NT would not contain all the books of the NT (for example, First and Second Timothy would be missing entirely), and not all the books would be complete (such as Matthew, Mark, Acts, James); but nearly every other book of the NT is extant—almost in full—in the early papyri, and in most cases the papyri give witness to readings that are very likely original—especially when supported by the evidence of other reliable MSS. The Greek texts of UBS[3] and NA[26] greatly reflect a text based on the early papyri, but not completely. For example, in a study I did on the Gospel of John, I discovered fifty-two readings found in the papyri (and supported by other Greek MSS) but not in the text of UBS[3] and NA[26] (see Comfort's article "The Greek Text of the Gospel of John According to the Early Papyri: As Compared to Nestle-Aland's *Novum Testamentum Graece*, 26th edition [NA[26]]," in *New Testament Studies*). It is my hope that future editions of the Greek text will incorporate even more of the readings found in the early papyri when such readings can in any way be vindicated by the principles of textual criticism.

With respect to significant variant readings (i.e., those usually indicated in the text of UBS[3]), modern translations do not fully reflect the evidence of the early papyri. For example, not one version followed the reading of 𝔭6 and 𝔭45 in John 11:45 ("seeing the things he did") or the reading of 𝔭21 in Matt. 12:25 ("seeing [or, perceiving] their thoughts"). And though noted in the margins of all the other translations, only the NJB adopted the reading of 𝔭13 and 𝔭46 in Heb. 4:2 ("they were not united in faith with those who heard"). And none of the versions I studied followed the reading of 𝔭46 in 1 Cor. 10:9 ("let us not tempt Christ") or the reading of 𝔭46 in 1 Cor. 13:3 ("if I give my body that I may boast"). And though noted in some margins, not one translation followed the shorter reading of 𝔭45 in Luke 10:21 ("he rejoiced in his spirit"), or the reading in 𝔭66 and 𝔭75 in John 5:44 ("the glory of the only One"), or the readings in 𝔭66 in John 19:35 and 20:31 ("that you might continue to believe"), or the reading of 𝔭72 in 2 Peter 1:3 ("called us through glory and virtue"), or the reading of 𝔭81 in 1 Peter 2:21 ("Christ died for you" instead of "Christ suffered for you").

Furthermore, translators have demonstrated a reluctance to omit portions of the text that are not found in the papyri and other early MSS. This is the case with Luke 22:43-44, which is not present in 𝔭69 𝔭75 ℵ¹ A B T W; Luke 23:34a, which is not present in 𝔭75 ℵ¹ B D* W; and the pericope about the adulteress (John 7:53–8:11), which is not present in 𝔭66 𝔭75 ℵ Avid B Cvid T W. And not one translation has a marginal note on one of several very interesting variants in the following papyri: 𝔭15, "the Spirit of Christ" in 1 Cor. 7:40; 𝔭23, "the Father of lights, with whom there is no variation or shadow of turning" in James 1:17; 𝔭72, "God, the Messiah, delivered his people out of Egypt" in Jude 5 (where the variant "Jesus" is cited in all the margins but not included in any version).

More examples could be given, but these should suffice to demonstrate that the papyri could and should be having more influence on future translations and revisions of the NT. Some of these changes will be found in The New Revised Standard Version (NRSV), appearing in 1990. It is the first modern English translation to have the reading "let us not tempt Christ" in 1 Cor. 10:9 and the reading "if I give my body that I may boast" in 1 Cor. 13:3. It also has the reading "they were not united in faith with those who listened" in Heb. 4:2, a reading supported by 𝔭13vid and 𝔭46.

THE CUMULATIVE EFFECT OF THE PAPYRI: FROM THE AMERICAN STANDARD VERSION TO A MODERN TRANSLATION

The most ideal way to conclude this book would be to print an English translation of the NT that reflects the evidence of the earliest papyrus manuscripts. However, it is far more practical and expedient to produce a compiled comparison to an already existing translation—a compilation which would demonstrate the need for revision. The ASV (1901) serves this purpose well because, as has been often noted in this book, it reflects the effect of the manuscripts discovered in the nineteenth century and at the same time provides a point of comparative reference for all manuscript discoveries in this century. Thus, if I were to produce a modern English translation which reflects only textual changes (as opposed to other kinds of revisions) based on the early manuscripts discovered in this century, I would suggest the following changes to the ASV. These changes, in effect, display most of the significant textual changes (extracted from the early manuscripts discovered in this century) that have affected English translations since the ASV. (The renderings given below follow those found in Section 3 of this book; they are not exact quotations from the ASV—yet they reflect the underlying textual variant.)

MATTHEW

5:25

change **lest the adversary hand you over to the judge, and the judge hand you over to the officer** to lest the adversary hand you over to the judge, and the judge to the officer

12:25

change **knowing their thoughts he said** to seeing [or, **perceiving**] their thoughts he said

26:20

change **the twelve disciples** to **the Twelve**

MARK

2:4

change **could not come near to him** to **could not bring him**

2:16

change **why does he eat and drink?** to **why does he eat?**

5:21

add mg. note saying **in the boat** is not included in some ancient MSS

6:23

add **with many** [vows] before **he swore to her**

7:4

add **and beds** [couches] after **bronze vessels**

7:28

delete **Yes** before **Lord**

7:35

add **immediately** before **his ears were opened**

8:15

add mg. note to **Herod,** saying some ancient MSS read **Herodians**

8:38a

add mg. note to **whoever is ashamed of me and my words,** saying some
    ancient MSS read **whoever is ashamed of me and mine**

8:38b

add mg. note to **the glory of his father with his holy angels,** saying some
    ancient MSS read **the glory of his father and of the holy angels**

9:24

delete mg. note which says some ancient MSS add **with tears** after **cried
    out**

LUKE

1:68

add mg. note to **Blessed be [the] Lord, the God of Israel,** saying some
    ancient MSS read **Blessed be the God of Israel**

4:44

change **the synagogues of Galilee** to **the synagogues of Judea**

6:1

change **on the second-first sabbath** to **on the sabbath**

7:11

change **on the next day** to **soon afterward**

8:43

delete **who had spent all her living on physicians and** from text; note in
    mg.

10:1, 17

change **seventy** to **seventy-two**; adjust mg. note accordingly

10:21

add mg. note to **in the Holy Spirit,** saying some ancient MSS read **in the Spirit**

10:38

change **received him into her house** to **received him**

11:10

delete **if his son asks for bread will he give him a stone?** from text; adjust mg. note accordingly

11:33

delete **or under a bushel** after **puts it in a hidden place [cellar]**

12:39

delete **he would have watched and** from the text

14:5

change **donkey or an ox** to **son or an ox**; adjust mg. note accordingly

22:43-44

omit verses; place in mg. note

23:34

delete **And Jesus said, "Father, forgive them, for they do not know what they are doing"** from text; place in mg. note with explanation

23:42

change **come in your kingdom** to **come into your kingdom**; adjust mg. note accordingly

24:3, 6, 9, 36, 40, 50, 52

The mg. notes on the omissions in these verses must make it clear that the omissions are not found in the most ancient MSS

24:32

delete **within us** from the text; add mg. note saying the words appear in some ancient MSS

JOHN

1:18

change **the only begotten Son** to **an only begotten, God**

1:34

add mg. note to **the Son of God,** saying that some ancient MSS read **the chosen One of God**

3:13

change **the Son of man who is in heaven** to **the Son of man**

5:2

change **Bethesda** to **Bethsaida**

5:44

change **glory from the only God** to **glory from the only One**

7:8

change **I am not going up to this feast** to **I am not yet going up to this feast**

7:39

change **the Spirit was not yet given** to **the Spirit was not yet**

7:52

add mg. note to **a prophet,** saying that one ancient MS reads "the prophet"

7:53–8:11

delete this portion and place in mg. note with explanation

8:57

add mg. note to **you have seen Abraham,** saying that some ancient MSS read **Abraham has seen you**

9:35

change **the Son of God** to **the Son of man;** adjust mg. note accordingly

12:17

add mg. note to **the crowd that had been with him when he called Lazarus out of the tomb and raised him from the dead was giving testimony,** saying that some ancient MSS read **the crowd that had been with him was testifying that he called Lazarus out of the tomb and raised him from the dead**

13:2

change **during supper** to **supper having ended** [or, **supper having been served**]

14:7

change **If you had known me, you would have known my Father also** to **If you have come to know me, you will know my Father also**

14:14

change **ask anything** to **ask me anything**; change mg. note accordingly

14:17

add mg. note to **because he abides with you and will be in you**, saying some ancient MSS read **because he abides with you and is in you**

16:22a

add mg. note to **you have sorrow**, saying some ancient MSS read **you will have sorrow**

16:22b

add mg. note to **no one takes your joy from you**, saying some ancient MSS read **no one will take your joy from you**

16:23

add mg. note to **whatever you ask the Father he will give it to you in my name**, saying some ancient MSS read **whatever you ask the Father in my name he will give it to you**

16:27

change **I came forth from the Father** to **I came forth from God**

ACTS

11:11

change **the house where we were** to **the house where I was**

11:12

change **making no distinction** [i.e., distinction between Gentiles and Jews] to **without doubting** [or, **with no hesitation**]

13:48

change **word of God** to **word of the Lord**

ROMANS

1:1

change **Jesus Christ** to **Christ Jesus**

8:28

change **everything works together for good** [or, **he works together everything for good**] to **God works all things together for good**; adjust mg. note accordingly

8:34

change **whom he raised from the dead** to **whom he raised**

11:31

change **they may now receive mercy** to **they may receive mercy**

15:19

change **the Holy Spirit** to **the Spirit of God**

1 CORINTHIANS

1:13

add mg. note to **has Christ been divided?**, saying some MSS read **Christ cannot be divided, can he?**

2:1

change **the testimony of God** to **the mystery of God**; adjust mg. note accordingly

5:5

change **Lord Jesus** to **Lord**; delete mg. note

7:15

change **called you** to **called us**; adjust mg. note accordingly

7:40

add mg. note to **Spirit of God**, saying some MSS read **Spirit of Christ**

10:2

change **were baptized** to **received baptism**

10:9

change **Lord** to **Christ**; adjust mg. note accordingly

13:3

change **if I give my body to be burned** to **if I give my body that I may boast**; adjust mg. note accordingly

15:54

change **when the perishable has been clothed with the imperishable, and the mortal with immortality** to **when the mortal has been clothed with immortality**; adjust mg. note accordingly

2 CORINTHIANS

1:10

add mg. note to **so great a death**, saying some MSS read **so great deaths**

2:1

change **But I decided** to **For I decided**; adjust mg. note accordingly

2:17

add mg. note to **the rest**, saying some MSS read **the many**

8:7

change **your love for us** to **our love for you**

GALATIANS

1:3

change **God our Father and Lord Jesus Christ** to **God the Father and our Lord Jesus Christ**; adjust mg. note accordingly

1:15

change **God was pleased** to **he was pleased**

4:28

change **we are** to **you are**; adjust mg. note accordingly

6:2

change **fulfill** (an imperative) to **you will fulfill**

EPHESIANS

1:1

omit **in Ephesus**; adjust mg. note accordingly

4:8

change **he led captivity captive, and he gave gifts** to **he led captivity captive, he gave gifts**

5:2

change **loved you** to **loved us**

5:5

change **one who is covetous, who is an idolater** to **one who is covetous, which is idolatry**

PHILIPPIANS

1:14

change **to speak the word of God** to **to speak the word**

3:3

add mg. note to **who worship by [or, in] the Spirit of God**, saying some MSS read **who worship God in spirit**, and some MSS read **who worship in spirit**

4:16

add mg. note to **you sent to my need**, saying some MSS read **you sent money to me**, and some MSS read **you contributed to my needs**

COLOSSIANS

3:6

omit **upon the sons of disobedience**; adjust mg. note accordingly

1 THESSALONIANS

2:7

perhaps change **gentle** to **babes**; adjust mg. note accordingly

PHILEMON

v. 25

omit **Amen**; adjust mg. note accordingly

HEBREWS

1:1

change **the fathers** to **our fathers**

2:7

omit **and did set him over the works of your hands**; adjust mg. note accordingly

3:2

change **in all his house** to **in his house**

3:6

omit **firm to the end**

4:2

change **those who heard did not combine it** [the word] **with faith** to **they were not united in faith with those who heard**; adjust mg. note accordingly

6:1-2

add mg. note to **not laying again a foundation of repentance from dead works and of faith toward God, of instruction about baptisms,** saying some MSS read **not laying again a foundation of repentance from dead works and of faith toward God, with** [or, even] **instruction about baptisms**

9:11

change **of the good things that are about to come** to **of the good things that have come**; adjust mg. note accordingly

11:4

add mg. note to **offered to God**, saying one early MS reads **offered**

11:11

change **by faith Sarah herself received power to conceive** to **by faith, even though Sarah was barren, he** [Abraham] **received power to beget**

12:3

change **against himself** to **against themselves**; adjust mg. note accordingly

JAMES

1:17

add mg. note to **the Father of lights with whom there is no variation or shadow of turning,** saying one early MS reads **the Father of lights with whom there is no variation or turning of the shadow**

1 PETER

1:22

change **heart** to **pure heart**; adjust mg. note accordingly

2:21

add mg. note to **suffered**, saying some MSS read **died**

3:18

change **suffered** to **died**; adjust mg. note accordingly

5:10

add mg. note to **perfect, establish, strengthen you**, saying some MSS
read **perfect, establish, confirm you**

2 PETER

1:3

change **called us by [or, to] his own glory and virtue** to **called us through
glory and virtue**; adjust mg. note accordingly

2:4

change **pits** to **chains**; adjust mg. note accordingly

2:20

change **the Lord and Savior, Jesus Christ** to **our Lord and Savior, Jesus
Christ**; adjust mg. note accordingly

3:10

add mg. note to **the earth and the works that are upon it will be burned
up**, saying one early MS reads **the earth and the works that are upon
it will be found dissolved**

JUDE

v. 5

change **the Lord delivered his people out of Egypt** to **Jesus delivered his
people out of Egypt** and to this add mg. note saying one early MS reads
God, the Messiah, delivered his people out of Egypt

vv. 22-23

add mg. note displaying textual variations of these verses and note reading
in 𝔭72 as follows: one early MS reads **and some snatch from fire,
and show mercy with fear to others who have doubts**

212

REVELATION

11:12

add mg. note to **they heard**, saying some MSS read **I heard**

13:6

add mg. note to **blaspheming his name and his dwelling place, that is, those who dwell in heaven**, saying some MSS read **blaspheming his name and those who dwell in heaven** and one early MS reads **blaspheming his name and his dwelling place in heaven**

14:3

change **they sing, as it were, a new song** to **they sing a new song**

15:6

change **stone** to **linen**; adjust mg. note accordingly

16:4

change **it became blood** to **they became blood**; adjust mg. note accordingly

The above list shows about 115 changes (and/or additions) to the ASV based upon the readings of the early MSS discovered in this century. This is a substantial number, which could be greatly increased if all manner of variant readings were included, not just those with obvious significance for translation. However, the number of changes is not phenomenally high because the early MSS discovered in this century have so often affirmed Codex Vaticanus and Codex Siniaticus, the MSS which the ASV greatly reflects. Thus, from a textual perspective, modern translations are much closer to the ASV than the ASV is to a version such as the KJV. (If one were to make a list of the differences between the ASV and the KJV due to the manuscript discoveries of the eighteenth century, it would very likely have a thousand or more significant changes.) Nonetheless, the early MSS discovered in the twentieth century have had a significant impact on our modern English versions and have helped modern translators produce versions that more closely reflect the earliest and best text of the Greek NT.

Bibliography

Abbott, Edwin A. *Johannine Grammar*. London: Adam and Charles Black, 1906.
Aland, Kurt. "Der Text des Johannesevangeliums im 2. Jahrhundert," in *Studien zum Text und zur Ethik des Neuen Testaments*, 1986.
———. "Neue neutestamentliche Papyri III," in *New Testament Studies* 20 (1974).
———. "Neue neutestamentliche Papyri III," in *New Testament Studies* 22 (1976).
———. "The Significance of the Papyri for Progress in New Testament Research," in *The Bible in Modern Scholarship*, ed. J. P. Hyatt. Nashville: Abingdon Press, 1965.
Aland, Kurt, and Barbara Aland. *The Text of the New Testament*, trans. Erroll F. Rhodes. Grand Rapids: Eerdmans, 1987.
Alford, Henry. *The Greek Testament*, 1852. Reprint. Grand Rapids: Guardian Press, 1976.
Amundsen, Leiv. "Christian Papyri from the Oslo Collection," in *Symbolae Osloenses* 24 (1945).

Baarda, Tj. "Gadarenes, Gerasenes, Gergesenes and the 'Diatessaron' Traditions," in *Neotestamentica et Semitica* (Studies in Honour of Principal Matthew Black); eds. E. Earle Ellis and Max Wilcox. Edinburgh: T. & T. Clark, 1969.
Barrett, C. K. *The Gospel according to St. John*. Philadelphia: Westminster Press, 1978.
Bartoletti, Vittorio. *Pubblicazioni della Società Italiana, Papiri Greci e Latini* XIV (1957).
Beasley-Murray, George R. *John* in the *Word Biblical Commentary*. Waco, Texas: Word, 1987.
Bell, Harold I. *The New Gospel Fragments*. Oxford: Oxford University Press, 1935, 1951.
Bilabel, Friedrich. "Römerbrieffragmente," in *Veröffentlichungen aus den Badischen Papyrussammlungen* IV (1924).
Birdsall, J. N. *The Bodmer Papyrus of the Gospel of John*. London: The Tyndale Press, 1960.
Birdsall, J. N. "The Text of Jude in 𝔓72," in *Journal of Theological Studies* 14 (1963).
Bratcher, Robert. "The T.E.V. and the Greek Text," in *The Bible Translator* 18 (1967).
———. *Translator's Guide to 2 Corinthians*. New York: United Bible Societies, 1983.
Bruce, F. F. *The Epistle to the Hebrews*. Grand Rapids: Eerdmans, 1964.
———. *This is That*. Exeter: Paternoster, 1968.

Caird, G. B. *Paul's Letters from Prison*. London: Oxford University Press, 1976.
Carson, D. A. "Matthew," in *The Expositor's Bible Commentary*. Grand Rapids: Zondervan, 1984.
Charalambakis, Hagedorn, Kaimakis, Thüngen, "Vier literarische Papyri der Kölner Sammlung," in *Zeitschrift für Papyrologie und Epigraphik*, 14 (1974).
Clark, Albert C. *The Acts of the Apostles*. London: Oxford University Press, 1933.
Cobern, Camden M. *The New Archeological Discoveries and Their Bearing upon the New Testament*. New York: Funk and Wagnalls, 1917.
Colwell, Earnest. "Hort Redivivus: A Plea and a Program," in *Studies in Methodology in Textual Criticism of the New Testament*. Leiden: E. J. Brill, 1969.
———. "Method in Evaluating Scribal Habits: A Study of 𝔓45, 𝔓66, 𝔓75" in *Studies in Methodology in Textual Criticism of the New Testament*. Leiden: E. J. Brill, 1969.
———. *What is the Best New Testament?* Chicago: University of Chicago Press, 1952.

Comfort, Philip W. "An Analysis of Five Modern Translations of the Gospel of John," in
Notes on Translation Vol. 3, No. 3, 1989.
————. "Exploring the Common Identification of Three New Testament Manuscripts: ℙ4,
ℙ64 and ℙ67," in *Tyndale Bulletin* 46 (1995): 43–54.
————. "Guide to the Ancient Manuscripts" in *Eight Translation New Testament*. Wheaton:
Tyndale House Publishers, 1988 (eighth edition).
————. "The Pericope of the Adulteress (John 7:53–8:11)," in *The Bible Translator* 40
(1989).
————. *The Quest for the Original Text of the New Testament*. Grand Rapids: Baker Book
House, 1992.

Daris, Sergio. "Papiri letterari dell' Università Cattolica di Milano," in *Aegyptus* 52
(1972).
————. "Uno nuovo frammento della prima lettera di Pietro," in *Papyrologica
Castroctaviana: Studia et Textus* 2 (Barcelona, 1967).

Deissmann, Adolf. "Ein Evangelienblatt aus den Tagen Hadrians," in *Deutsche allgemeine
Zeitung* 564 (3 December 1935).

Douglas, J. D., ed. *Illustrated Bible Dictionary*. Wheaton, Il.: Tyndale House Publishers,
1980.

Ellison, H. L. "Ebionites," in *New International Dictionary of the Christian Church*, ed. J.
D. Douglas. Grand Rapids: Zondervan, 1974.

Epp, Eldon J. "A Continuing Interlude in New Testament Textual Criticism?," in *Harvard
Theological Review* 73 (1980).
————. "The Twentieth Century Interlude in New Testament Textual Criticism," in *Jour-
nal of Biblical Literature* 93:3 (1974).
————. "The New Testament Papyrus Manuscripts in Historical Perspective," in *To Touch
the Text: Studies in Honor of Joseph A. Fitzmyer, S. J.* New York: Crossroad, 1989.
————. "The Significance of the Papyri for Determining the Nature of the New Testament
Text in the Second Century: A Dynamic View of Textual Transmission," in *Gospel Tra-
ditions in the Second Century*, ed. William M. Petersen. Notre Dame, Indiana: University of Notre Dame Press, 1989.
————. "Toward the Clarification of the Term 'Textual Variant,'" in *Studies in New Testament Language and Text*, ed. J. K. Elliott. Leiden: E. J. Brill, 1976.

Fee, Gordon. *First Corinthians* in the *New International Commentary on the New Testa-
ment*. Grand Rapids: Zondervan, 1988.
————. "'One Thing Is Needful'? Luke 10:42," in *New Testament Textual Criticisim: Its
Significance for Exegesis*, eds. Eldon Epp and Gordon Fee. London: Oxford University
Press, 1981.
————. "ℙ66, ℙ75, and Origen: The Myth of the Early Textual Recension in Alexandria,"
in *New Dimensions in New Testament Study*, eds. Longenecker and Tenney. Grand Ra-
pids: Zondervan, 1974.
————. *Papyrus Bodmer II (ℙ66): Its Textual Relationships and Scribal Characteristics*, in
Studies and Documents 34 (1968). Salt Lake City: University of Utah Press.

Finegan, Jack. *Encountering New Testament Manuscripts*. Grand Rapids: Eerdmans, 1974.

Gallazzi, Claudio. "Frammenti di un Codice con le Epistole di Paolo," in *Zeitschrift für
Papyrologie und Epigraphik* 46 (1982).
————. "P. Mil. Vogl. Inv. 1224: Novum Testamentum, Act. 2,30-37 E 2,46-3,2," in *Bul-
letin of American Society of Papyrologists* 19 (1982).

Gerstinger, Hans. "Ein Fragment des Chester Beatty-Evangelienkodex in der Papyrussammlung der Nationalbibliothek in Wien," in *Aegyptus* 13 (1933).

Grant, F. C. *An Introduction to the Revised Standard Version of the New Testament*. Published by the International Council of Religious Education, 1946.

Gregory, Caspar R. *Textkritik des Neuen Testaments III*. Leipzig: 1909.

Grenfell, B. P., and A. S. Hunt. *Amherst Papyri*. London, 1900.
————. *Oxyrhynchus Papyri* I (1898), II (1899), III (1903), IV (1904), VII (1910), VIII
(1911), IX (1912), X (1914), XI (1915), XIII (1919), XV (1922). London, 1898-1922.

Harrison, Everett F. "Romans," in *The Expositor's Bible Commentary*. Grand Rapids: Zondervan, 1976.

Hatch, W. H. P. *The Principal Uncial Manuscripts of the New Testament*. Chicago: University Press, 1939.

Hatch, W. H. P., and C. B. Wells. "A Hitherto Unpublished Fragment of the Epistle to the Ephesians," in *Harvard Theological Review*, 51 (1958).

Hawthorne, Gerald F. *Philippians*, in the *Word Biblical Commentary*. Waco, Texas: Word, 1983.

Hodges Z., and A. Farstad. *The Greek New Testament according to the Majority Text*. Nashville: Nelson, 1982.

Hort, Fenton. *Two Dissertations*. Cambridge: MacMillan, 1876.

Hunger, Herbert. "Zur Datierung des Papyrus Bodmer II (𝔓66)," in *Anzeiger der österreichischen Akademie der Wissenschaften*, philologisch-historischen Klasse, 1960, no. 4:12–23.

Hunt, A. S. *Catalogue of the Greek Papyri in the John Rylands Library* I. Manchester, 1911.

Ingrams, Kingston, Parsons, Rea, *Oxyrhynchus Papyri*, XXXIV. London, 1968.

Kasser, Rudolf, and Victor Martin. *Papyrus Bodmer XIV-XV*, I: *XIV: Luc chap 3-24*; II: XV: *Jean chap. 1-15*. Cologny/Geneva: Bibliotheca Bodmeriana, 1961.

Kelly, J. N. D. *Early Christian Creeds*. 2d ed. London: Longmans, 1960.

Kent, Homer. "Philippians," in *The Expositor's Bible Commentary*. Grand Rapids: Zondervan, 1978.

Kenyon, Frederic G. *Chester Beatty Biblical Papyri* II/1: *The Gospels and Acts, Text* (London: Emery Walker Ltd., 1933); II/2: *The Gospels and Acts, Plates* (1934); *Chester Biblical Papyri* III/1: *Pauline Epistles and Revelation, Text* (1934); III/2: *Revelation, Plates* (1936); III/3 (Supplement): *Pauline Epistles, Text* (1936); III/4: *Pauline Epistles, Plates* (1937).

—————. *Recent Developments in the Textual Criticism of the Greek Bible*. London: Oxford University Press, 1933.

Kim, Young Kyu. "Palaeographical Dating of 𝔓46 to the Later First Century," in *Biblica* 69 (1988): 248–57.

Kraeling, Carl H. "𝔓50: Two Selections from Acts," in *Quantulacumque: Studies Presented to Kirsopp Lake*, eds. R. Casey, S. Lake, A. K. Lake. London, 1937.

Kramer, Römer, and Hagedorn. *Kölner Papyri 4: Papyrologica Coloniensa* Vol. VII (1982).

Kubo, Sakae. "Jude 22-3: Two-division form or Three?," in *New Testament Textual Criticism: Its Significance for Exegesis*, eds. Eldon Epp and Gordon Fee. London: Oxford University Press, 1981.

—————. 𝔓72 *and the Codex Vaticanus*, in *Studies and Documents* 27 (1965), University of Utah Press.

Kubo, Sakae, and Walter Specht. *So Many Versions?* Grand Rapids: Zondervan, 1975.

Lenaerts, Jean. "Un papyrus l'Evangile de Jean: PL II/31," in *Chronique d'Egypte* LX (1985).

Lewis, Jack P. *The English Bible, From KJV to NIV: A History and Evaluation*. Grand Rapids: Baker Book House, 1981.

Lightfoot, J. B. *St. Paul's Epistle to the Philippians*. London: Macmillan, 1894.

Lobel, Edgar, Colin H. Roberts, and E. P. Wegener. *Oxyrhynchus Papyri* XVIII (1941), XXIV (1957).

Martin, Ralph P. *2 Corinthians*, in the *Word Biblical Commentary*. Waco, Texas: Word, 1986.

—————. *James*, in the *Word Biblical Commentary*. Waco, Texas: Word, 1988.

Martin, Victor. *Papyrus Bodmer II: Evangile de Jean, 1-14*. Cologny/Geneva: Bibliotheca Bodmeriana, 1956.

—————. *Papyrus Bodmer II: Supplément, Evangile de Jean, 14-21*. Cologny/Geneva: Bibliotheca Bodmeriana, 1958.

Martin, Victor and J. W. B. Barns. *Papyrus Bodmer II: Supplément, Evangile de Jean, 14-21* (with photographic reproductions of John 1–21). Cologny/Geneva: Bibliotheca Bodmeriana, 1962.

Martin, Victor and Rudolfe Kasser. *Papyrus Bodmer XIV: Evangile du Luc chap. 3-24; and Papyrus Bodmer XV, Evangile de Jean chap. 1-15.* Cologny/Geneva: Bibliotheca Bodmeriana, 1961.

Martini, Carlo M. *Beati Petri Apostoloi Epistulae, Ex Papyro Bodmeriano VIII.* Milan, 1968.

Merell, J. "Nouveaux fragments papyrus IV," in *Revue Biblique* 47 (1938).

Merk, Augustine. "Codex Evangeliorum et Actum ex collectione P Chester Beatty," in *Miscellanea Biblica* II. Rome, 1934.

Metzger, Bruce M. *The Text of the New Testament.* 1968. Reprint. Oxford: Oxford University Press, 1980.

———. *A Textual Commentary on the Greek New Testament.* New York: United Bible Societies, 1971.

Morris, Leon. "Hebrews," in *The Expositor's Bible Commentary.* Grand Rapids: Zondervan, 1981.

Naldini, M. "Nuovi frammenti del vangelo di Matteo," in *Prometheus* 1 (1975).

Nestle, Eberhard. *Introduction to the Textual Criticism of the Greek New Testament;* trans. William Edie. London: Williams and Norgate, 1901.

Newman, Barclay, and Eugene Nida. *A Translator's Handbook on the Gospel of John.* New York: United Bible Societies, 1980.

Osburn, Carroll D. "The Text of 1 Corinthians 10:9," in *New Testament Textual Criticism: Its Significance for Exegesis,* eds. Eldon Epp and Gordon Fee. London: Oxford University Press, 1981.

Pfeiffer, Charles F.,,H. V. Vos, and John Rea, eds. *Wycliffe Bible Encyclopedia.* Chicago: Moody Press, 1975.

Pickering, S. R. "The Macquarie Papyrus of the Acts of the Apostles," a preliminary report (Aug. 30, 1984, from Macquarie University).

———. "P. Macquarie Inv. 360 (+ P. Mil. Vogl. Inv. 1224): Acta Apostolorum 2.30-37, 2.46–3.2," in *Zeitschrift für Papyrologie und Epigraphik* 65 (1986).

Pintaudi, Rosario. "N.T. Ad Hebraeos VI, 7-9; 15-17 (PL III/292)," in *Zeitschrift für Papyrologie und Epigraphik* 42 (1981).

Pistelli, E. *Papiri greci e latini della Società Italiana* I (1912).

Porter, Calvin. "Papyrus Bodmer XV (𝔓75) and the Text of Codex Vaticanus," in the *Journal of Biblical Literature,* 81 (1962).

Roberts, Colin H. "An Early Papyrus of the First Gospel," in *Harvard Theological Review,* 46 (1953).

———. *An Unpublished Fragment of the Fourth Gospel in the John Rylands Library.* Manchester: Manchester University Press, 1935.

———. *Bulletin of the John Rylands Library* XX (1936).

———. *Catalogue of the Greek and Latin Papyri in the John Rylands Library* iii. Manchester, 1938.

———. *Manuscript, Society, and Belief in Early Christian Egypt.* London: Oxford University Press, 1979.

Robinson, James M. "The Discovering and Marketing of Coptic Manuscripts: The Nag Hammadi Codices and the Bodmer Papyri," in *The Roots of Egyptian Christianity,* ed. Birger A. Pearson and James E. Goehring. Philadelphia: Fortress, 1986.

Roca-Puig, P. "Nueva publicacion del papiro numero uno de Barcelona," in *Helmantica* 37 (1961).

———. "Papiro del evangelio de San Juan con 'Hermeneia,' " in *Atti dell' XI Congresso Internazionale di Papirologia.* Milan, 1966.

———. *Un Papiro Griego del Evangelio de San Mateo.* Barcelona, 1957.

Rösch, Friedrich, ed. *Bruchstücke des ersten Clemensbrief nach dem achmimischen Papyrus der Strassburger Universitäts- und Landesbibliothek.* Strasbourg, 1910.

Sanders, Henry A. "A Papyrus Fragment of Acts in the Michigan Collection," in *Harvard Theological Review* 20 (1927).

Sanders, Henry A. *A Third-century Papyrus Codex of the Epistles of Paul*. Ann Arbor: University of Michigan Press, 1935.

Sanders, Henry A. "A Third Century Papyrus of Matthew and Acts," in *Quantulacumque: Studies Presented to Kirsopp Lake*, eds. R. Casey, S. Lake, A. K. Lake. London, 1937.

Sanders, Henry A. "An Early Papyrus Fragment of the Gospel of Matthew in the Michigan Collection," in *Harvard Theological Review*, 19 (1926).

Scanlin, Harold P. "Bible Translation as a Means of Communicating New Testament Textual Criticism to the Public," in *The Bible Translator*, 39 (1988).

Schnackenburg, Rudolph. *The Gospel According to St. John*; trans. Kevin Smyth. New York: Crossroad Publishing Co., 1982.

Schofield, Ellwood M. "The Papyrus Fragments of the Greek New Testament" (dissertation, Southern Baptist Theological Seminary, 1936).

Schwartz, J. "Fragment d'évangile sur papyrus," in *Zeitschrift für Papyrologie und Epigraphik* 3 (1968).

———. "Fragment d'evangile sur papyrus," in *Zeitschrift für Papyrologie und Epigraphik* 4 (1969).

Scrivener, F. H. A. *A Plain Introduction to the Criticism of the New Testament*. Cambridge: Deighton, Bell, and Co., 1883.

Skeat, Theodore A. *Oxyrhynchus Papyri 2* (= vol. 50). London, 1983.

Stegmüller, Otto. "Ein Bruchstück aus dem griechischen Diatessaron," in *Zeitschrift für Papyrologie und Epigraphik* 37 (1938).

Tasker, R. V. G. "Notes on Variant Readings," in *The Greek New Testament* (being the Text Translated in the New English Bible, 1961). London: Oxford University Press, 1964.

Testuz, Michael. *Papyrus Bodmer VII-IX: L'Epître de Jude, Les deux Epîtres de Pierre, Les Psaumes 33 et 34*. Cologny/Geneva: Bibliotheca Bodmeriana, 1959.

Thiede, Carsten Peter. "Papyrus Magdalen Greek 17 (Gregory-Aland 𝔓64): A Reappraisal," in *Tyndale Bulletin* 46 (1995): 29–42.

Thrall, Margaret E. "2 Corinthians 1:12: ἁγιότητι or ἁπλότητι," in *Studies in New Testament Language and Text*, ed. J. K. Elliott. Leiden: E. J. Brill, 1976.

Tregelles, Samuel P. *An Account of the Printed Text of the Greek New Testament*. London: Samuel Bagster and Sons, 1854.

Turner, Eric G. *Greek Papyri: An Introduction*. Princeton: Princeton University Press, 1968.

———. *The Typology of the Early Codex*. Philadelphia: University of Pennsylvania Press, 1977.

Vitelli, G., and S. G. Mercati. *Pubblicazioni della Società Italiana, Papiri Greci e Latini*, 10 (1932).

Wessely, Karl. "Les plus anciens monuments du christianisme," in *Patrologia Orientalis* 4/2 (1907).

Westcott, B. F. *Gospel According to St. John*, 1881. Reprint. Grand Rapids: Zondervan, 1973.

Westcott, B. F. and F. J. A. Hort, *Introduction to the New Testament in the Original Greek* (with "Notes on Select Readings"). New York: Harper and Brothers, 1882.

Wikgren, Allen. "Some Problems in Jude 5," in *Studies and Documents*, 29, eds. B. L. Daniels and J. M. Suggs. Salt Lake City: University of Utah Press, 1967.

Williams, James. "Renderings from Some Johannine Passages," in *The Bible Translator*, 25:3 (1974).

Zuntz, Günther. "Reconstruction of one Leaf of the Chester Beatty Papyrus of the Gospels and Acts (Mt 25:41–26:39)," in *Chronique d'Egypte* 26 (1951).

———. *The Text of the Epistles*. London: Oxford University Press, 1953.

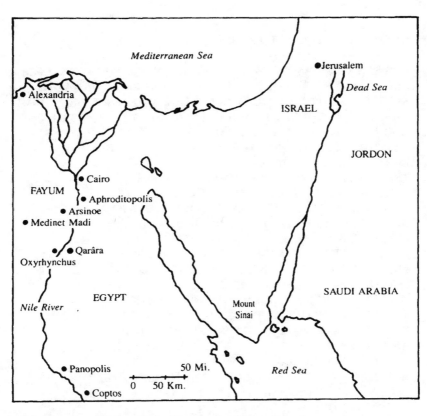

Places in Egypt Where Early Manuscripts Were Found
Aphroditopolis (Atfih) or Panopolis (Akmim): 𝔭45, 46, 47, 66, 72, 75
Arsinoe: 𝔭12
Coptos (Qift): 𝔭4, 64/67
Fayum: 𝔭37, 38, (52?), 53
Medinet Madi (Narmouthis): 𝔭92
Oxyrhynchus (El-Bahnasa): 𝔭1, 5, 9, 10, 13, 15, 16, 17, 18, 20, 21, 22, 23, 24,
    27, 28, 29, 30, (32?), 35, 39, 48, 51, (52?), 69, 70, 71, 77, 78, (82?), 85,
    90, 0162
Qarâra: 𝔭40

Note: modern names of certain locations are given within parentheses

GOSPEL ACCORDING TO JOHN

IN BEGINNING WAS THE WORD, AND THE WORD WAS WITH [GOD]
AND GOD WAS THE WORD. THIS ONE WAS IN BEGINNING WITH [GOD]
ALL THINGS THROUGH HIM WERE MADE, AND APART FROM [HIM]
WAS MADE NOTHING WHICH HAS BEEN MADE(.) IN HIM LIFE [WAS]
AND THE LIFE WAS THE LIGHT OF MEN
AND THE LIGHT IN THE DARKNESS SHINES, AND THE
DARKNESS IT DID NOT GRASP.
THERE WAS A MAN HAVING BEEN SENT FROM
GOD(,) NAME TO HIM(,) JOHN. THIS ONE
CAME FOR A TESTIMONY THAT HE MIGHT TESTIFY
ABOUT THE LIGHT, THAT ALL MEN MIGHT BE-
LIEVE THROUGH HIM. NOT HE WAS THAT
LIGHT BUT THAT HE MIGHT TESTIFY ABOUT THE
LIGHT(.) IT WAS THE LIGHT(,) THE TRUE ONE(,) WHICH EN-
LIGHTENS EVERY MAN COMING
INTO THE WORLD. IN THE WORLD HE WAS AND
THE WORLD THROUGH HIM WAS MADE AND THE WORLD
HIM NOT RECOGNIZED(.) TO HIS OWN [HE CAME]
AND HIS OWN HIM NOT RECEIVED. [BUT] AS MANY AS
RECEIVED HIM HE GAVE THEM
AUTHORITY CHILDREN OF GOD TO BECOME, TO THE ONES
BELIEVING IN THE NAME OF HIM(,) WHO
NOT OF BLOODS NOR OF WILL
OF FLESH NOR OF WILL OF A HUSBAND
BUT OF GOD WERE BORN. AND

Note: Words in brackets reflect words missing in the manuscript due to a lacuna.
Punctuation in parentheses was supplied to help the intelligibility of the
translation; all other punctuation marks reflect those in the manuscript, p66.

PHOTO 1

𝔭66 (Bodmer Papyrus II), showing John 1:1-14. The facing page gives a literal line-for-line translation of the text.

Photo credit: Foundation Bodmer; Geneva, Switzerland.

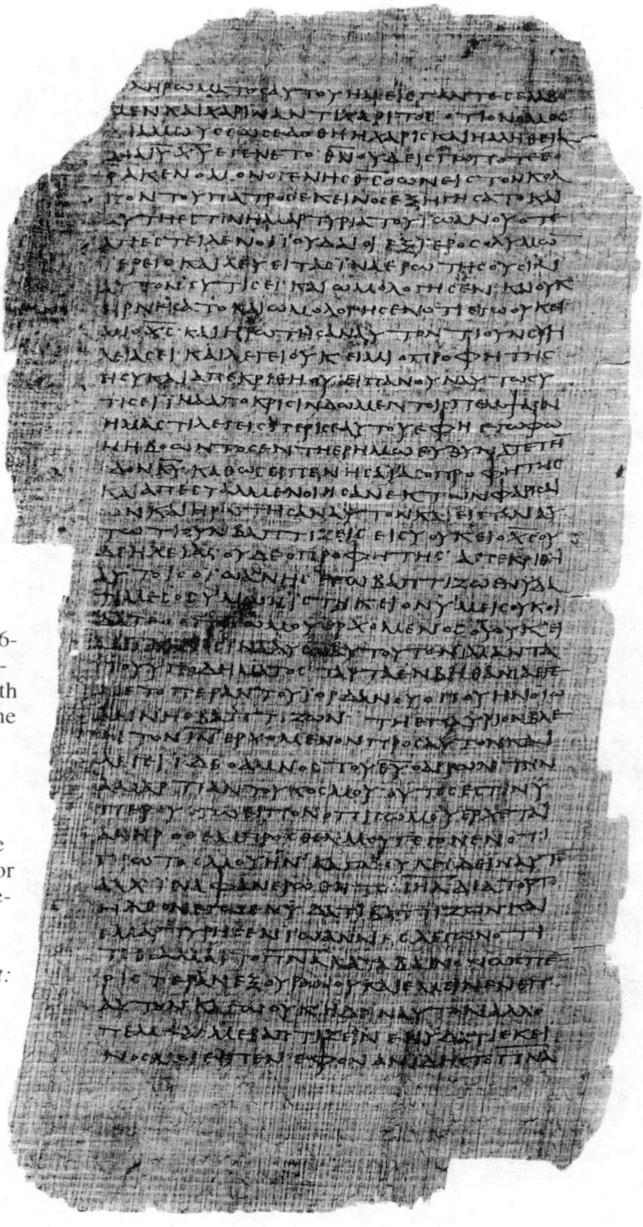

PHOTO 2
𝔓75 (Bodmer Papyrus XIV–XV), showing John 1:16-33. Notice the expression in the fifth line down from the top: ΟΜΟΝΟΓΕΝΗΣΘΣ = ὁ μονογενὴς θεός, which can be translated, "the Only One, God" or "God, the only begotten." See discussion on John 1:18. *Photo credit:* Foundation Bodmer; Geneva, Switzerland.

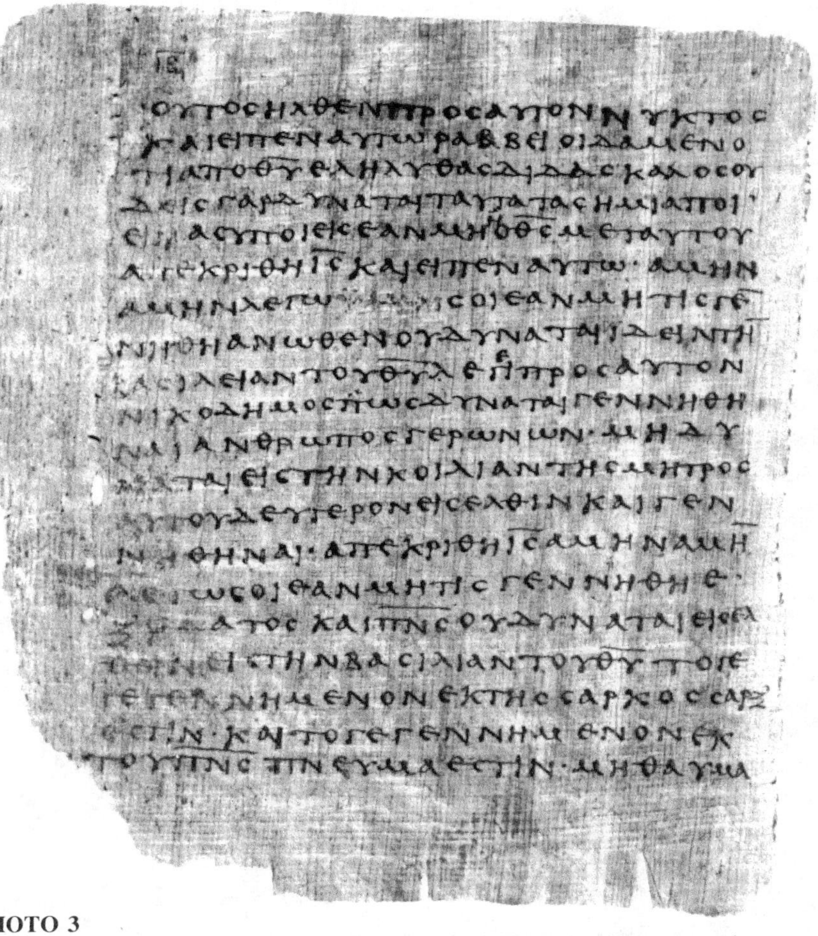

PHOTO 3

𝔓66 (Bodmer Papyrus II), showing John 3:2-7. Notice the last line where the scribe wrote ΠΝΕΥΜΑ in two ways: ΠΝΣ (abbreviated as a nomen sacrum, indicating the divine Spirit) and ΠΝΕΥΜΑ (written out, indicating the human spirit). See discussion on John 3:6. *Photo credit:* Foundation Bodmer; Geneva, Switzerland.

225

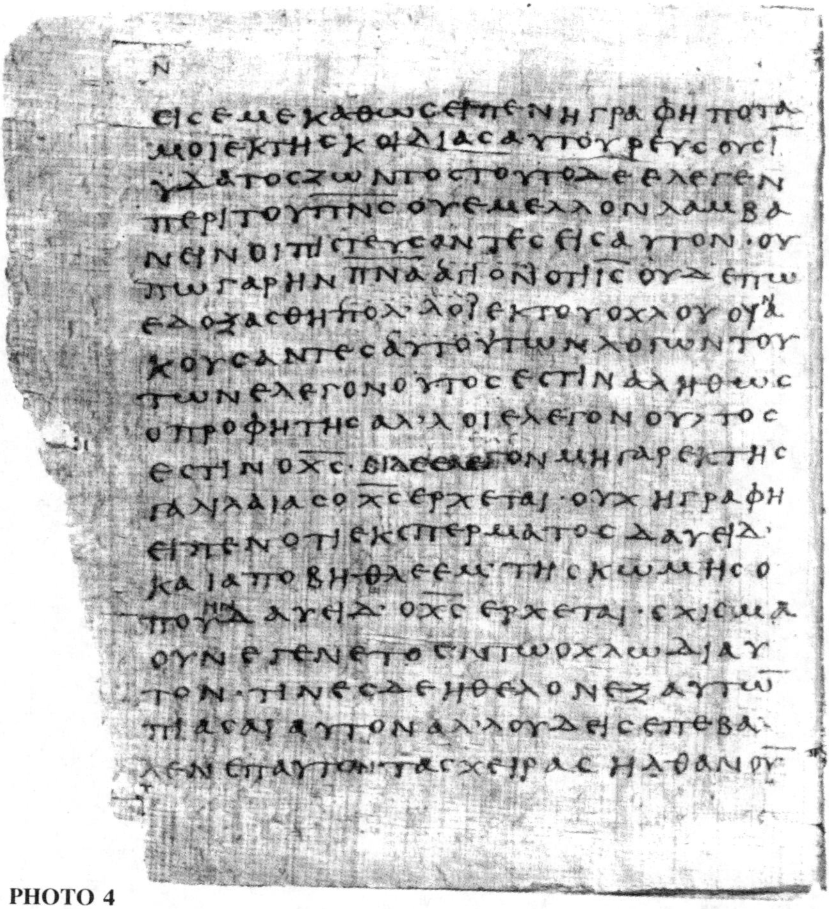

PHOTO 4

𝔓66 (Bodmer Papyrus II), showing John 7:38-45. Notice the sixth line down from the top, where it is written ΠΝΑ ΑΓΙΟΝ (lit. "Spirit Holy"). The markings above the word ΑΓΙΟΝ ("Holy") show that the scribe decided to delete this word after he wrote it—giving the reading "[the] Spirit was not yet," as opposed to "[the] Holy Spirit was not yet." See discussion on John 7:39. *Photo credit:* Foundation Bodmer; Geneva, Switzerland.

PHOTO 5

𝔓66 (Bodmer Papyrus II), showing John 7:52–8:16, lacking John 7:53–8:11. Notice in the second line from the top that the first two words read ΟΠΡΟΦΗΤΗΣ = ὁ προφήτης ("the prophet"). This is the only MS that clearly has this reading in John 7:52. (Some have thought 𝔓75 also reads ὁ προφήτης, but the lacuna in 𝔓75 is too large to determine if the article ὁ was present or not—see photo 6, line 9). But notice the slanted line after the definite article ὁ; this indicates that the scribe of 𝔓66 decided to delete the article—giving the reading found in all other MSS: "a prophet."

Note also in the same line in 𝔓66 that it ends with the last word of John 7:52 and begins with the first word of John 8:12 (ΕΓΙΡΕΤΑΙ.ΠΑΛΙΝ). This provides the earliest testimony to the absence of the pericope about the adulteress (see discussion on John 7:53–8:11). *Photo credit:* Foundation Bodmer; Geneva, Switzerland.

PHOTO 6
𝔓75 (Bodmer Papyrus XIV-XV), showing John 7:49–8:22, lacking John 7:53–8:11. Notice in the tenth line from the top that the first two words read ΕΓΕΡΕΤΑΙ.ΠΑ [ΛΙΝ—the last word of John 7:52 and the first word of John 8:12. This, with 𝔓66 (see photo 4), provides early testimony to support the position that John did not write the pericope of the adulteress (see discussion on John 7:53–8:11). *Photo credit:* Foundation Bodmer; Geneva, Switzerland.

228

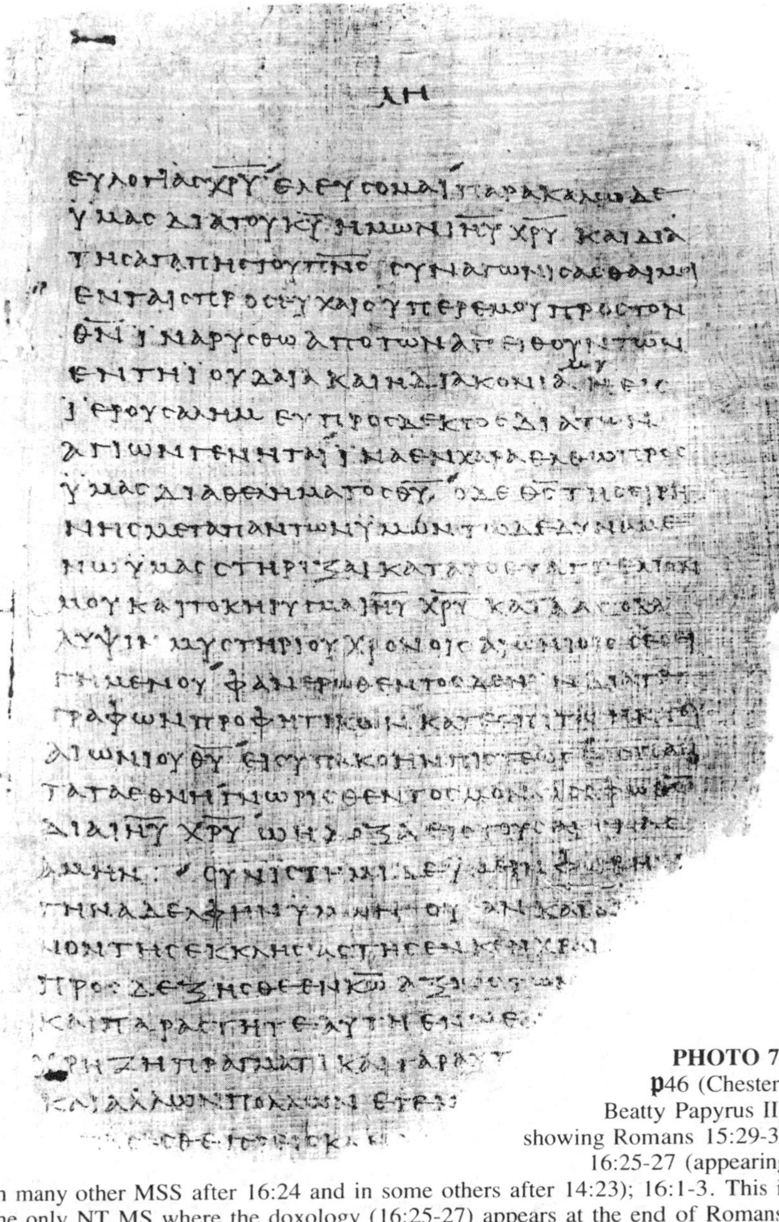

PHOTO 7
𝔓46 (Chester Beatty Papyrus II), showing Romans 15:29-33; 16:25-27 (appearing in many other MSS after 16:24 and in some others after 14:23); 16:1-3. This is the only NT MS where the doxology (16:25-27) appears at the end of Romans 15. See discussion on Rom. 16:25-27. *Photo credit:* Department of Rare Books and Special Collections, The University of Michigan Library.

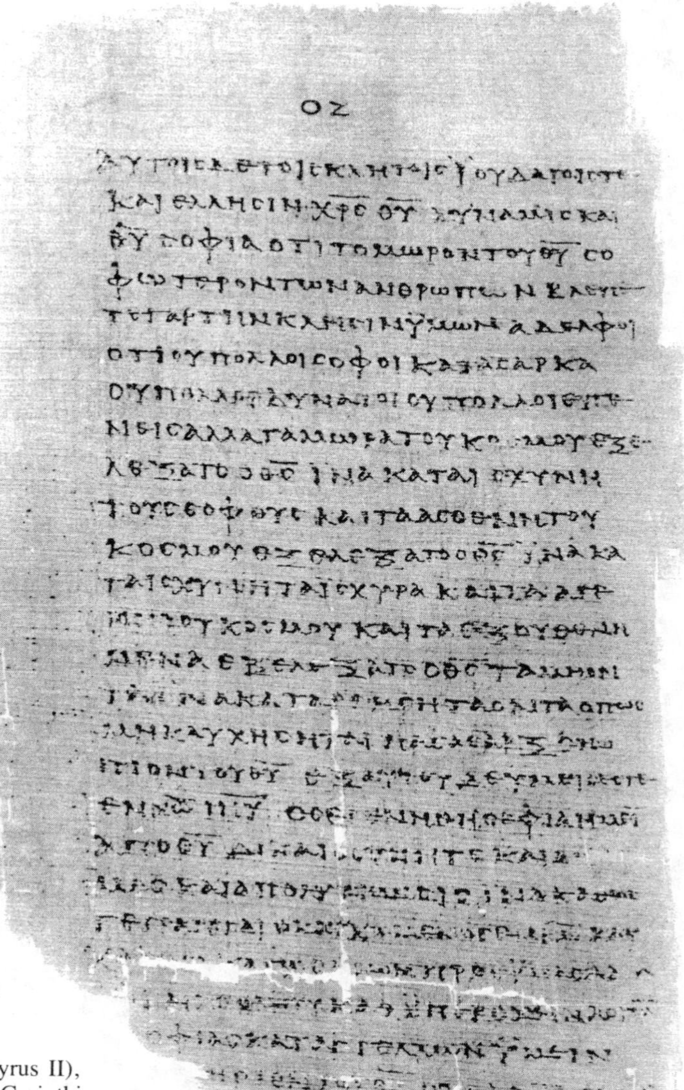

PHOTO 8
𝔓46
(Chester
Beatty Papyrus II),
showing 1 Corinthians
1:24–2:2. Notice the last
line, which at the beginning clearly shows the last four letters (PION) of one of
two words: ΜΥΣΤΗΡΙΟΝ ("mystery") or ΜΑΡΤΥΡΙΟΝ ("testimony"). If the
letter before these last four letters is *eta* (H), then 𝔓46 reads ΜΥΣΤΗΡΙΟΝ
("mystery"); if it is *upsilon* (Y), then 𝔓46 reads ΜΑΡΤΥΡΙΟΝ ("testimony").
From my observation, the letter appears to be an *eta* (H). Thus, 𝔓46 provides the
earliest witness to the reading, "the mystery of God," as opposed to the reading,
"the testimony of God." See discussion on 1 Cor. 2:2. *Photo credit:* Chester
Beatty Library; Dublin, Ireland.

230

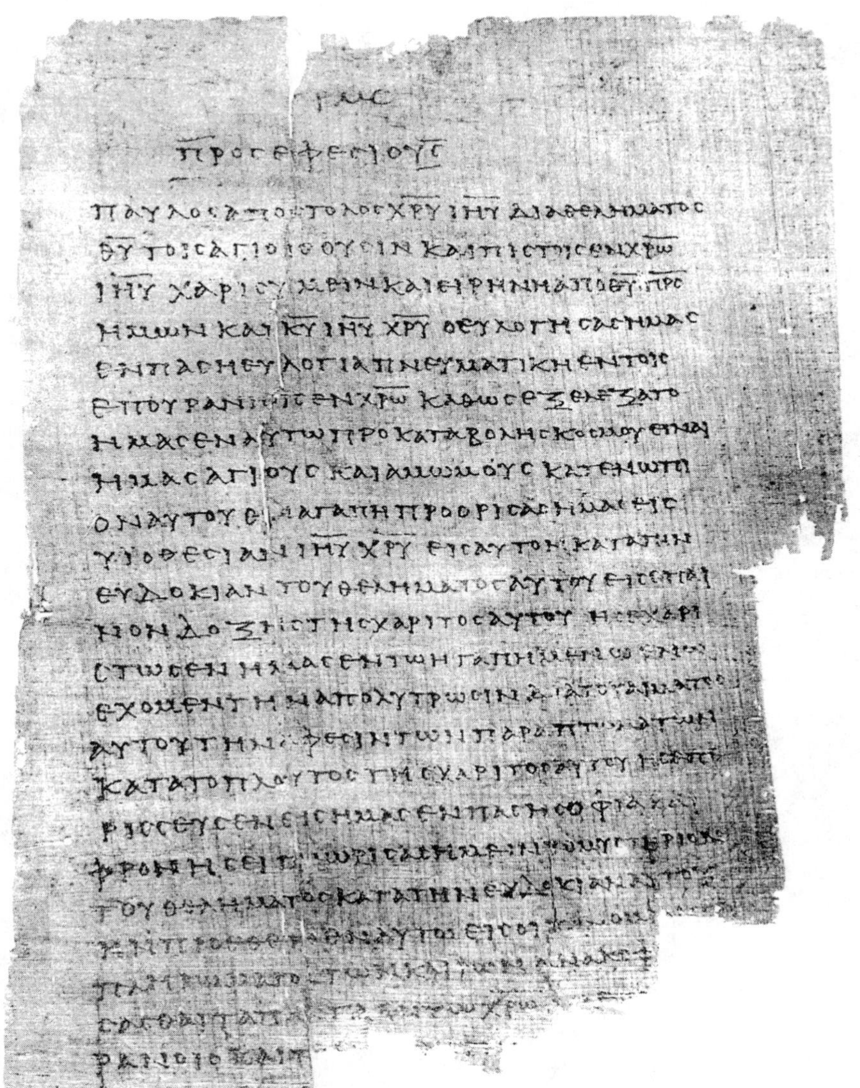

PHOTO 9

𝔓46 (Chester Beatty Papyrus II), showing Ephesians 1:1-11. The first verse does not include the words ἐν Ἐφέσῳ ("in Ephesus"); the same is true in ℵ and B. For this reason, many scholars believe that this epistle of Paul was addressed to several churches, one of which was Ephesus. See discussion on Eph. 1:1. *Photo credit:* Department of Rare Books and Special Collections, The University of Michigan Library.

231

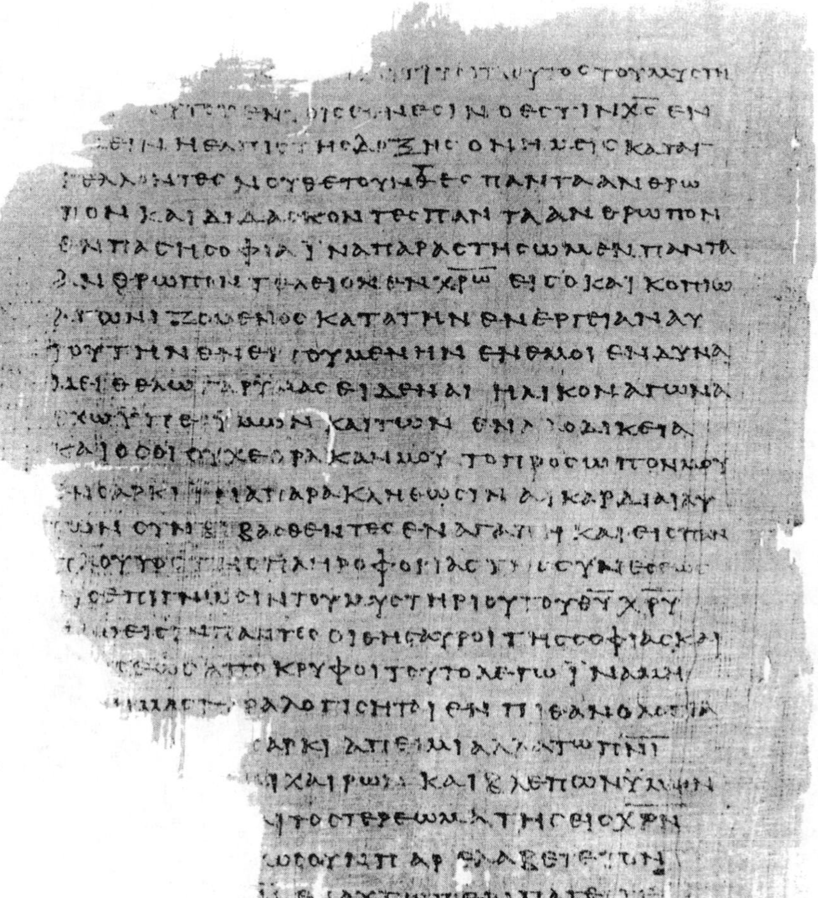

PHOTO 10

𝔓46 (Chester Beatty Papyrus II), showing Colossians 1:27–2:2. The sixteenth line has the phrase ΤΟΥΜΥΣΤΗΡΙΟΥΘΥΧΡΥ = τοῦ μυστηρίου τοῦ θεοῦ χριστοῦ ("the mystery of God, [namely] Christ"). This reading, found only in 𝔓46 and B, is considered by most scholars to be the one Paul originally wrote. See discussion on Col. 2:2. *Photo credit:* Chester Beatty Library; Dublin, Ireland.

PHOTO 11

𝔭13 (Oxyrhynchus Papyrus 657), showing Hebrews 4:2-11. Notice the last word of the second line, ΣΥΝΚΕΚΕΡΑΣΜΕΝΟΥΣ ("being joined together"); it agrees grammatically with ΕΚΕΙΝΟΥΣ ("those [who heard]"), not Ο ΛΟΓΟΣ ("the word"). Thus, 𝔭13 gives support to the reading, "they were not united in faith with those who heard." See discussion on Heb. 4:2. *Photo credit:* British Library, London.

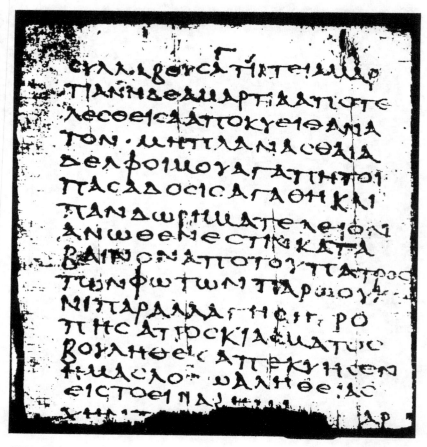

PHOTO 12

𝔓23 (Papyrus Oxyrhynchus 1229), showing James 1:15-18. The eleventh and twelfth lines have the phrase ΠΑΡΑΛΛΑΓΗΣΗΤΡΟ/ΠΗΣΑΠΟΣΚΙΑΣΜΑ-ΤΟΣ = παραλλαγῆς ἢ τροπῆς ἀποσκιάσματος ("variation or turning of the shadow"). This reading is not found in any other MS. See discussion on James 1:17. Courtesy, World Heritage Museum, University of Illinois Photo.

234

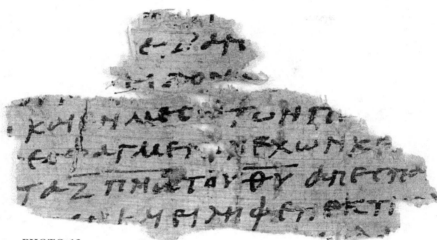

PHOTO 13

𝔓24 (Papyrus Oxyrhynchus 1230), showing Revelation 5:5-8 on recto. Notice on the sixth line the reading TA$\overline{\text{ZIINATOY}}\overline{\text{ΘY}}$ = τὰ ζ[zeta = ἑπτά] πνεύματα τοῦ θεοῦ ("the seven Spirits of God"). By writing the entire title as a *nomen sacrum,* the scribe of 𝔓24 was indicating that he considered the words "the seven" to be part of the title for the divine Spirit. See discussion on Rev. 5:6. *Photo credit:* Trask Library, Andover Newton Theological Seminary.

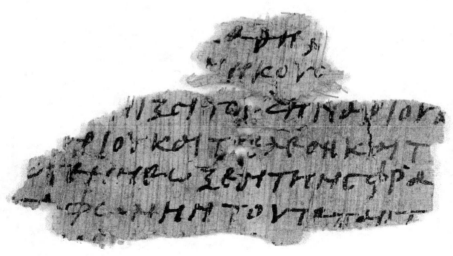

PHOTO 14

𝔓24 (Papyrus Oxyrhynchus 1230), showing Revelation 6:5-8 on verso. *Photo credit:* Trask Library, Andover Newton Theological Seminary.